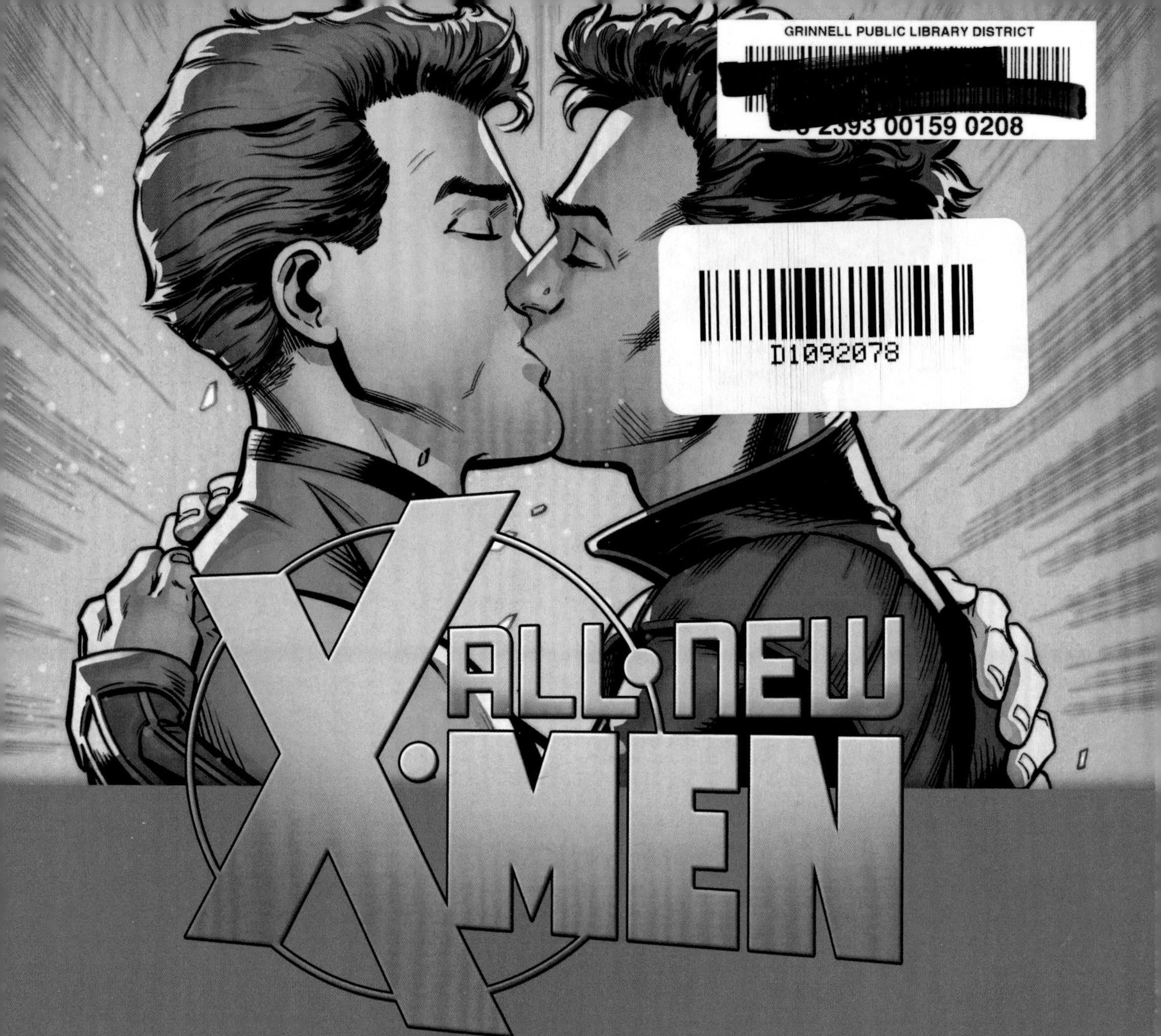
ALL-NEW
X-MEN

IVX

PLUCKED FROM THE PAST, THE ORIGINAL X-MEN — CYCLOPS, BEAST, ICEMAN AND ANGEL — ARE NOW TRAPPED IN THE PRESENT, IN A TIME WHEN MUTANTS ARE HATED AND FEARED MORE THAN EVER. DETERMINED NOT TO LET THE WORLD GET THE BETTER OF THEM, THEY'VE SET OUT TO WRITE THEIR OWN FUTURES AND BUILD A LEGACY THEY CAN BE PROUD OF.

ON A RECENT ADVENTURE IN MIAMI, BOBBY DRAKE MADE THE ACQUAINTANCE OF A YOUNG INHUMAN TEENAGER NAMED ROMEO. THEY QUICKLY HIT IT OFF AND HAVE BEEN SEEING EACH OTHER WHEN THEY CAN.

SINCE THEN, THE X-MEN HAVE DISCOVERED THAT THE TERRIGEN CLOUD CIRCLING THE EARTH IS ON THE VERGE OF DISSIPATING INTO THE ATMOSPHERE, RENDERING EARTH UNINHABITABLE FOR MUTANTS WHILE CREATING NEW INHUMANS. DIPLOMACY HAS BROKEN DOWN BETWEEN THE TWO CAMPS AND TENSIONS ARE ON THE RISE...

COLLECTION EDITOR: **MARK D. BEAZLEY**
ASSISTANT EDITOR: **CAITLIN O'CONNELL**
ASSOCIATE MANAGING EDITOR: **KATERI WOODY**
SENIOR EDITOR, SPECIAL PROJECTS: **JENNIFER GRÜNWALD**

VP PRODUCTION & SPECIAL PROJECTS: **JEFF YOUNGQUIST**
SVP PRINT, SALES & MARKETING: **DAVID GABRIEL**
BOOK DESIGNER: **JAY BOWEN**

EDITOR IN CHIEF: **AXEL ALONSO**
CHIEF CREATIVE OFFICER: **JOE QUESADA**
PRESIDENT: **DAN BUCKLEY**
EXECUTIVE PRODUCER: **ALAN FINE**

ALL-NEW X-MEN: INEVITABLE VOL. 4 — IVX. Contains material originally published in magazine form as ALL-NEW X-MEN #17-19 and ANNUAL #1, and X-MEN PRIME #1. First printing 2017. ISBN# 978-1-302-90523-1. Published by MARVEL WORLDWIDE, INC., a subsidiary of MARVEL ENTERTAINMENT, LLC. OFFICE OF PUBLICATION: 135 West 50th Street, New York, NY 10020. Copyright © 2017 MARVEL No similarity between any of the names, characters, persons, and/or institutions in this magazine with those of any living or dead person or institution is intended, and any such similarity which may exist is purely coincidental. **Printed in Canada.** DAN BUCKLEY, President, Marvel Entertainment; JOE QUESADA, Chief Creative Officer; TOM BREVOORT, SVP of Publishing; DAVID BOGART, SVP of Business Affairs & Operations, Publishing & Partnership; C.B. CEBULSKI, VP of Brand Management & Development, Asia; DAVID GABRIEL, SVP of Sales & Marketing, Publishing; JEFF YOUNGQUIST, VP of Production & Special Projects; DAN CARR, Executive Director of Publishing Technology; ALEX MORALES, Director of Publishing Operations; SUSAN CRESPI, Production Manager; STAN LEE, Chairman Emeritus. For information regarding advertising in Marvel Comics or on Marvel.com, please contact Vit DeBellis, Integrated Sales Manager, at vdebellis@marvel.com. For Marvel subscription inquiries, please call 888-511-5480. **Manufactured between 6/30/2017 and 8/1/2017 by SOLISCO PRINTERS, SCOTT, QC, CANADA.**

10 9 8 7 6 5 4 3 2 1

ALL-NEW X-MEN IVX

DENNIS HOPELESS
WRITER

MARK BAGLEY & PACO DIAZ (#19)
PENCILERS

**ANDREW HENNESSY
& PACO DIAZ** (#19)
INKERS

NOLAN WOODARD
COLORIST

VC's CORY PETIT
LETTERER

MARK BAGLEY, ANDREW HENNESSY & NOLAN WOODARD
COVER ART

+

ANNUAL #1

IDIE GOES ON A DATE

SINA GRACE
WRITER

CORY SMITH
ARTIST

ANDRES MOSSA
COLOR ARTIST

VC's CORY PETIT
LETTERER

THE LAST OF US, THE LAST OF X

REX OGLE
WRITER

ANDREA BROCCARDO
ARTIST

RACHELLE ROSENBERG
COLOR ARTIST

VC's CORY PETIT
LETTERER

CORY SMITH & ANDRES MOSSA
COVER ART

X-MEN PRIME #1

**MARC GUGGENHEIM, GREG PAK
& CULLEN BUNN**
WRITERS

**KEN LASHLEY, IBRAIM ROBERSON
& LEONARD KIRK** WITH GUILLERMO ORTEGO
ARTISTS

**MORRY HOLLOWELL,
FRANK D'ARMATA
& MICHAEL GARLAND**
COLORISTS

VC's CORY PETIT
LETTERER

**ARDIAN SYAF, JAY LEISTEN
& LAURA MARTIN**
COVER ART

CHRIS ROBINSON & DANIEL KETCHUM
EDITORS

MARK PANICCIA
X-MEN GROUP EDITOR

X-MEN CREATED BY **STAN LEE** & **JACK KIRBY**

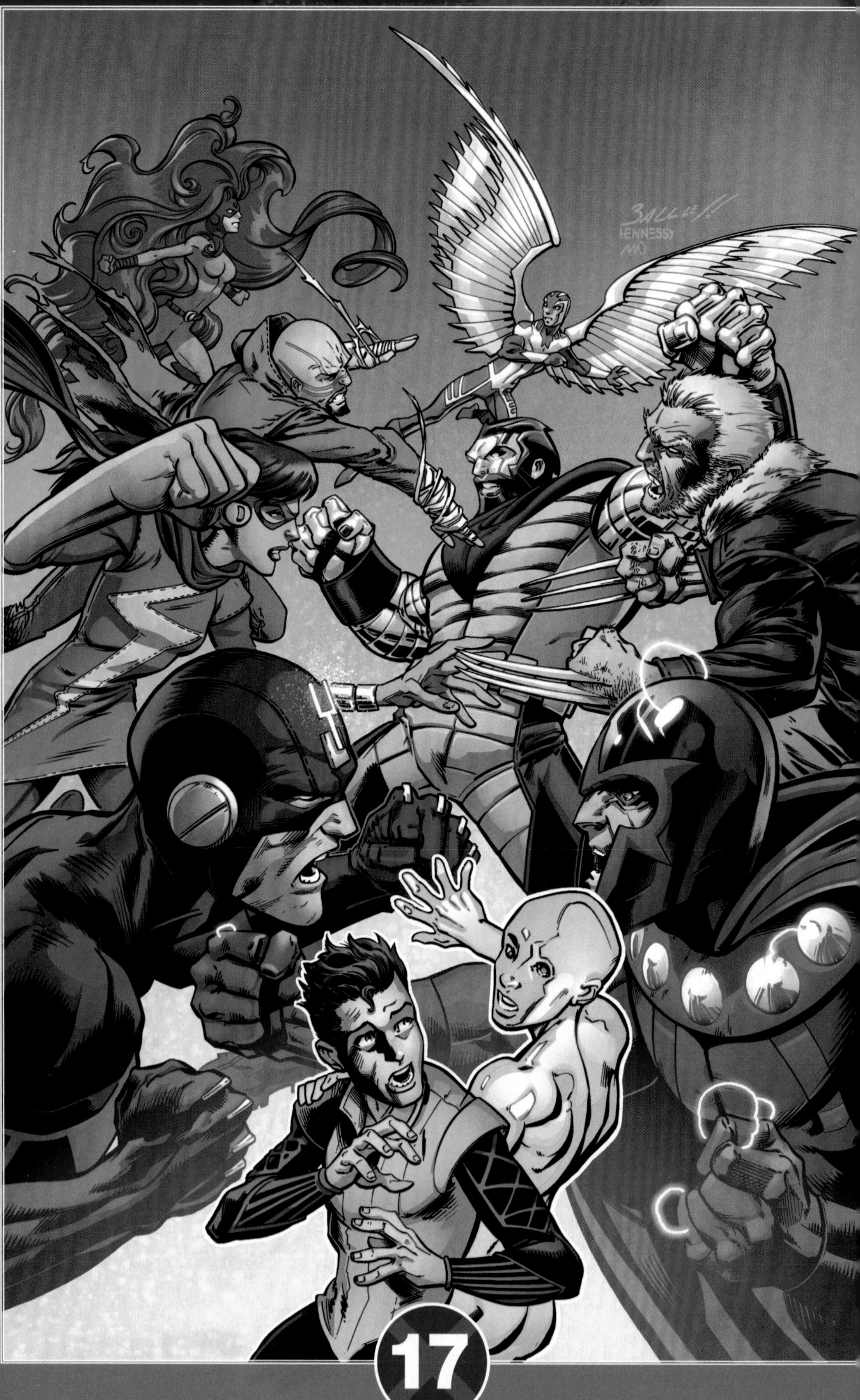
17

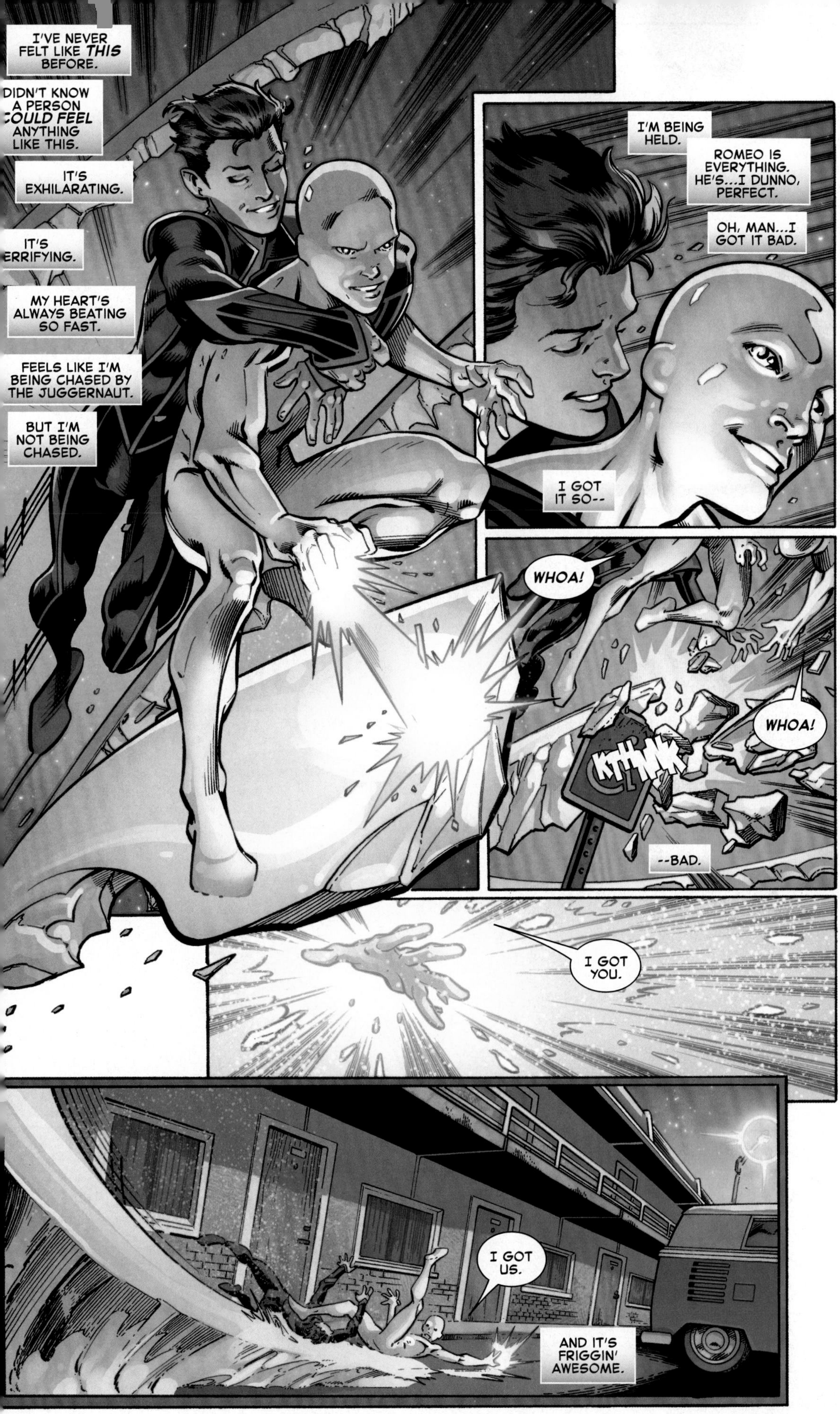
I'VE NEVER FELT LIKE THIS BEFORE.
DIDN'T KNOW A PERSON COULD FEEL ANYTHING LIKE THIS.
IT'S EXHILARATING.
IT'S ERRIFYING.
MY HEART'S ALWAYS BEATING SO FAST.
FEELS LIKE I'M BEING CHASED BY THE JUGGERNAUT.
BUT I'M NOT BEING CHASED.
I'M BEING HELD.
ROMEO IS EVERYTHING. HE'S...I DUNNO, PERFECT.
OH, MAN...I GOT IT BAD.
I GOT IT SO--
WHOA!
WHOA!
KTHNK
--BAD.
I GOT YOU.
I GOT US.
AND IT'S FRIGGIN' AWESOME.

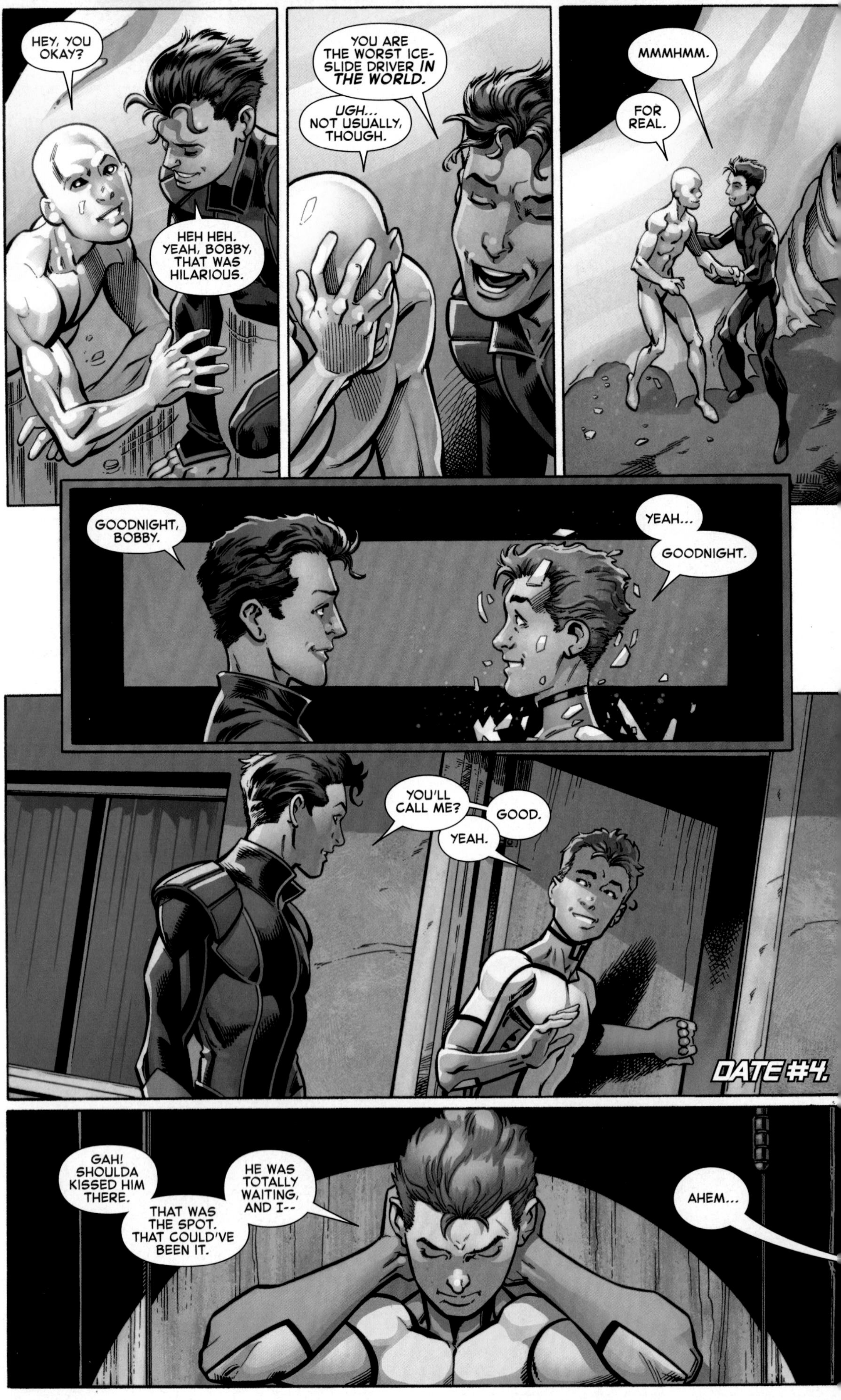
HEY, YOU OKAY?
HEH HEH. YEAH, BOBBY, THAT WAS HILARIOUS.
YOU ARE THE WORST ICE-SLIDE DRIVER IN THE WORLD.
UGH... NOT USUALLY, THOUGH.
MMMHMM.
FOR REAL.
GOODNIGHT, BOBBY.
YEAH...
GOODNIGHT.
YOU'LL CALL ME?
YEAH.
GOOD.
DATE #4.
GAH! SHOULDA KISSED HIM THERE.
THAT WAS THE SPOT. THAT COULD'VE BEEN IT.
HE WAS TOTALLY WAITING, AND I--
AHEM...

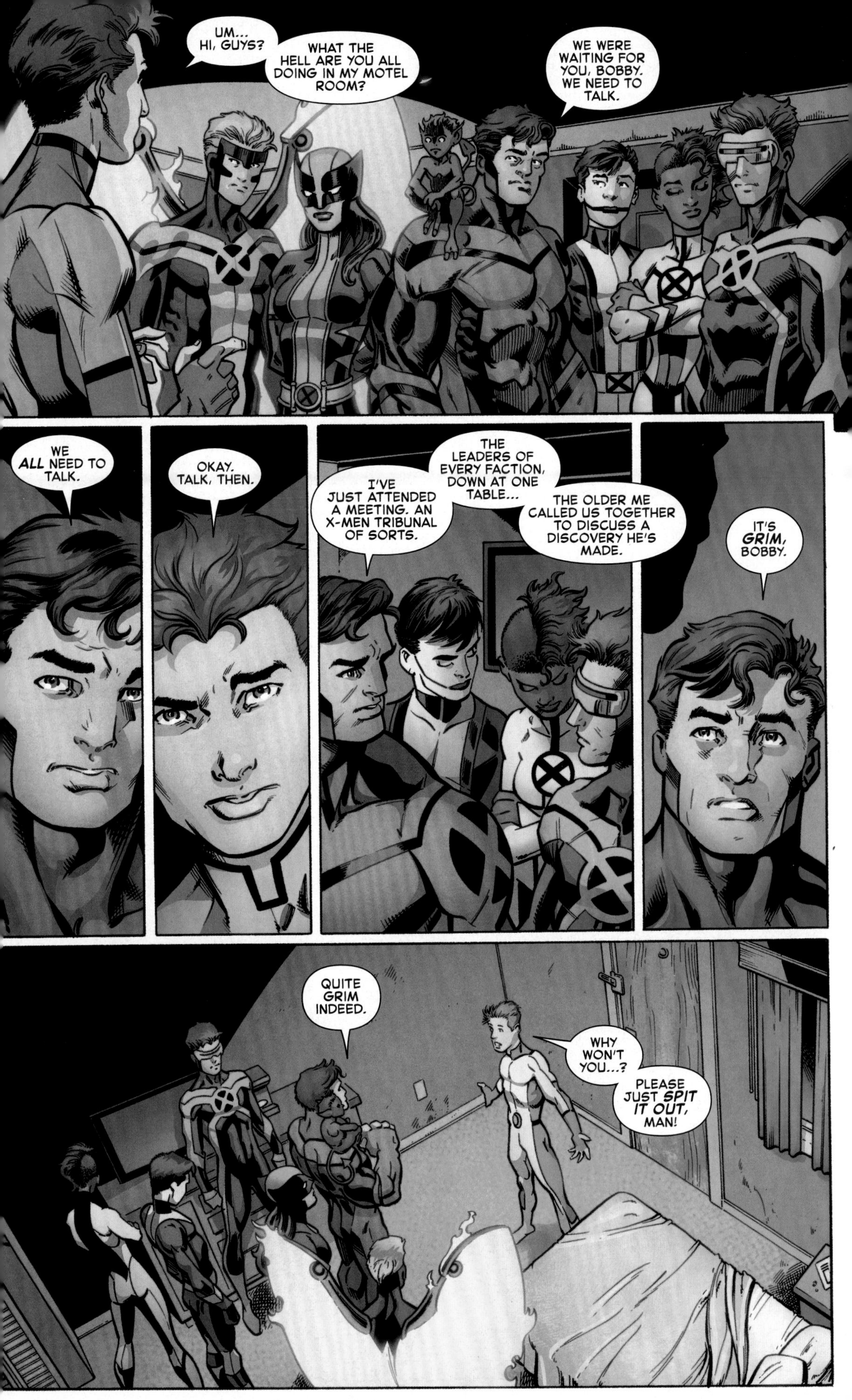
UM... HI, GUYS?
WHAT THE HELL ARE YOU ALL DOING IN MY MOTEL ROOM?
WE WERE WAITING FOR YOU, BOBBY. WE NEED TO TALK.
WE ALL NEED TO TALK.
OKAY. TALK, THEN.
I'VE JUST ATTENDED A MEETING. AN X-MEN TRIBUNAL OF SORTS.
THE LEADERS OF EVERY FACTION, DOWN AT ONE TABLE...
THE OLDER ME CALLED US TOGETHER TO DISCUSS A DISCOVERY HE'S MADE.
IT'S GRIM, BOBBY.
QUITE GRIM INDEED.
WHY WON'T YOU...?
PLEASE JUST SPIT IT OUT, MAN!

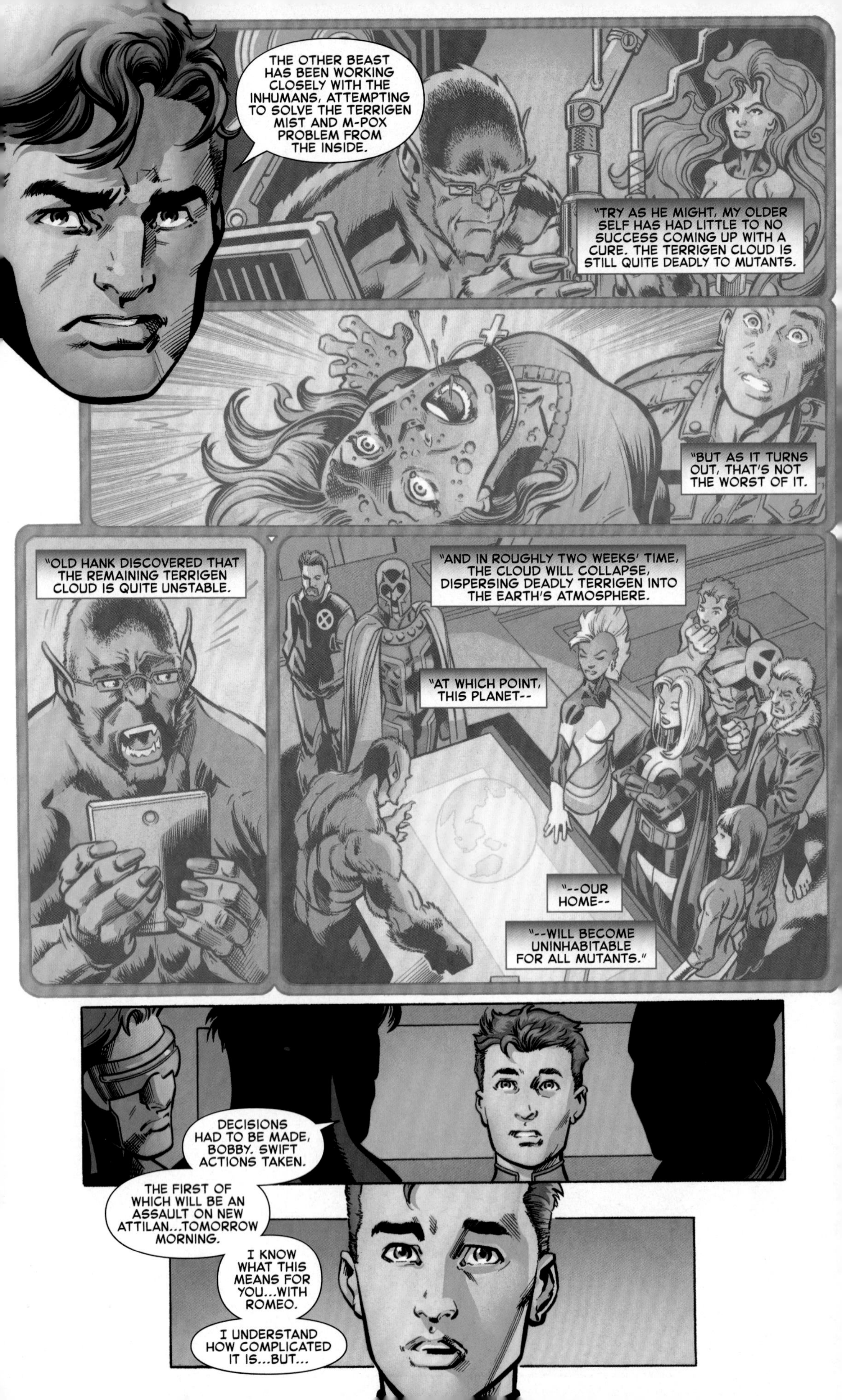

THE OTHER BEAST HAS BEEN WORKING CLOSELY WITH THE INHUMANS, ATTEMPTING TO SOLVE THE TERRIGEN MIST AND M-POX PROBLEM FROM THE INSIDE.
"TRY AS HE MIGHT, MY OLDER SELF HAS HAD LITTLE TO NO SUCCESS COMING UP WITH A CURE. THE TERRIGEN CLOUD IS STILL QUITE DEADLY TO MUTANTS.
"BUT AS IT TURNS OUT, THAT'S NOT THE WORST OF IT.
"OLD HANK DISCOVERED THAT THE REMAINING TERRIGEN CLOUD IS QUITE UNSTABLE.
"AND IN ROUGHLY TWO WEEKS' TIME, THE CLOUD WILL COLLAPSE, DISPERSING DEADLY TERRIGEN INTO THE EARTH'S ATMOSPHERE.
"AT WHICH POINT, THIS PLANET--
"--OUR HOME--
"--WILL BECOME UNINHABITABLE FOR ALL MUTANTS."
DECISIONS HAD TO BE MADE, BOBBY. SWIFT ACTIONS TAKEN.
THE FIRST OF WHICH WILL BE AN ASSAULT ON NEW ATTILAN...TOMORROW MORNING.
I KNOW WHAT THIS MEANS FOR YOU...WITH ROMEO.
I UNDERSTAND HOW COMPLICATED IT IS...BUT...

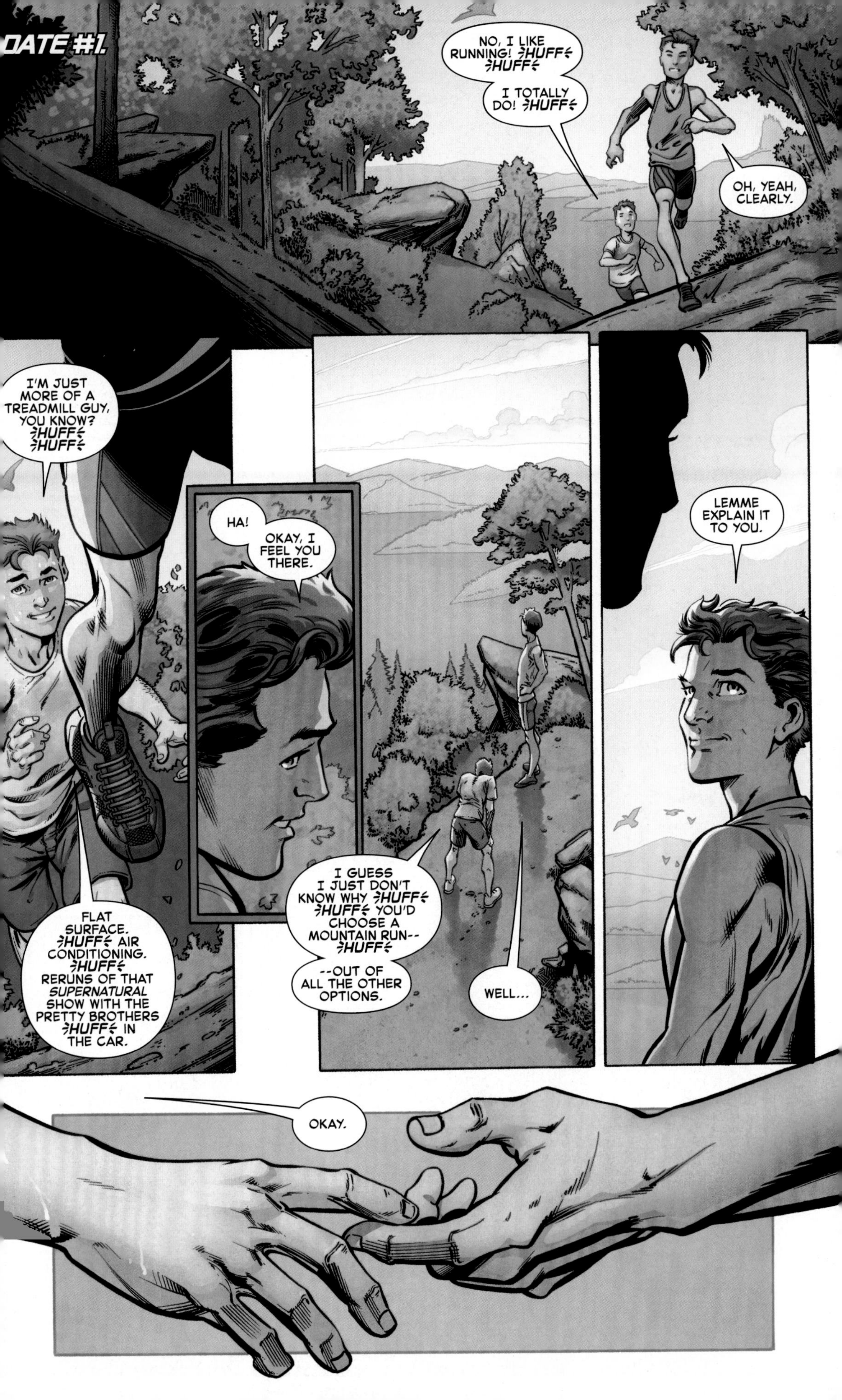
DATE #1.
NO, I LIKE RUNNING! HUFF HUFF
I TOTALLY DO! HUFF
OH, YEAH, CLEARLY.
I'M JUST MORE OF A TREADMILL GUY, YOU KNOW? HUFF HUFF
FLAT SURFACE. HUFF AIR CONDITIONING. HUFF RERUNS OF THAT SUPERNATURAL SHOW WITH THE PRETTY BROTHERS HUFF IN THE CAR.
HA!
OKAY, I FEEL YOU THERE.
I GUESS I JUST DON'T KNOW WHY HUFF HUFF YOU'D CHOOSE A MOUNTAIN RUN-- HUFF
--OUT OF ALL THE OTHER OPTIONS.
WELL...
LEMME EXPLAIN IT TO YOU.
OKAY.

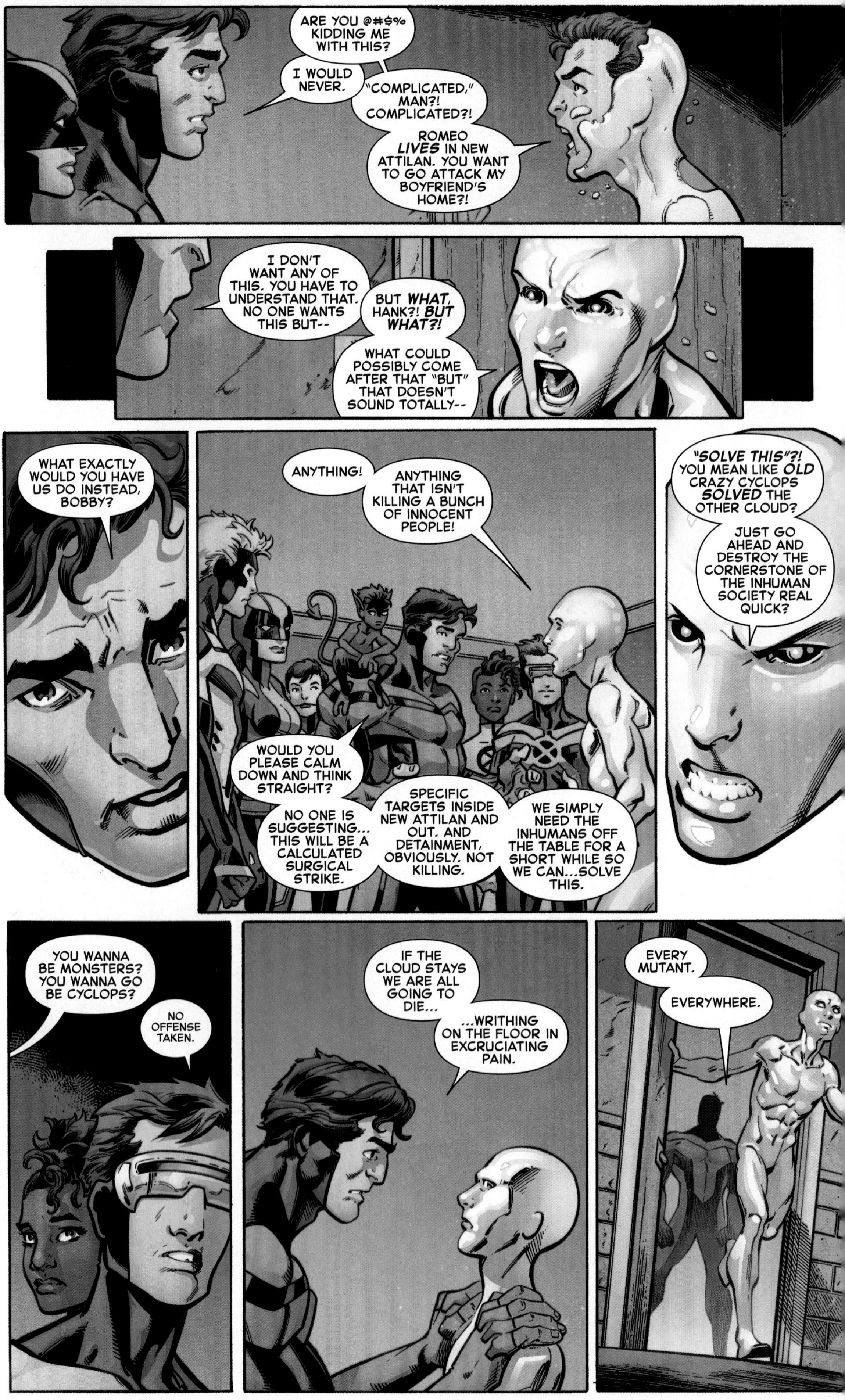

ARE YOU @#$% KIDDING ME WITH THIS?
I WOULD NEVER.
"COMPLICATED," MAN?! COMPLICATED?!
ROMEO LIVES IN NEW ATTILAN. YOU WANT TO GO ATTACK MY BOYFRIEND'S HOME?!
I DON'T WANT ANY OF THIS. YOU HAVE TO UNDERSTAND THAT. NO ONE WANTS THIS BUT--
BUT WHAT, HANK?! BUT WHAT?!
WHAT COULD POSSIBLY COME AFTER THAT "BUT" THAT DOESN'T SOUND TOTALLY--
WHAT EXACTLY WOULD YOU HAVE US DO INSTEAD, BOBBY?
ANYTHING!
ANYTHING THAT ISN'T KILLING A BUNCH OF INNOCENT PEOPLE!
WOULD YOU PLEASE CALM DOWN AND THINK STRAIGHT?
NO ONE IS SUGGESTING... THIS WILL BE A CALCULATED SURGICAL STRIKE.
SPECIFIC TARGETS INSIDE NEW ATTILAN AND OUT. AND DETAINMENT, OBVIOUSLY. NOT KILLING.
WE SIMPLY NEED THE INHUMANS OFF THE TABLE FOR A SHORT WHILE SO WE CAN...SOLVE THIS.
"SOLVE THIS"?! YOU MEAN LIKE OLD CRAZY CYCLOPS SOLVED THE OTHER CLOUD?
JUST GO AHEAD AND DESTROY THE CORNERSTONE OF THE INHUMAN SOCIETY REAL QUICK?
YOU WANNA BE MONSTERS? YOU WANNA GO BE CYCLOPS?
NO OFFENSE TAKEN.
IF THE CLOUD STAYS WE ARE ALL GOING TO DIE...
...WRITHING ON THE FLOOR IN EXCRUCIATING PAIN.
EVERY MUTANT.
EVERYWHERE.

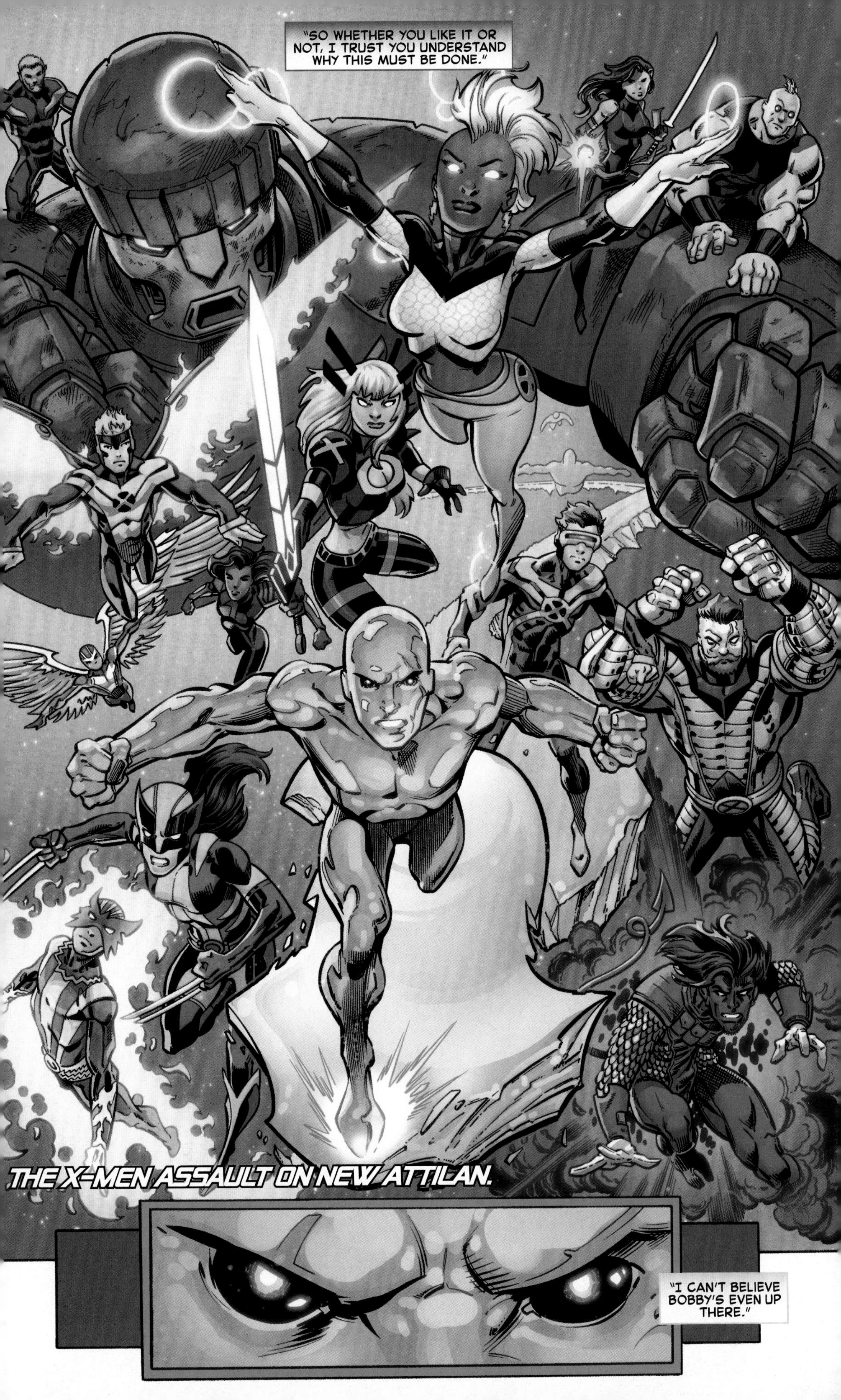

"SO WHETHER YOU LIKE IT OR NOT, I TRUST YOU UNDERSTAND WHY THIS MUST BE DONE."
THE X-MEN ASSAULT ON NEW ATTILAN.
"I CAN'T BELIEVE BOBBY'S EVEN UP THERE."

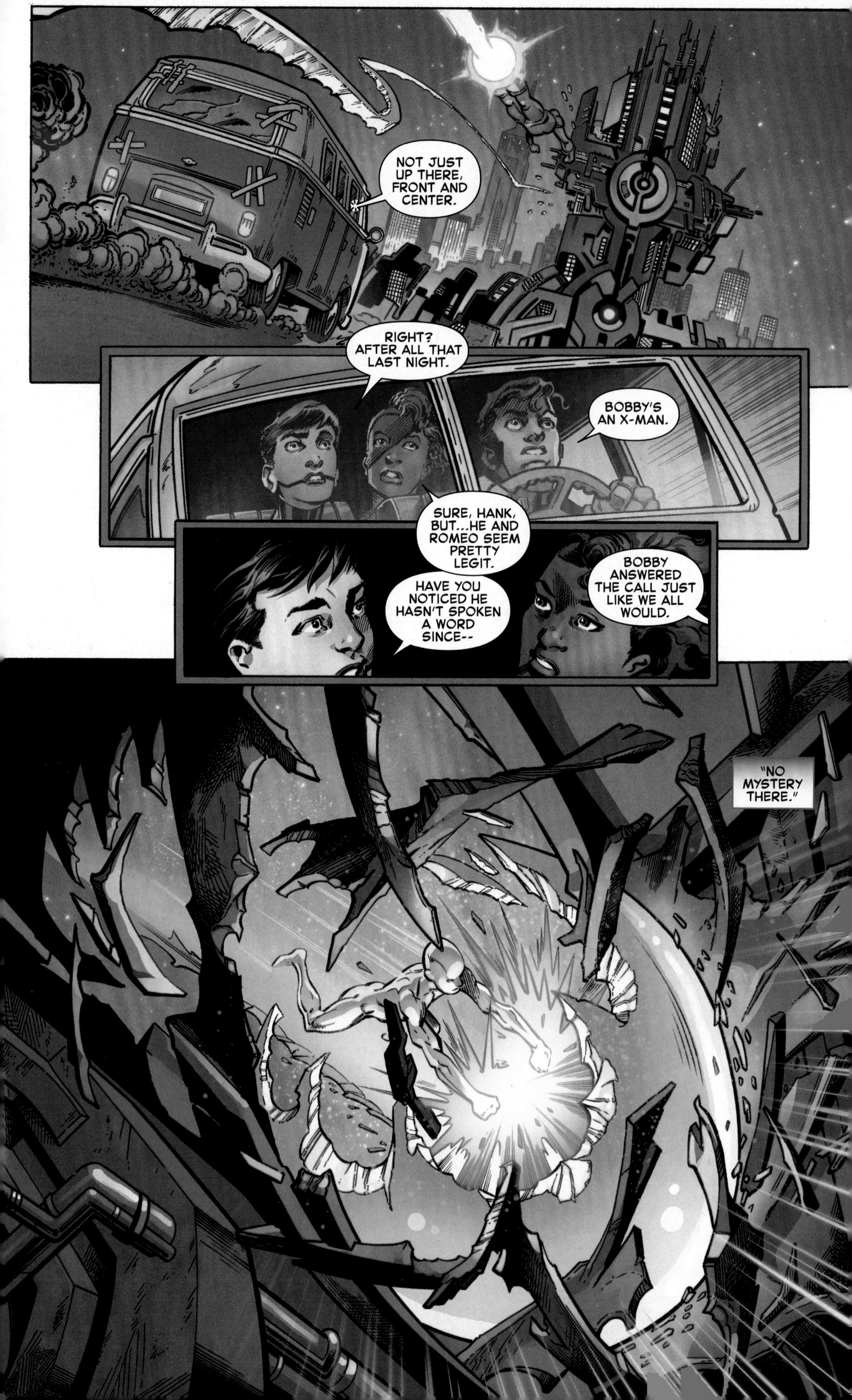
NOT JUST UP THERE, FRONT AND CENTER.
RIGHT? AFTER ALL THAT LAST NIGHT.
BOBBY'S AN X-MAN.
SURE, HANK, BUT...HE AND ROMEO SEEM PRETTY LEGIT.
BOBBY ANSWERED THE CALL JUST LIKE WE ALL WOULD.
HAVE YOU NOTICED HE HASN'T SPOKEN A WORD SINCE--
"NO MYSTERY THERE."

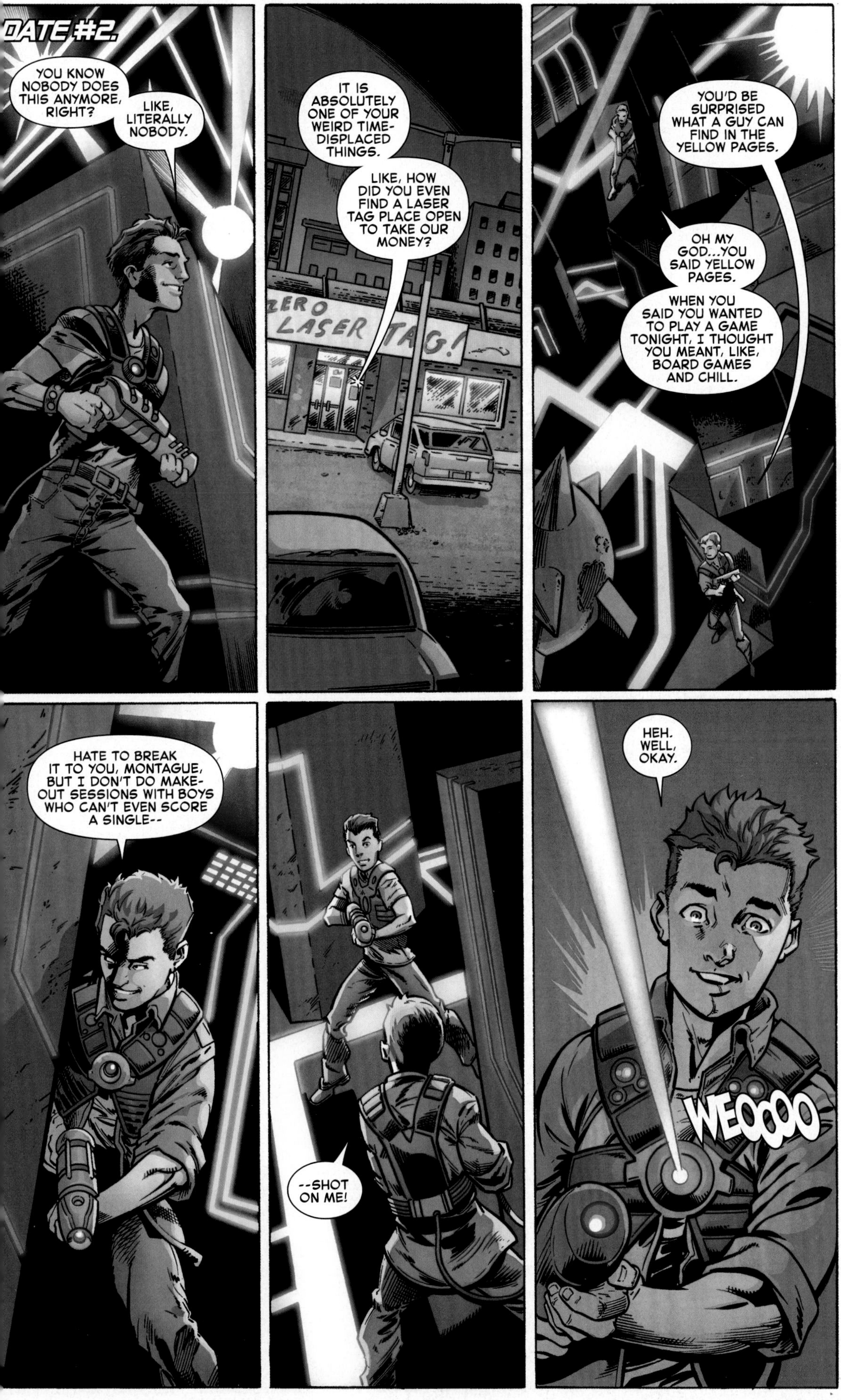
DATE #2.
YOU KNOW NOBODY DOES THIS ANYMORE, RIGHT?
LIKE, LITERALLY NOBODY.
IT IS ABSOLUTELY ONE OF YOUR WEIRD TIME-DISPLACED THINGS.
LIKE, HOW DID YOU EVEN FIND A LASER TAG PLACE OPEN TO TAKE OUR MONEY?
ZERO LASER TAG!
YOU'D BE SURPRISED WHAT A GUY CAN FIND IN THE YELLOW PAGES.
OH MY GOD...YOU SAID YELLOW PAGES.
WHEN YOU SAID YOU WANTED TO PLAY A GAME TONIGHT, I THOUGHT YOU MEANT, LIKE, BOARD GAMES AND CHILL.
HATE TO BREAK IT TO YOU, MONTAGUE, BUT I DON'T DO MAKE-OUT SESSIONS WITH BOYS WHO CAN'T EVEN SCORE A SINGLE--
--SHOT ON ME!
HEH. WELL, OKAY.
WEOOOO

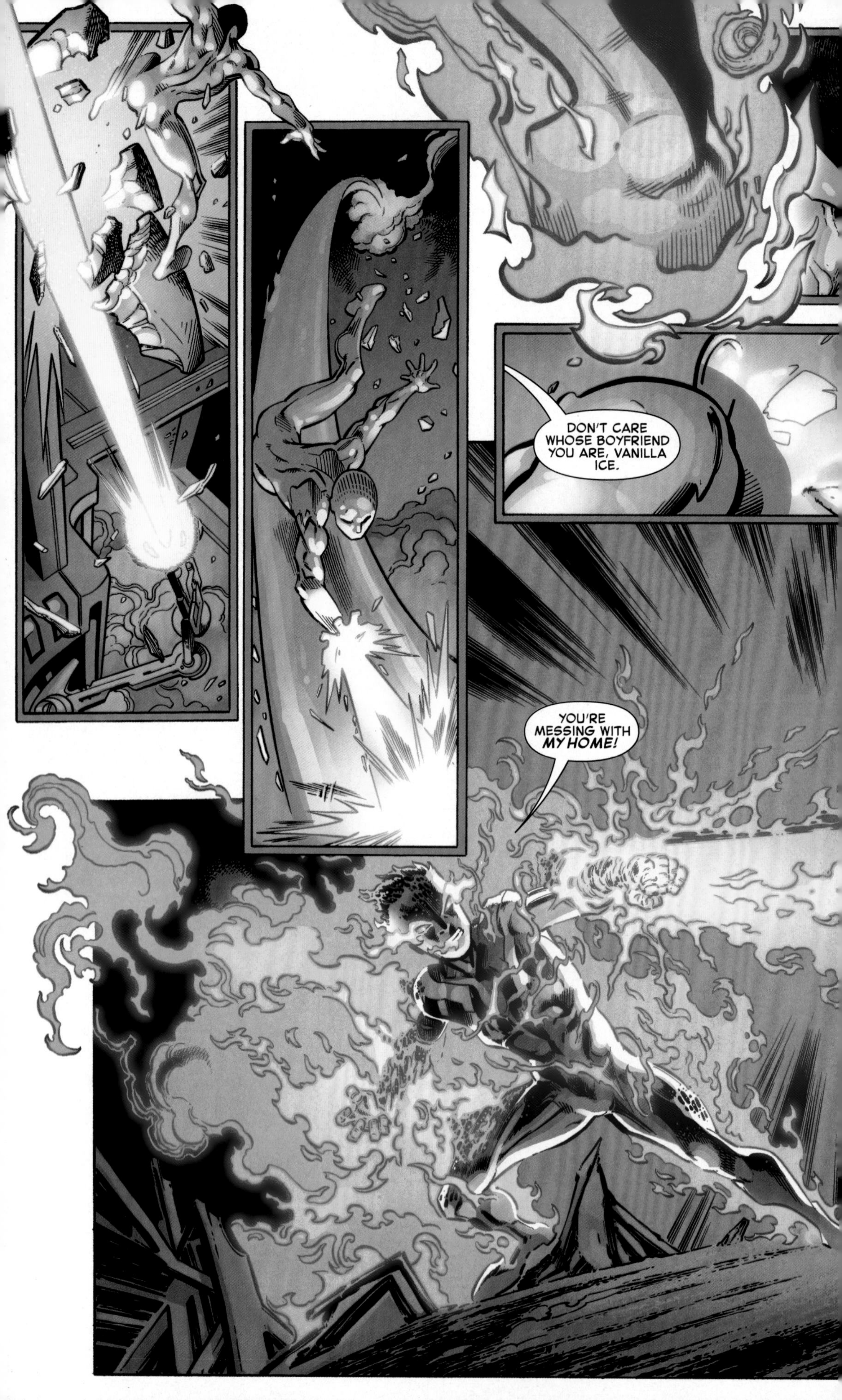
DON'T CARE WHOSE BOYFRIEND YOU ARE, VANILLA ICE.
YOU'RE MESSING WITH MY HOME!

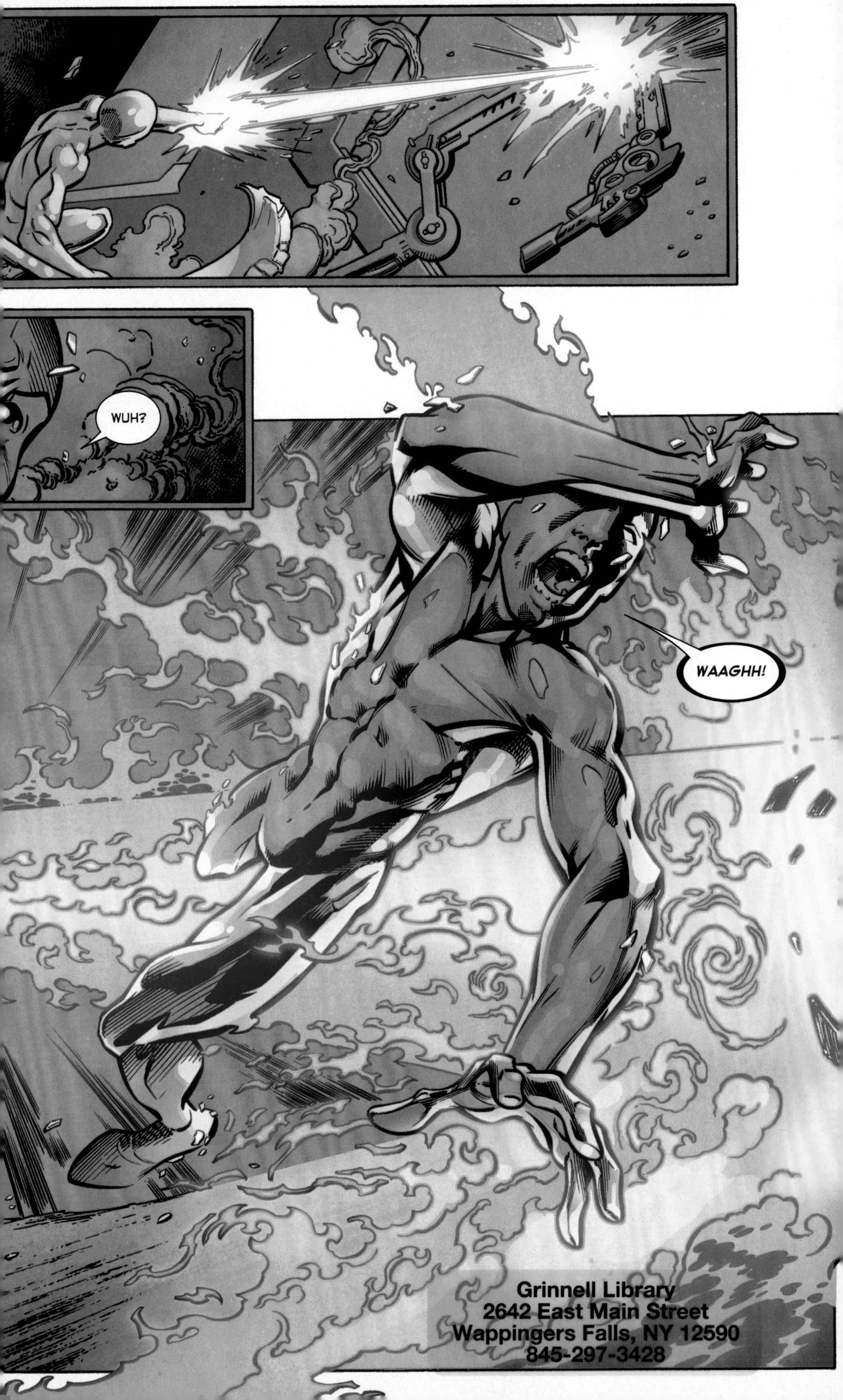
WUH?
WAAGHH!

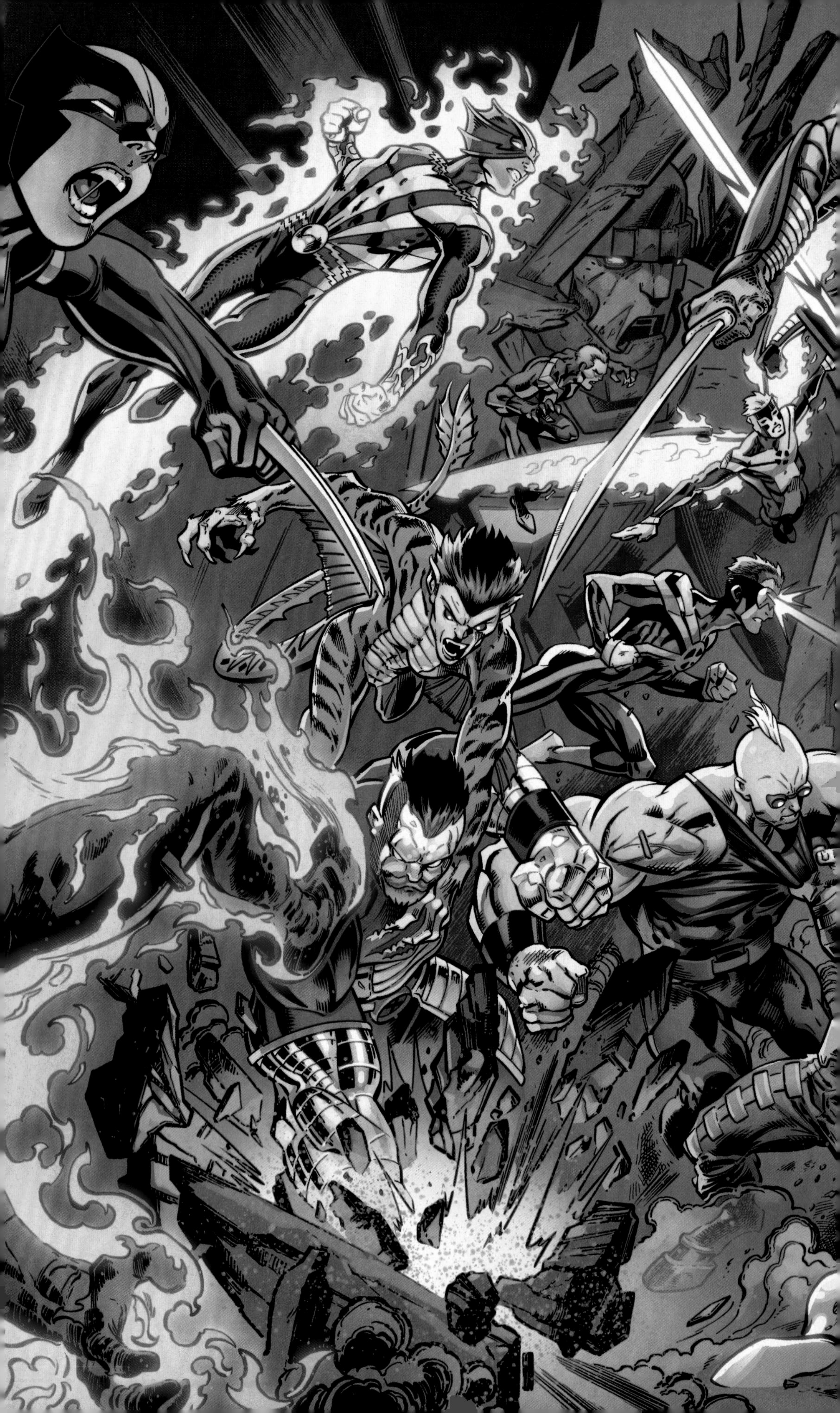

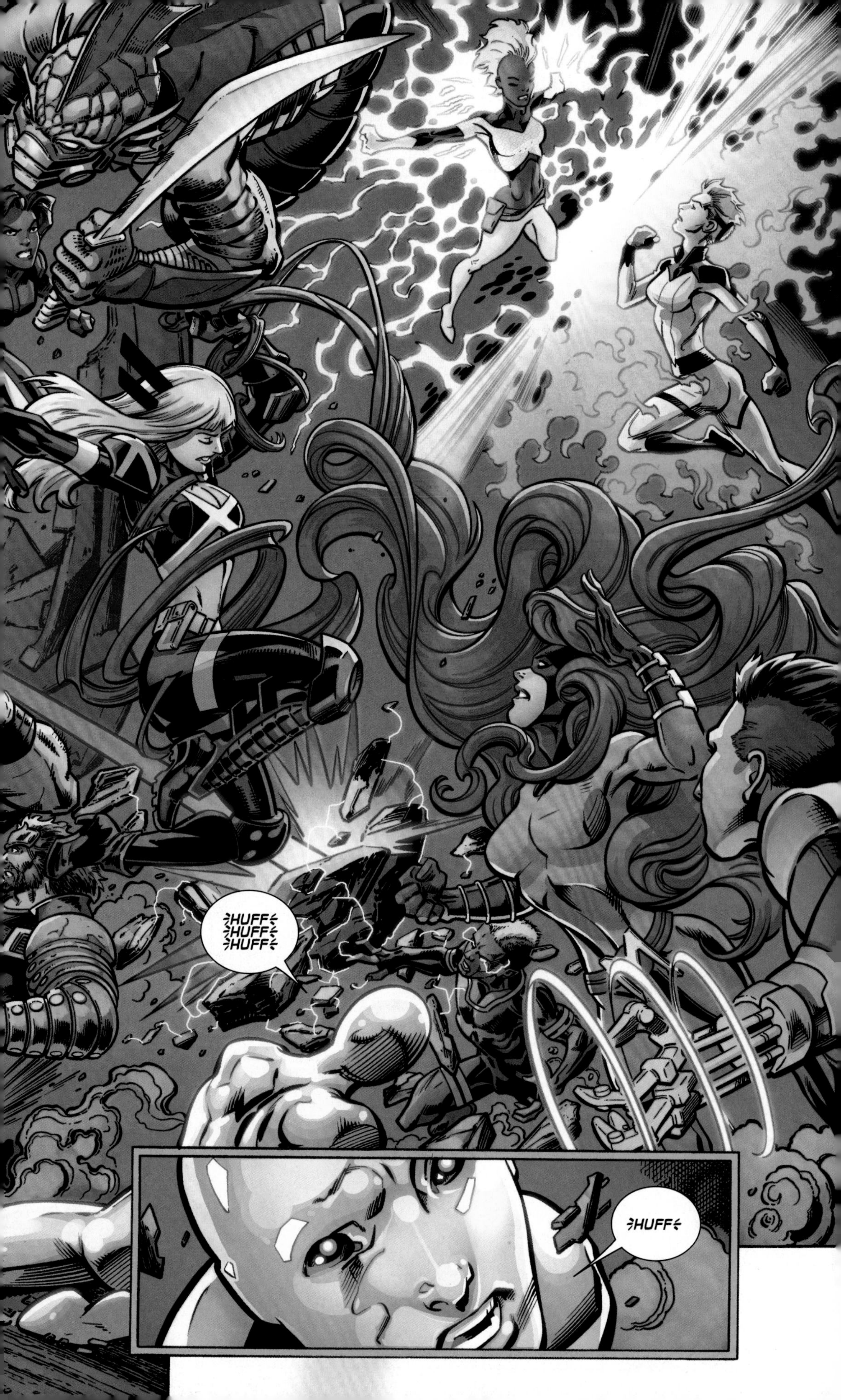
HUFF HUFF HUFF
HUFF

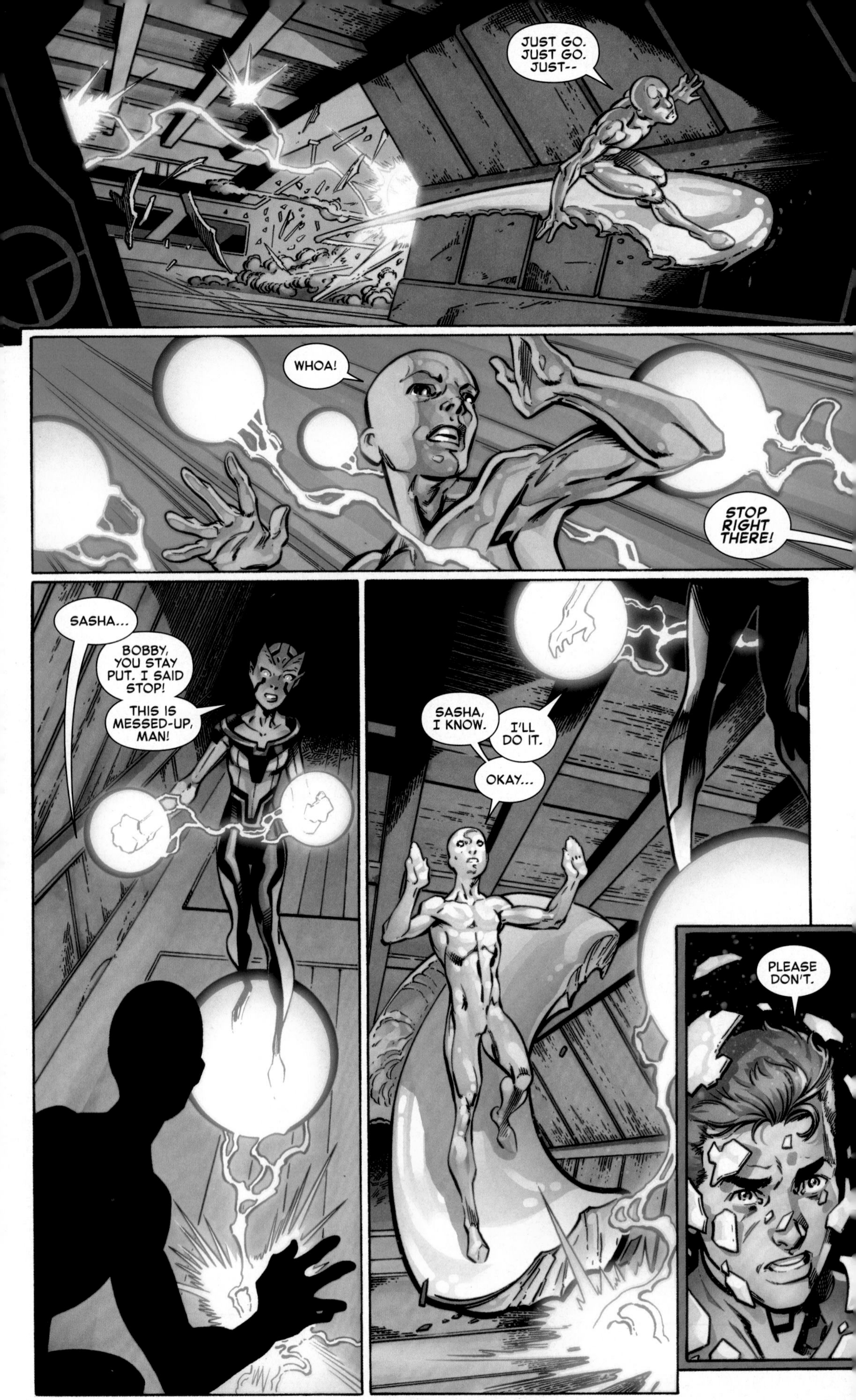
JUST GO. JUST GO. JUST--
WHOA!
STOP RIGHT THERE!
SASHA...
BOBBY, YOU STAY PUT. I SAID STOP!
THIS IS MESSED-UP, MAN!
SASHA, I KNOW.
I'LL DO IT.
OKAY...
PLEASE DON'T.

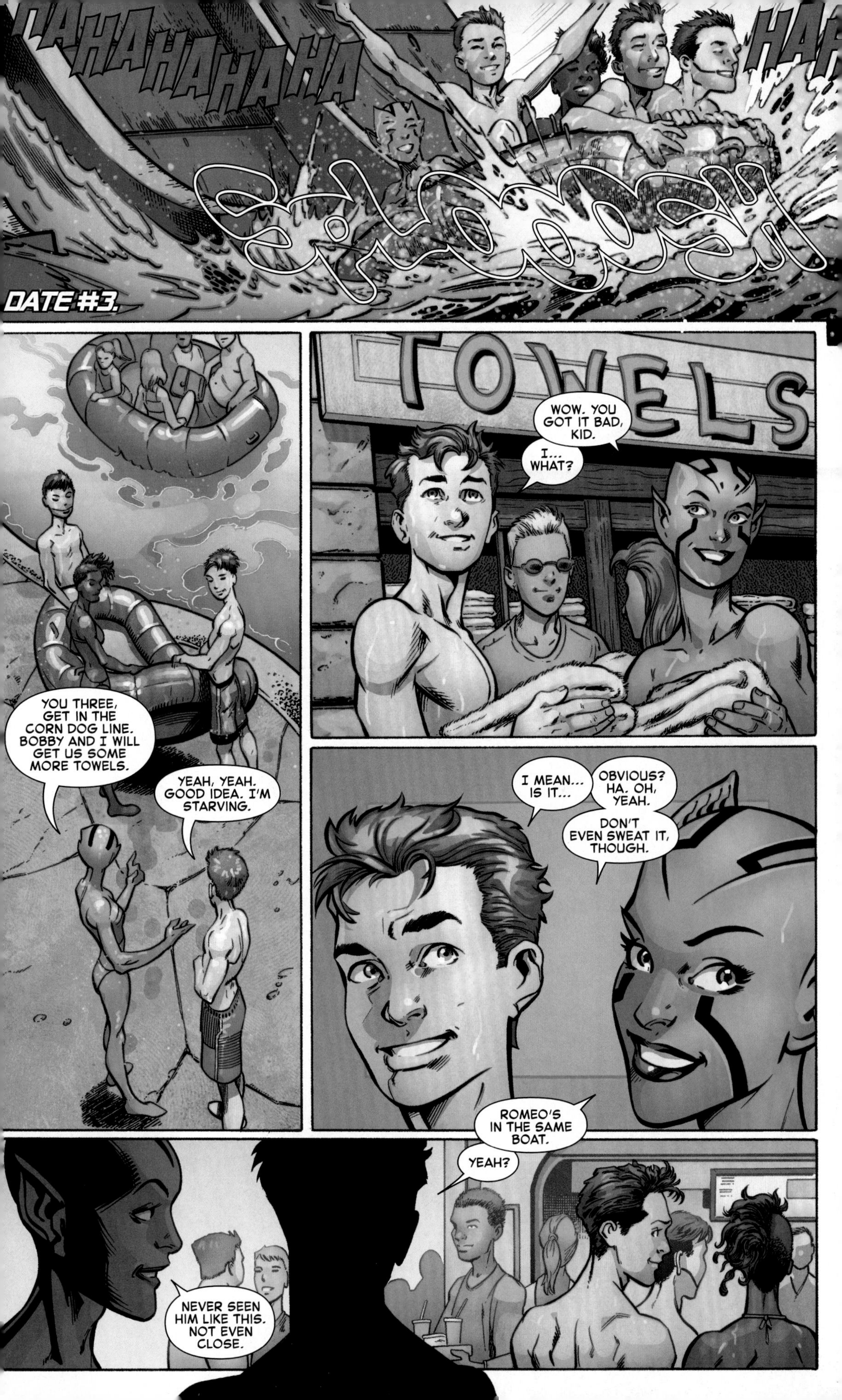
HAHAHAHAHA
HAH
SPLOOOSH
DATE #3.
YOU THREE, GET IN THE CORN DOG LINE. BOBBY AND I WILL GET US SOME MORE TOWELS.
YEAH, YEAH. GOOD IDEA. I'M STARVING.
TOWELS
WOW. YOU GOT IT BAD, KID.
I... WHAT?
I MEAN... IS IT...
OBVIOUS? HA. OH, YEAH.
DON'T EVEN SWEAT IT, THOUGH.
ROMEO'S IN THE SAME BOAT.
YEAH?
NEVER SEEN HIM LIKE THIS. NOT EVEN CLOSE.

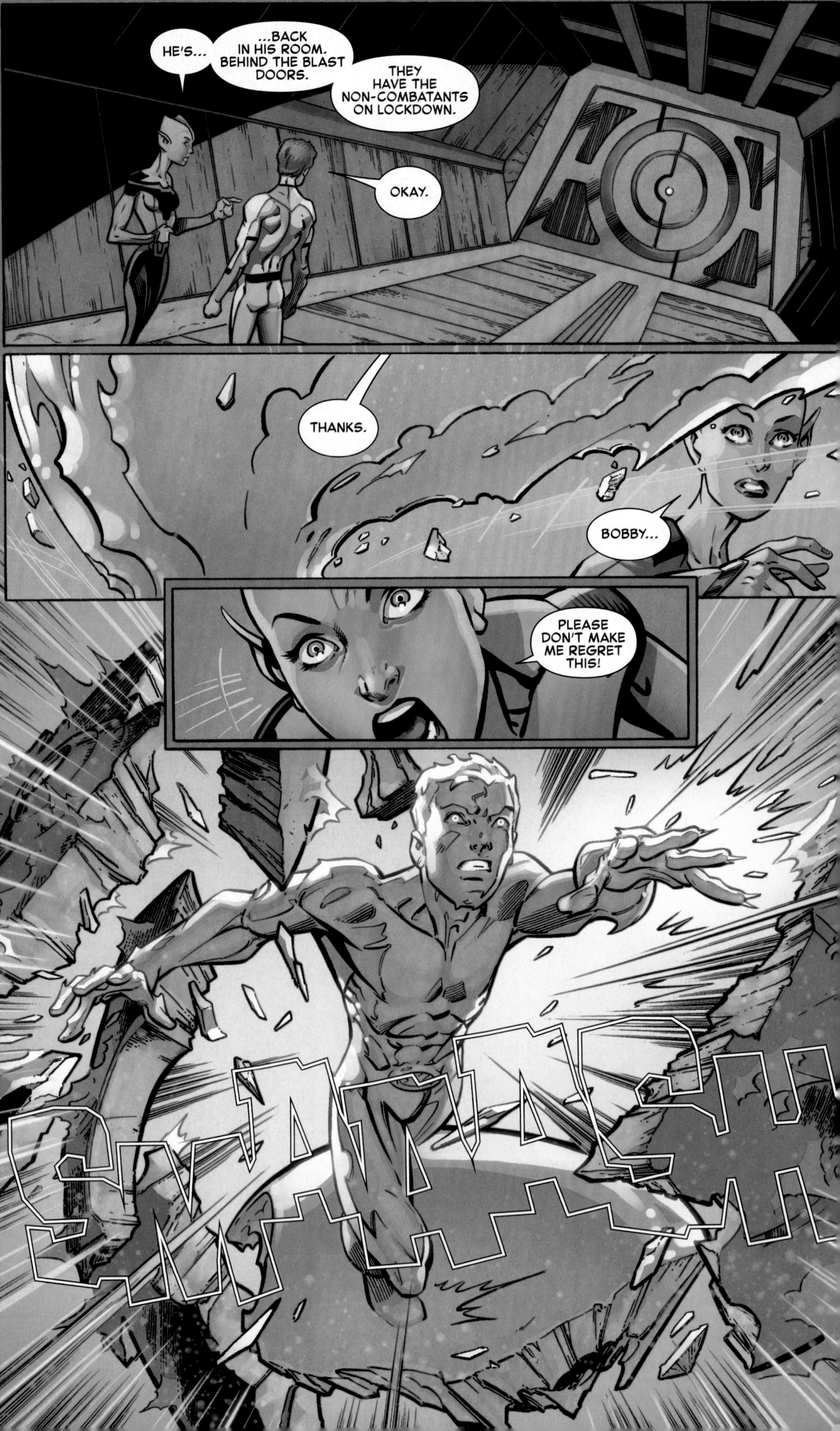

HE'S...
...BACK IN HIS ROOM. BEHIND THE BLAST DOORS.
THEY HAVE THE NON-COMBATANTS ON LOCKDOWN.
OKAY.
THANKS.
BOBBY...
PLEASE DON'T MAKE ME REGRET THIS!

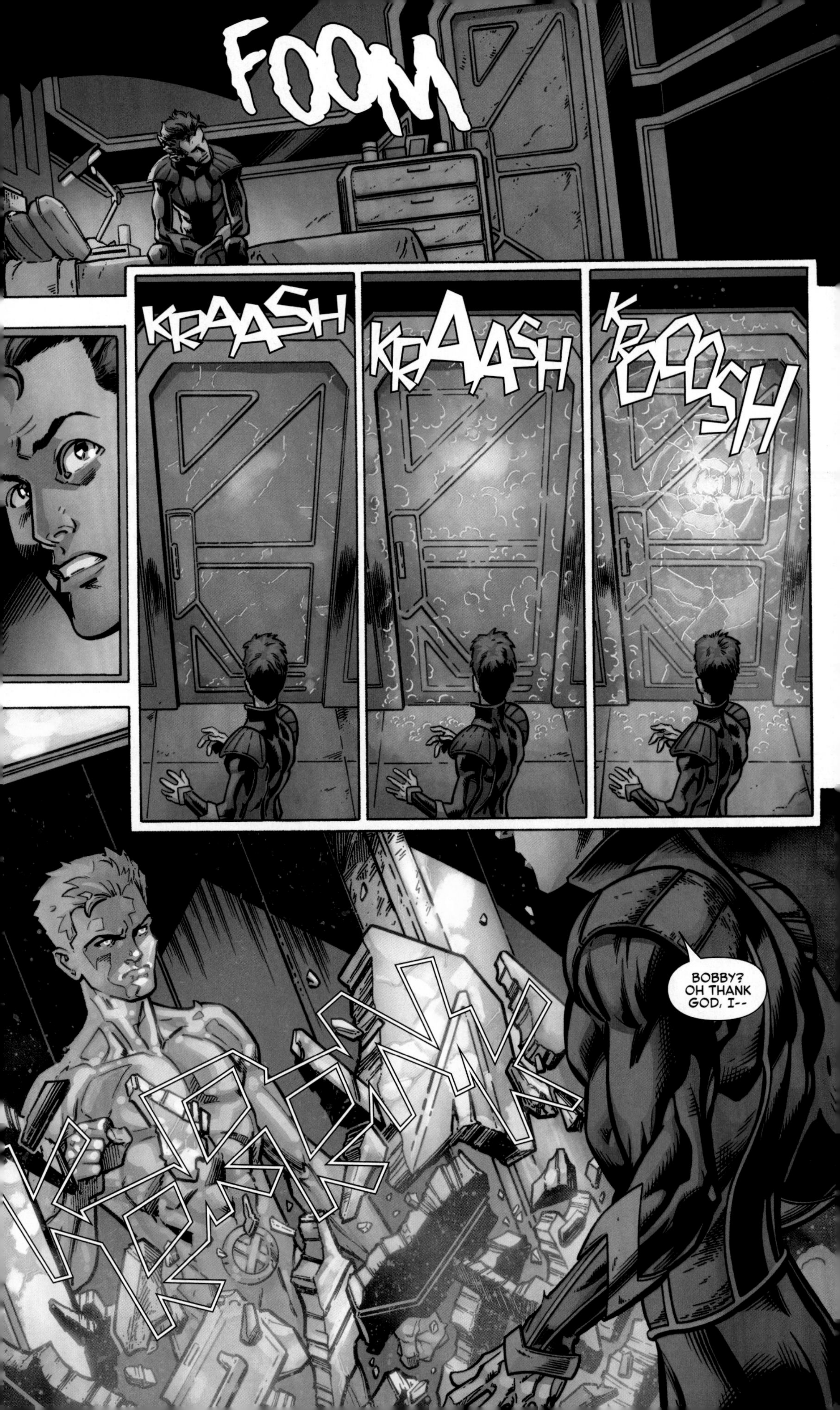
FOOM
KRAASH
KRAAASH
KROOOSH
BOBBY? OH THANK GOD, I--
KRRRAKK

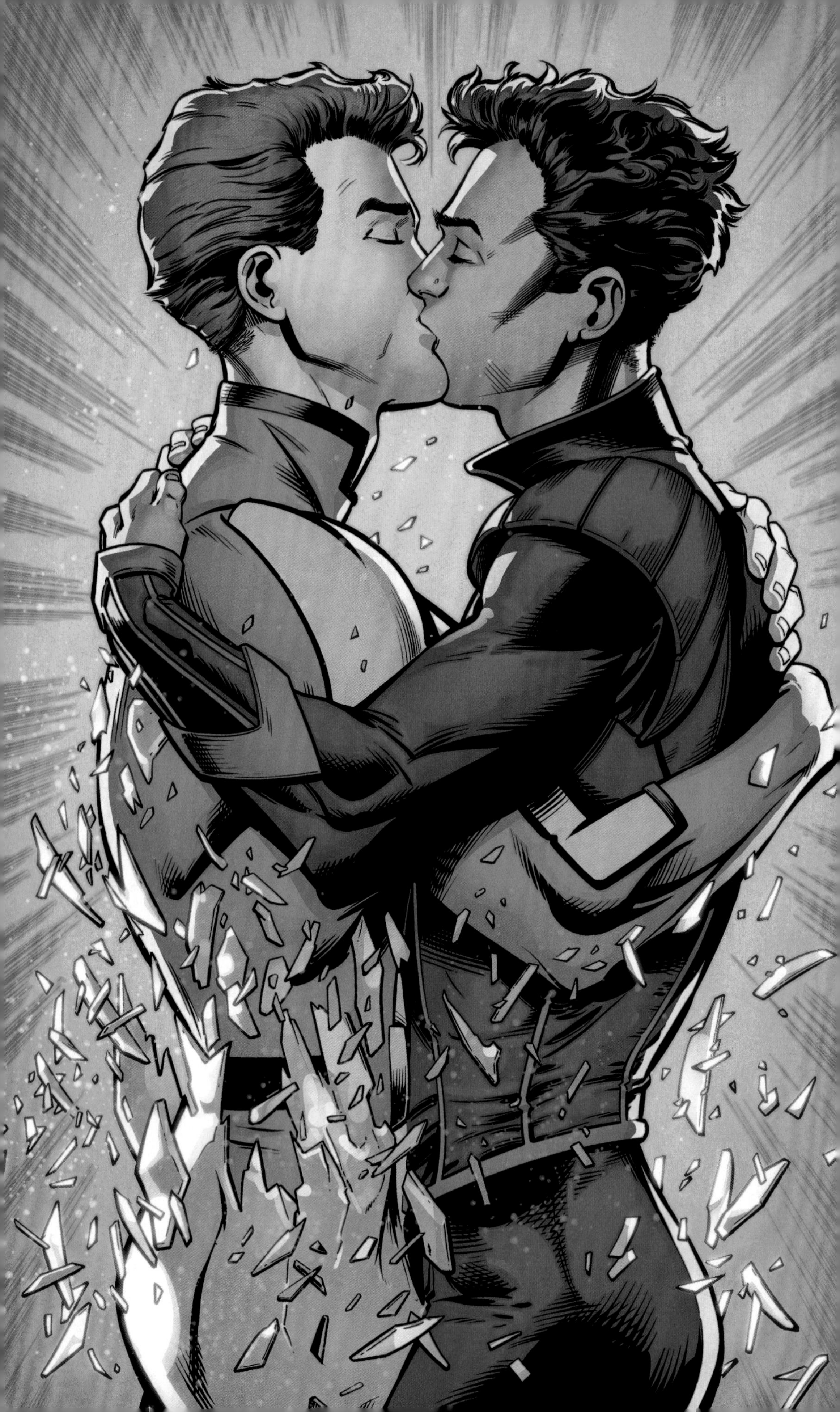

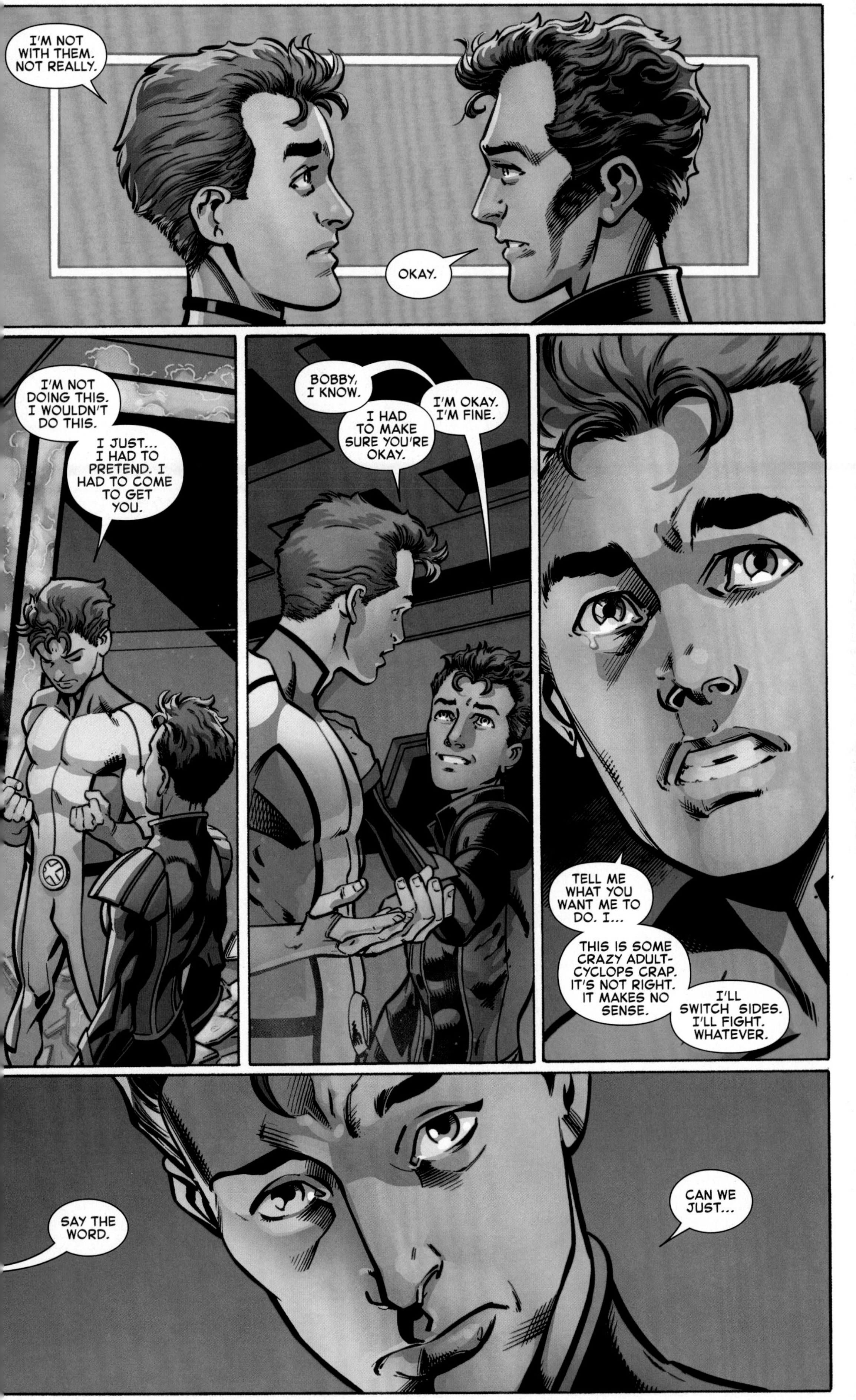
I'M NOT WITH THEM. NOT REALLY.
OKAY.
I'M NOT DOING THIS. I WOULDN'T DO THIS.
I JUST... I HAD TO PRETEND. I HAD TO COME TO GET YOU.
BOBBY, I KNOW.
I HAD TO MAKE SURE YOU'RE OKAY.
I'M OKAY. I'M FINE.
TELL ME WHAT YOU WANT ME TO DO. I...
THIS IS SOME CRAZY ADULT-CYCLOPS CRAP. IT'S NOT RIGHT. IT MAKES NO SENSE.
I'LL SWITCH SIDES. I'LL FIGHT. WHATEVER.
SAY THE WORD.
CAN WE JUST...

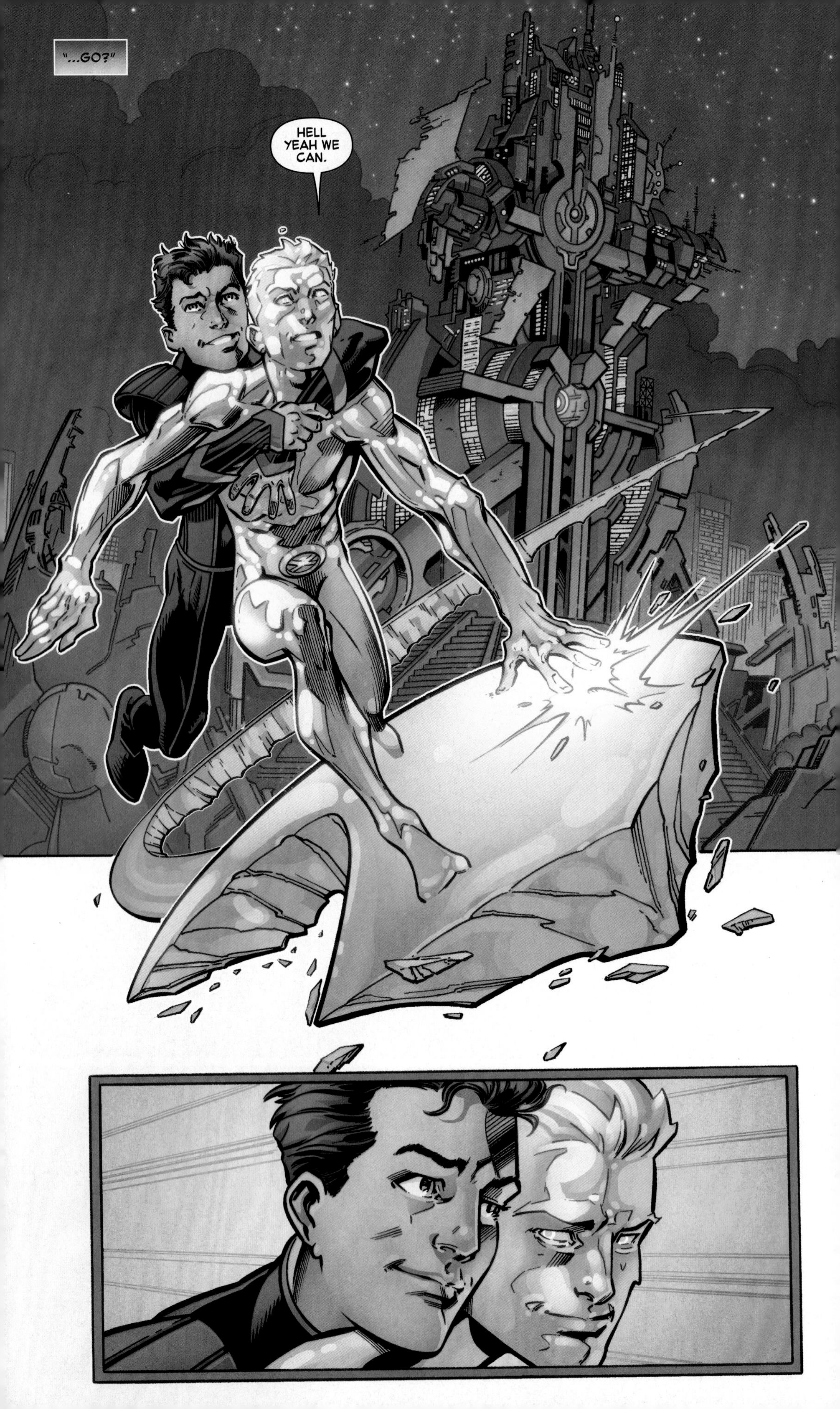
"...GO?"
HELL YEAH WE CAN.

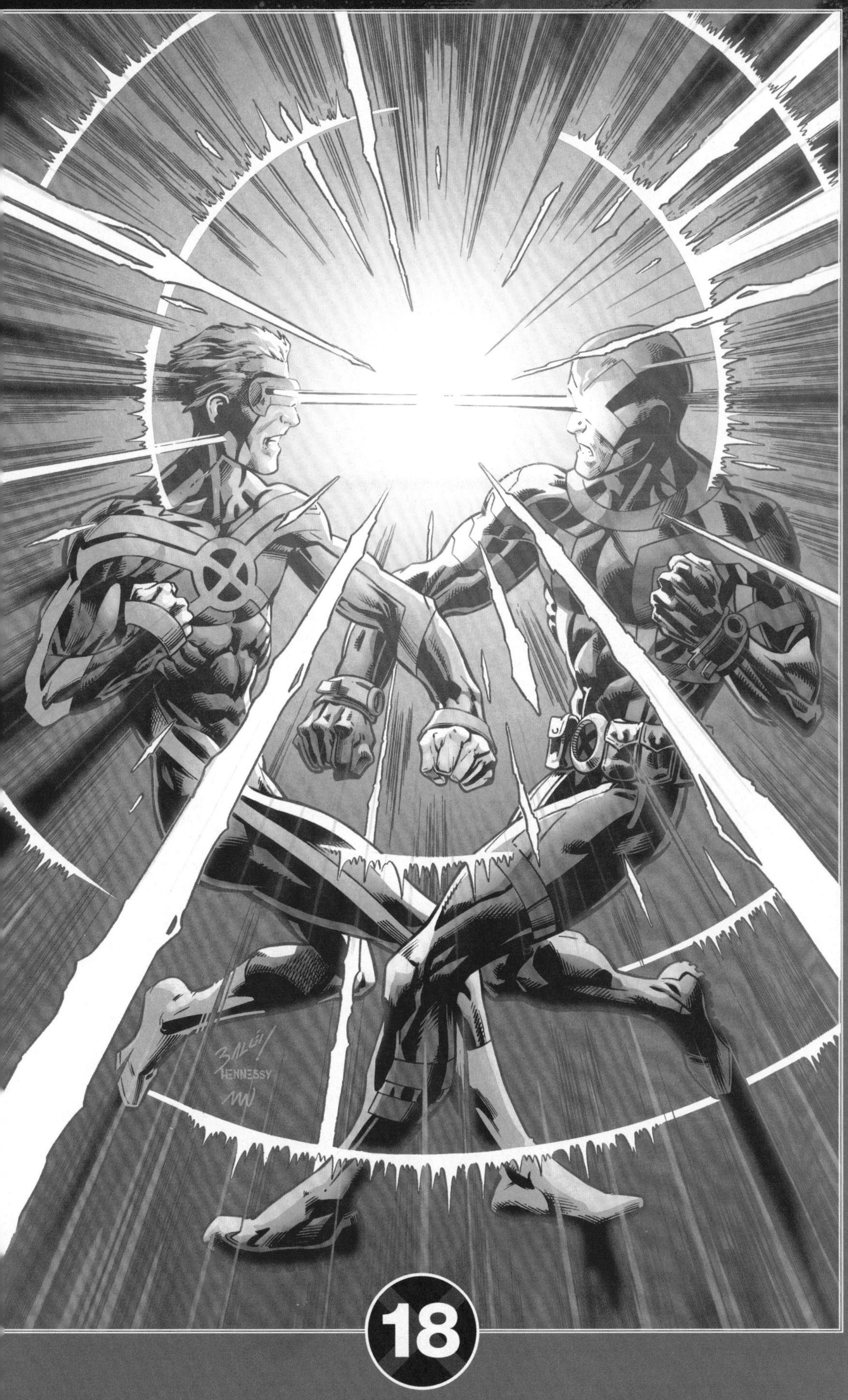
HENNESSY
18

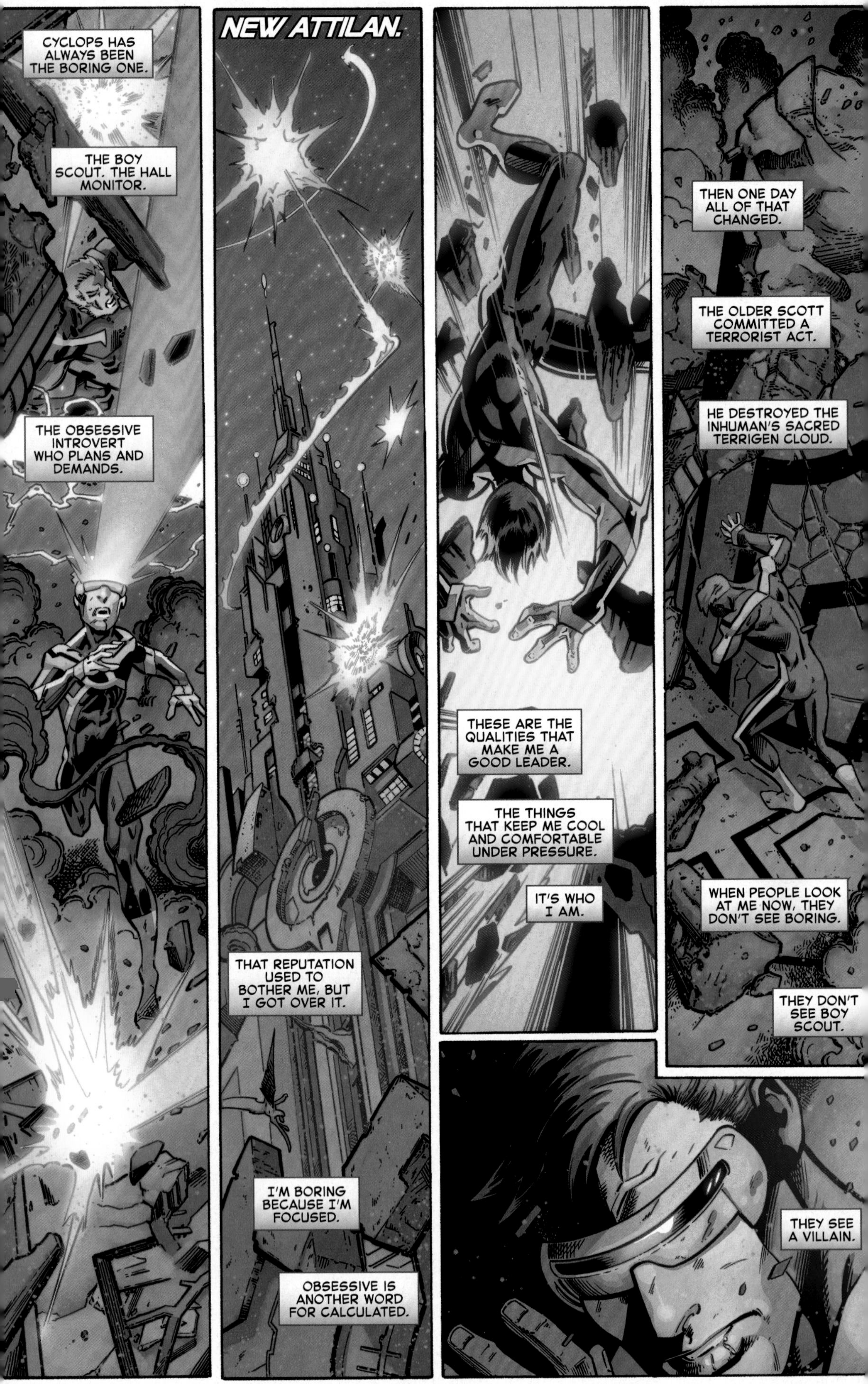
CYCLOPS HAS ALWAYS BEEN THE BORING ONE.
THE BOY SCOUT. THE HALL MONITOR.
THE OBSESSIVE INTROVERT WHO PLANS AND DEMANDS.
NEW ATTILAN.
THAT REPUTATION USED TO BOTHER ME, BUT I GOT OVER IT.
I'M BORING BECAUSE I'M FOCUSED.
OBSESSIVE IS ANOTHER WORD FOR CALCULATED.
THESE ARE THE QUALITIES THAT MAKE ME A GOOD LEADER.
THE THINGS THAT KEEP ME COOL AND COMFORTABLE UNDER PRESSURE.
IT'S WHO I AM.
THEN ONE DAY ALL OF THAT CHANGED.
THE OLDER SCOTT COMMITTED A TERRORIST ACT.
HE DESTROYED THE INHUMAN'S SACRED TERRIGEN CLOUD.
WHEN PEOPLE LOOK AT ME NOW, THEY DON'T SEE BORING.
THEY DON'T SEE BOY SCOUT.
THEY SEE A VILLAIN.

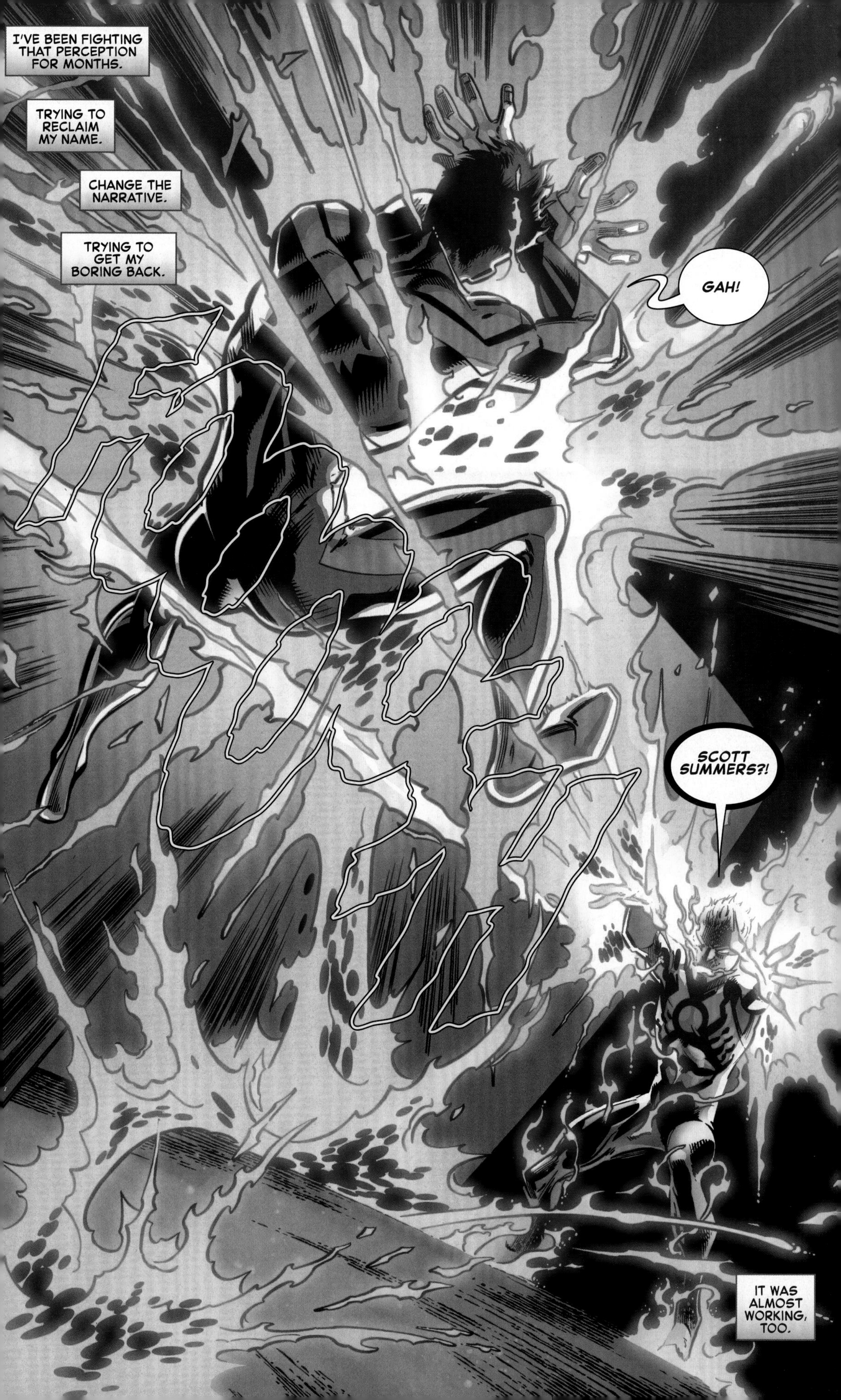
I'VE BEEN FIGHTING THAT PERCEPTION FOR MONTHS.
TRYING TO RECLAIM MY NAME.
CHANGE THE NARRATIVE.
TRYING TO GET MY BORING BACK.
GAH!
SCOTT SUMMERS?!
IT WAS ALMOST WORKING, TOO.

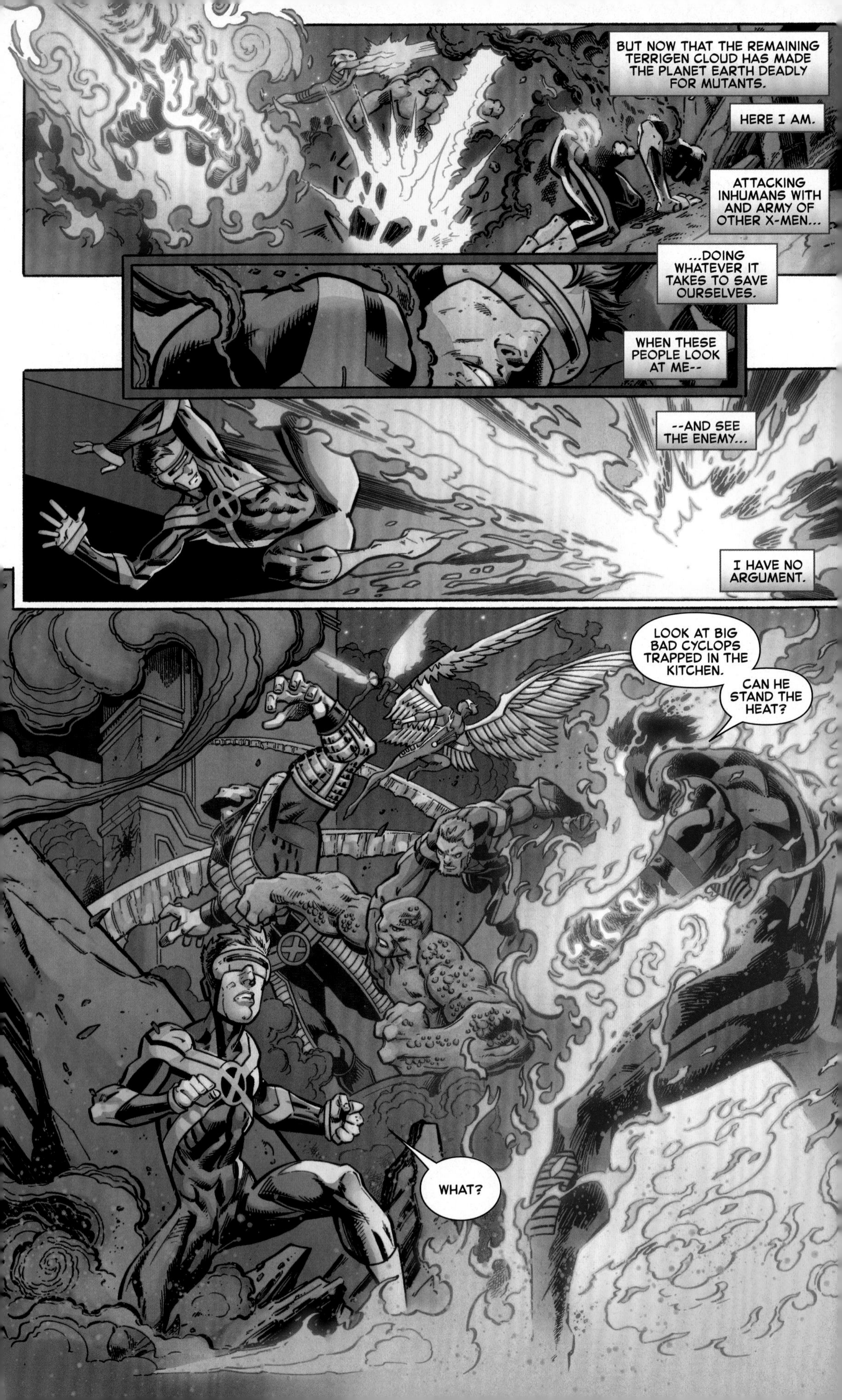

BUT NOW THAT THE REMAINING TERRIGEN CLOUD HAS MADE THE PLANET EARTH DEADLY FOR MUTANTS.
HERE I AM.
ATTACKING INHUMANS WITH AND ARMY OF OTHER X-MEN...
...DOING WHATEVER IT TAKES TO SAVE OURSELVES.
WHEN THESE PEOPLE LOOK AT ME--
--AND SEE THE ENEMY...
I HAVE NO ARGUMENT.
LOOK AT BIG BAD CYCLOPS TRAPPED IN THE KITCHEN.
CAN HE STAND THE HEAT?
WHAT?

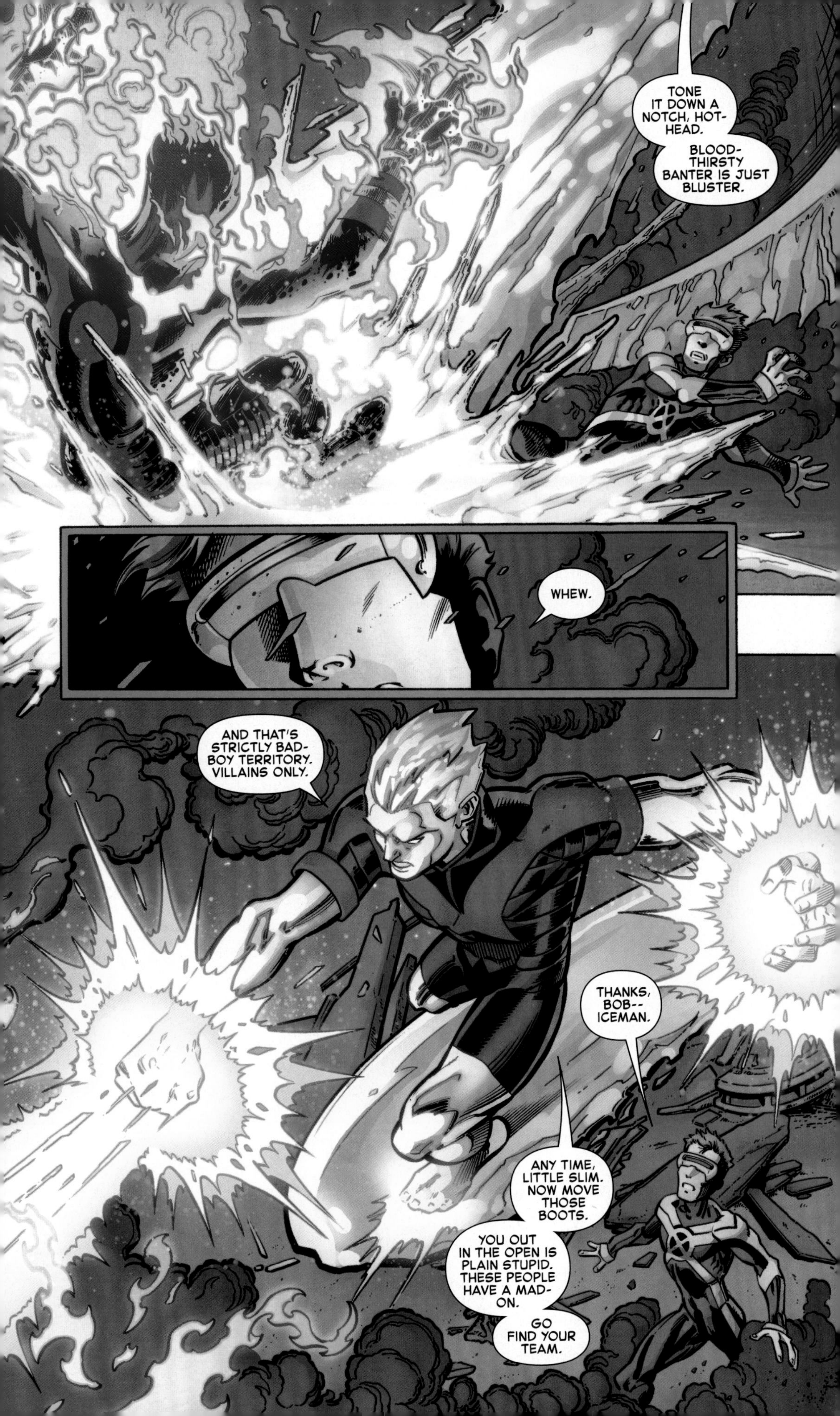
TONE IT DOWN A NOTCH, HOT-HEAD.
BLOOD-THIRSTY BANTER IS JUST BLUSTER.
WHEW.
AND THAT'S STRICTLY BAD-BOY TERRITORY. VILLAINS ONLY.
THANKS, BOB--ICEMAN.
ANY TIME, LITTLE SLIM. NOW MOVE THOSE BOOTS.
YOU OUT IN THE OPEN IS PLAIN STUPID. THESE PEOPLE HAVE A MAD-ON.
GO FIND YOUR TEAM.

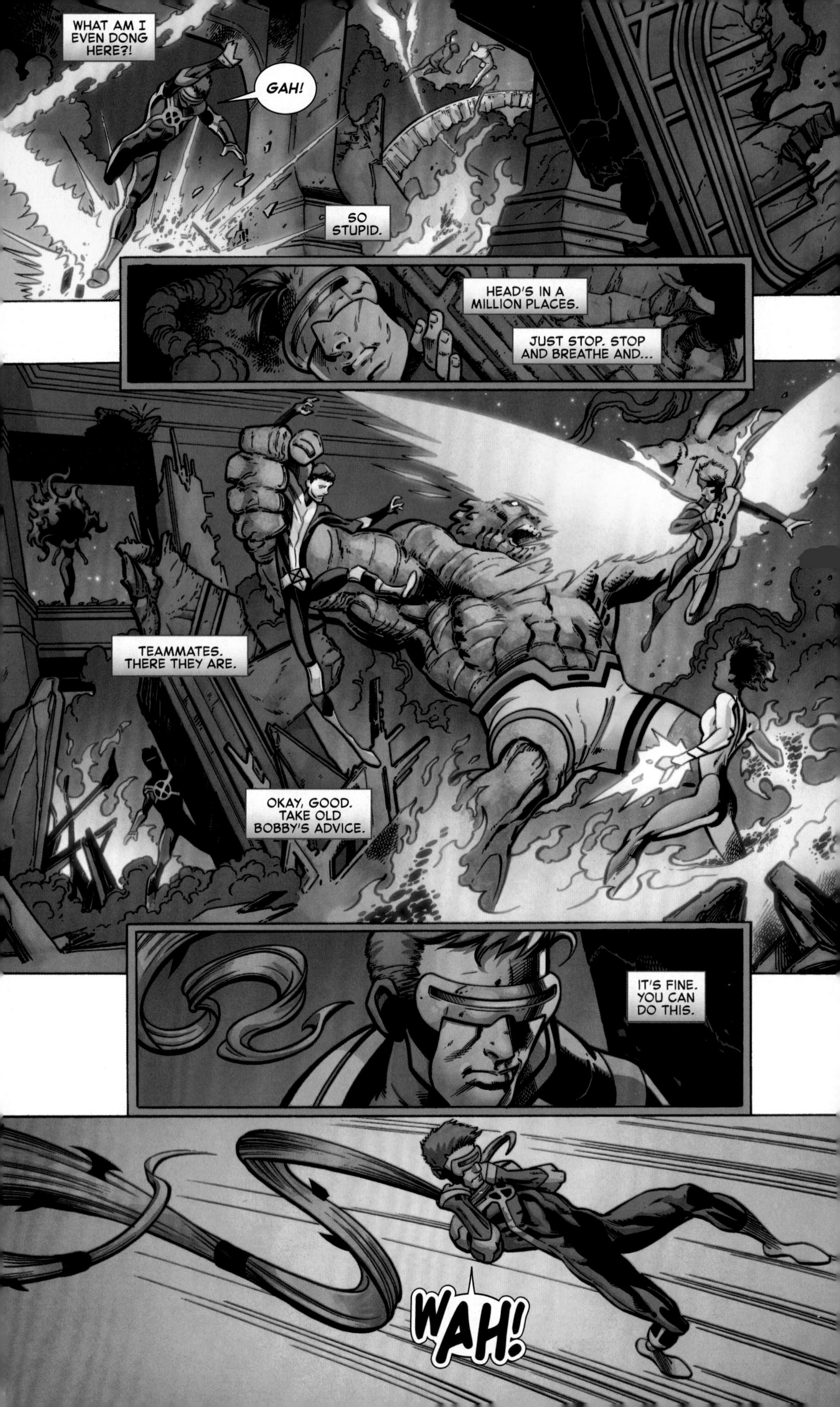
WHAT AM I
EVEN DONG
HERE?!
GAH!
SO
STUPID.
HEAD'S IN A
MILLION PLACES.
JUST STOP. STOP
AND BREATHE AND...
TEAMMATES.
THERE THEY ARE.
OKAY, GOOD.
TAKE OLD
BOBBY'S ADVICE.
IT'S FINE.
YOU CAN
DO THIS.
WAH!

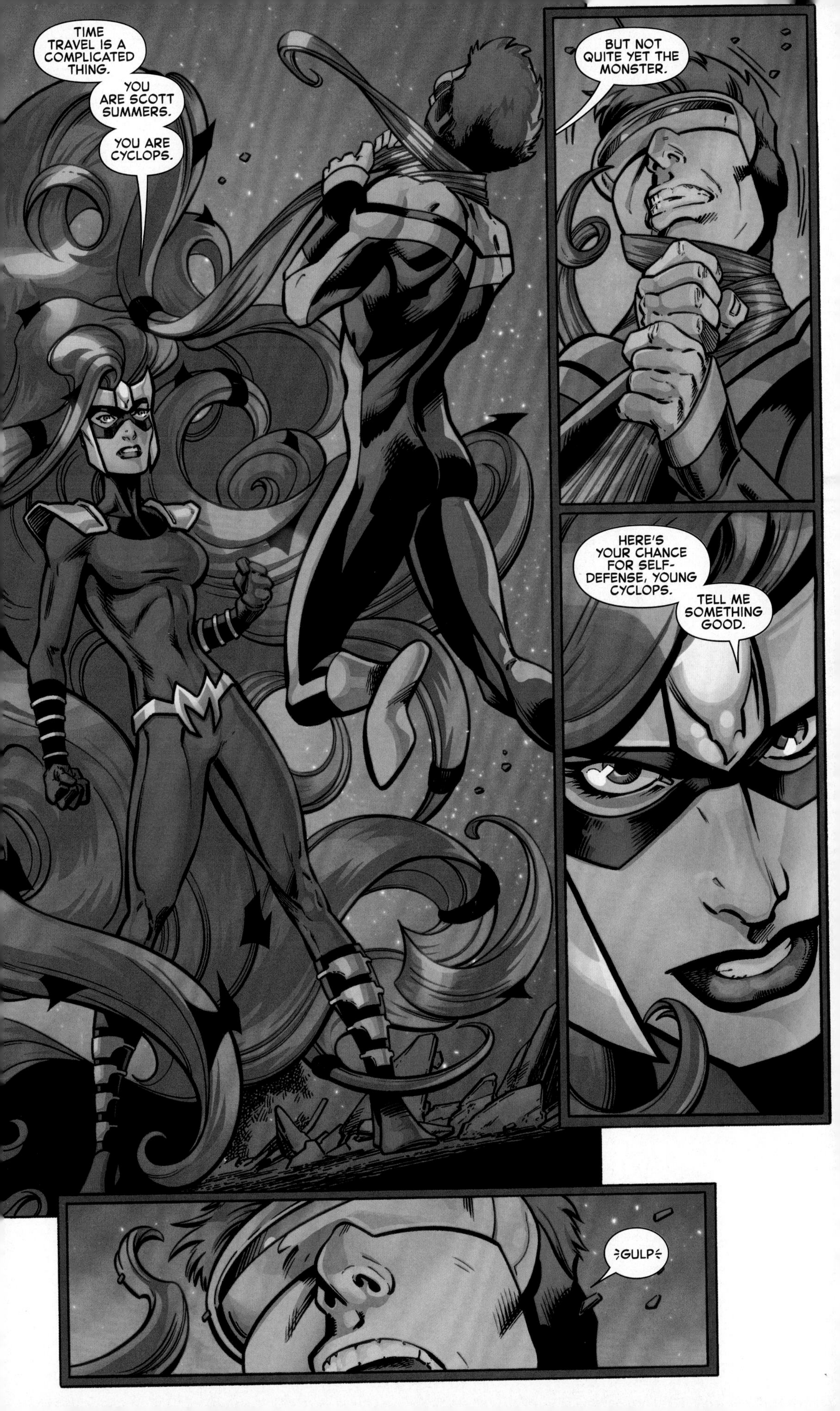
TIME TRAVEL IS A COMPLICATED THING.
YOU ARE SCOTT SUMMERS.
YOU ARE CYCLOPS.
BUT NOT QUITE YET THE MONSTER.
HERE'S YOUR CHANCE FOR SELF-DEFENSE, YOUNG CYCLOPS.
TELL ME SOMETHING GOOD.
GULP

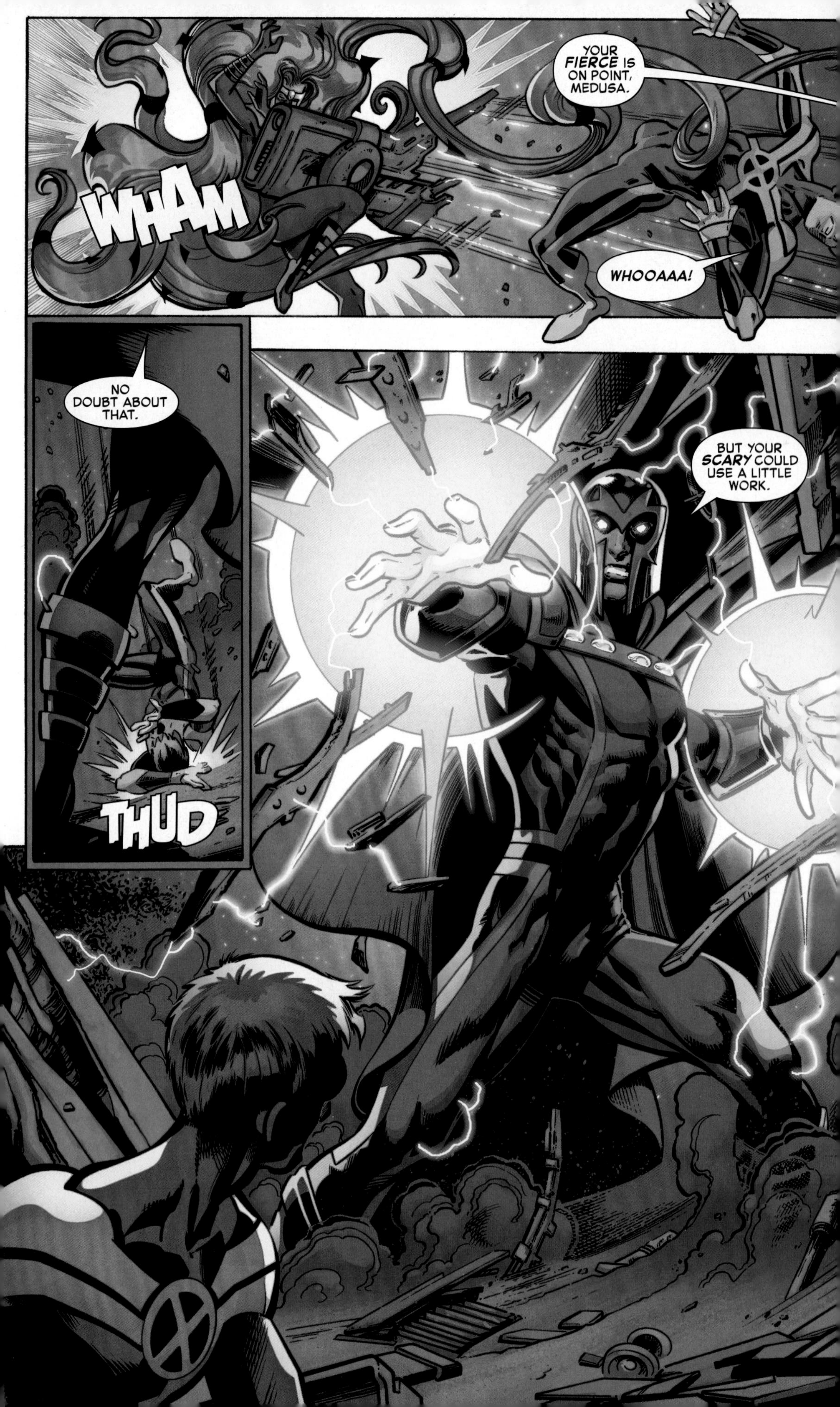
WHAM
YOUR *FIERCE* IS ON POINT, MEDUSA.
WHOOAAA!
NO DOUBT ABOUT THAT.
THUD
BUT YOUR *SCARY* COULD USE A LITTLE WORK.

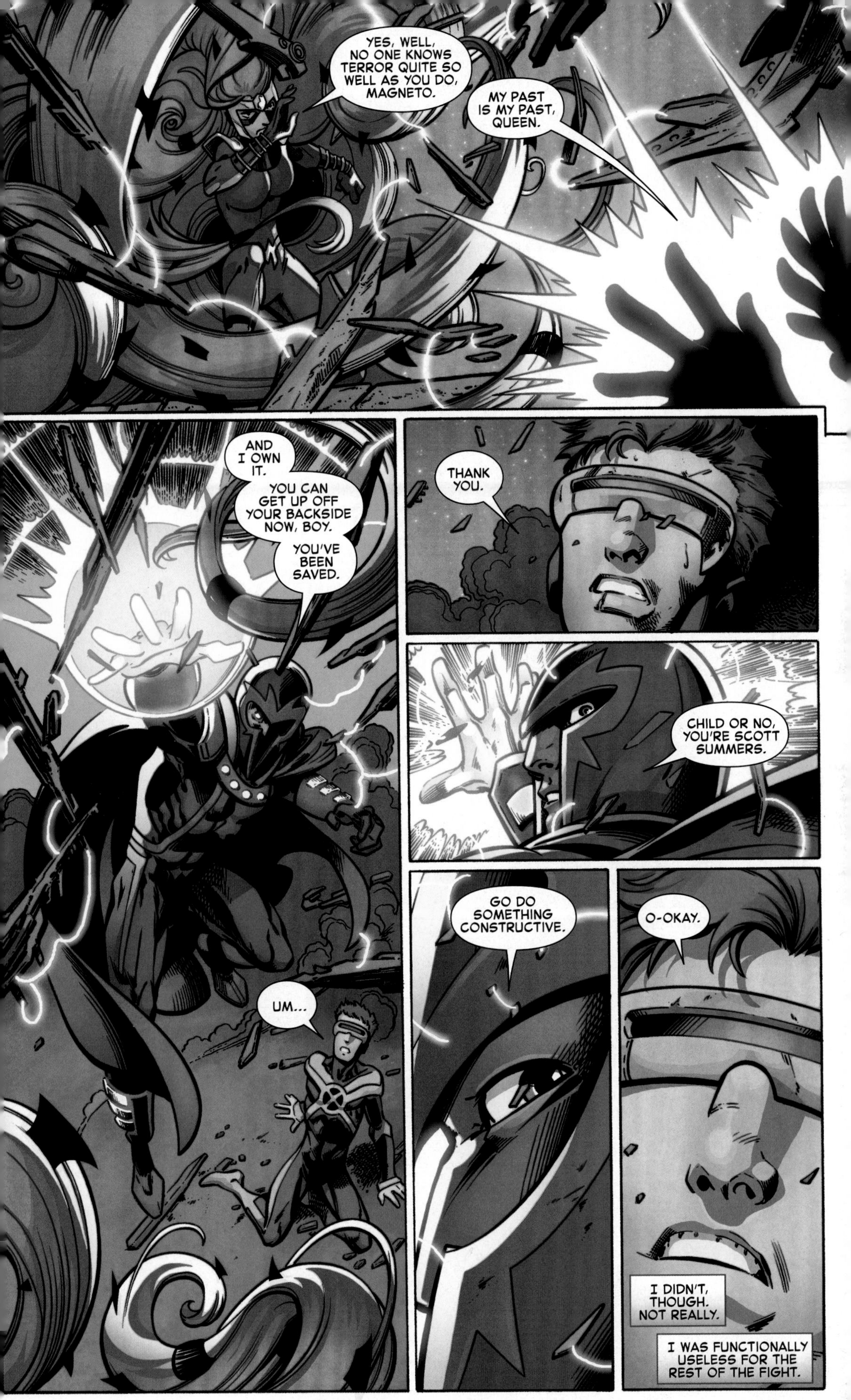
YES, WELL, NO ONE KNOWS TERROR QUITE SO WELL AS YOU DO, MAGNETO.
MY PAST IS MY PAST, QUEEN.
AND I OWN IT.
YOU CAN GET UP OFF YOUR BACKSIDE NOW, BOY.
YOU'VE BEEN SAVED.
UM...
THANK YOU.
CHILD OR NO, YOU'RE SCOTT SUMMERS.
GO DO SOMETHING CONSTRUCTIVE.
O-OKAY.
I DIDN'T, THOUGH. NOT REALLY.
I WAS FUNCTIONALLY USELESS FOR THE REST OF THE FIGHT.

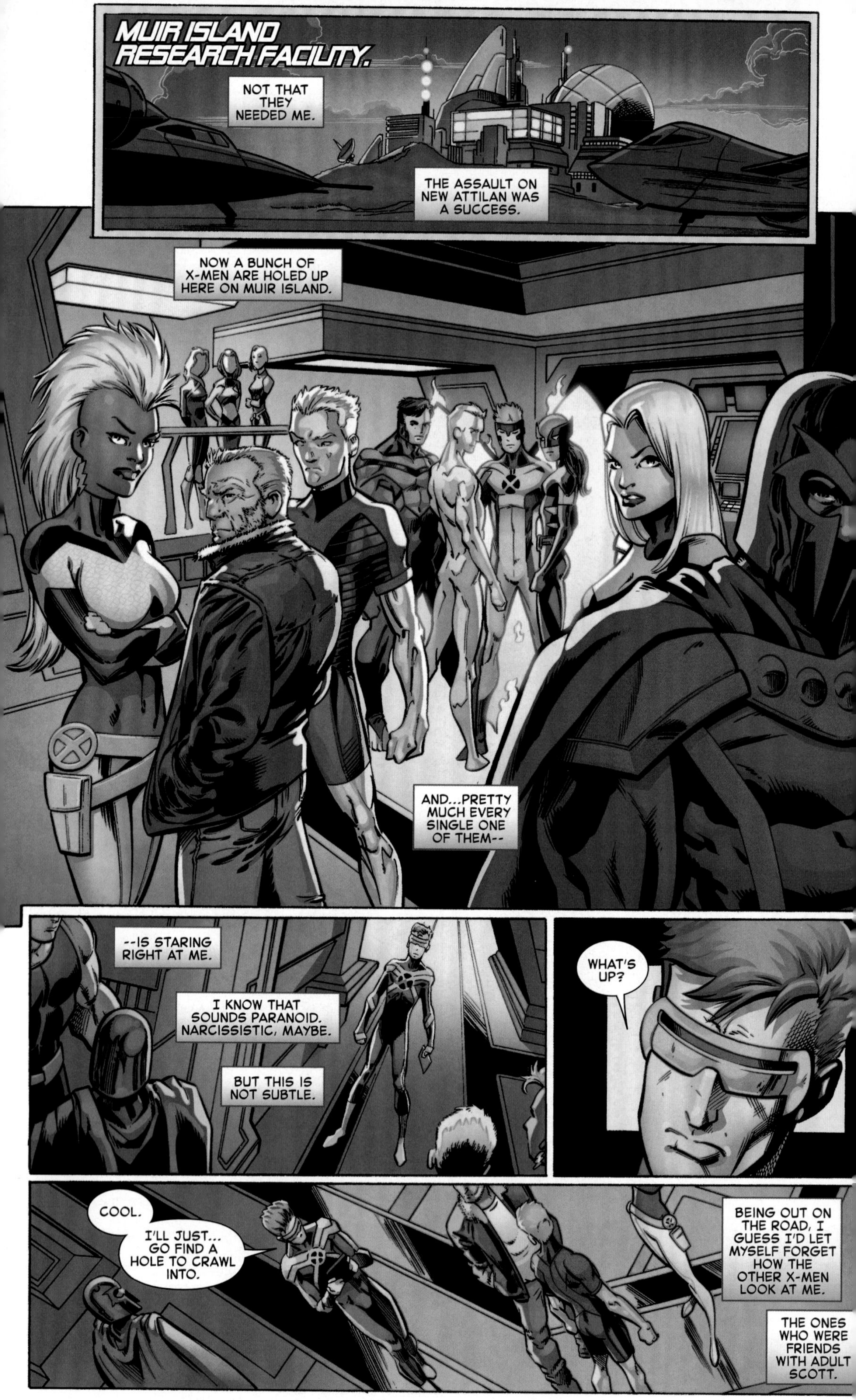
MUIR ISLAND RESEARCH FACILITY.
NOT THAT THEY NEEDED ME.
THE ASSAULT ON NEW ATTILAN WAS A SUCCESS.
NOW A BUNCH OF X-MEN ARE HOLED UP HERE ON MUIR ISLAND.
AND...PRETTY MUCH EVERY SINGLE ONE OF THEM--
--IS STARING RIGHT AT ME.
I KNOW THAT SOUNDS PARANOID. NARCISSISTIC, MAYBE.
BUT THIS IS NOT SUBTLE.
WHAT'S UP?
COOL.
I'LL JUST... GO FIND A HOLE TO CRAWL INTO.
BEING OUT ON THE ROAD, I GUESS I'D LET MYSELF FORGET HOW THE OTHER X-MEN LOOK AT ME.
THE ONES WHO WERE FRIENDS WITH ADULT SCOTT.

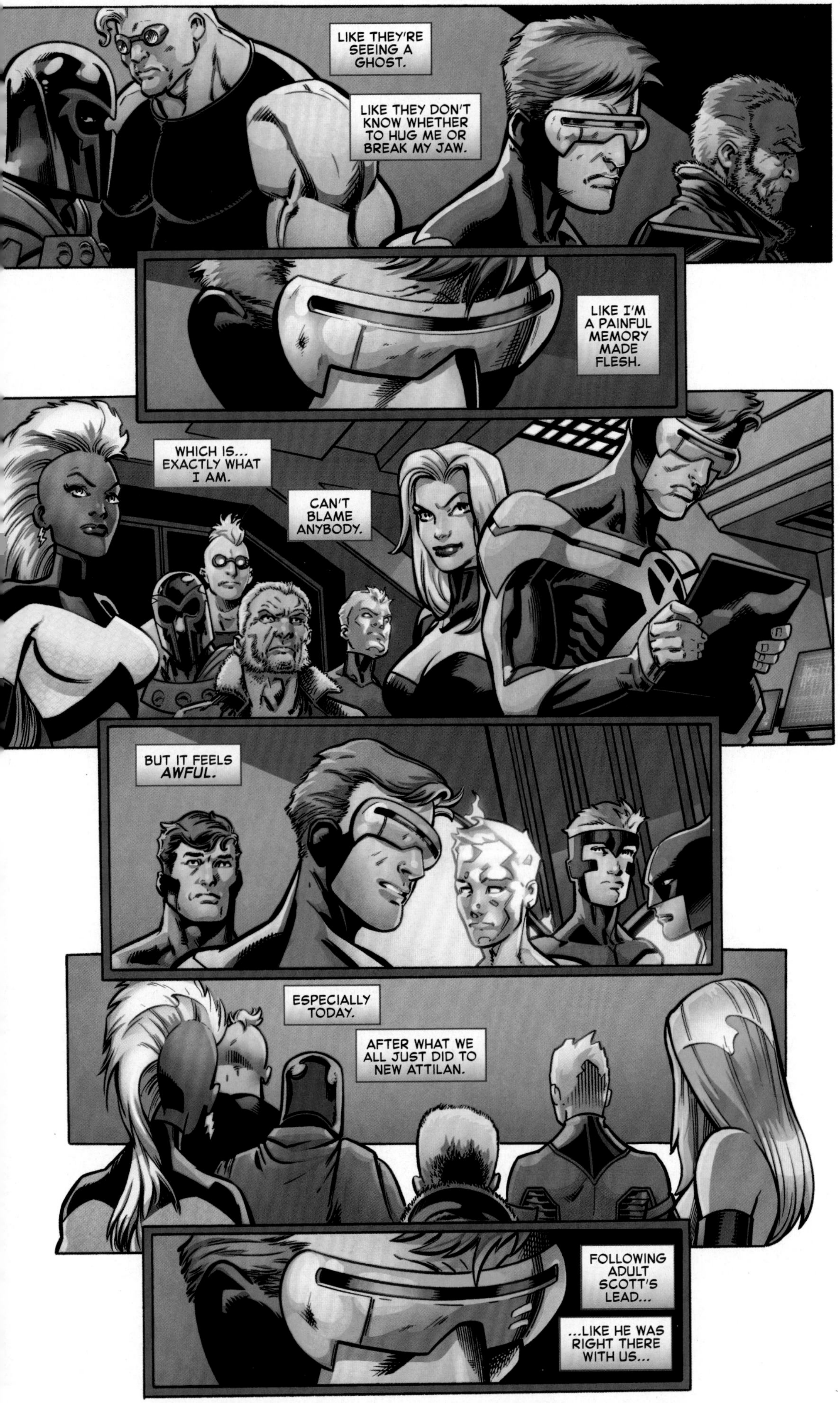
LIKE THEY'RE SEEING A GHOST.
LIKE THEY DON'T KNOW WHETHER TO HUG ME OR BREAK MY JAW.
LIKE I'M A PAINFUL MEMORY MADE FLESH.
WHICH IS... EXACTLY WHAT I AM.
CAN'T BLAME ANYBODY.
BUT IT FEELS AWFUL.
ESPECIALLY TODAY.
AFTER WHAT WE ALL JUST DID TO NEW ATTILAN.
FOLLOWING ADULT SCOTT'S LEAD...
...LIKE HE WAS RIGHT THERE WITH US...

...PULLING STRINGS FROM BEYOND THE GRAVE.

GRUDE HERE IT'S WAR INHUMAN VS MUTANT

...N MIST

INHUWA... CYCLOPS: MUTANT HITLER?

CYCLOPS.

COLON.

"THE MUTANT MENACE MADE FLESH."

DAMN, MAN...

THAT'S SOME GRIM INTERNETTING.

I THOUGHT... YOU'D, UM...

YOU KNOW, SORTA MOVED PAST ALL THAT.

YEAH, I THOUGHT SO, TOO, WARREN.

HAVEN'T WALLOWED IN MONTHS.

IT WAS GETTING BETTER, YOU KNOW.

APPROACHING ZEN OR WHATEVER. I'M NOT OLD CYCLOPS AND I DON'T HAVE TO OWN HIS MISTAKES. NOT FULLY.

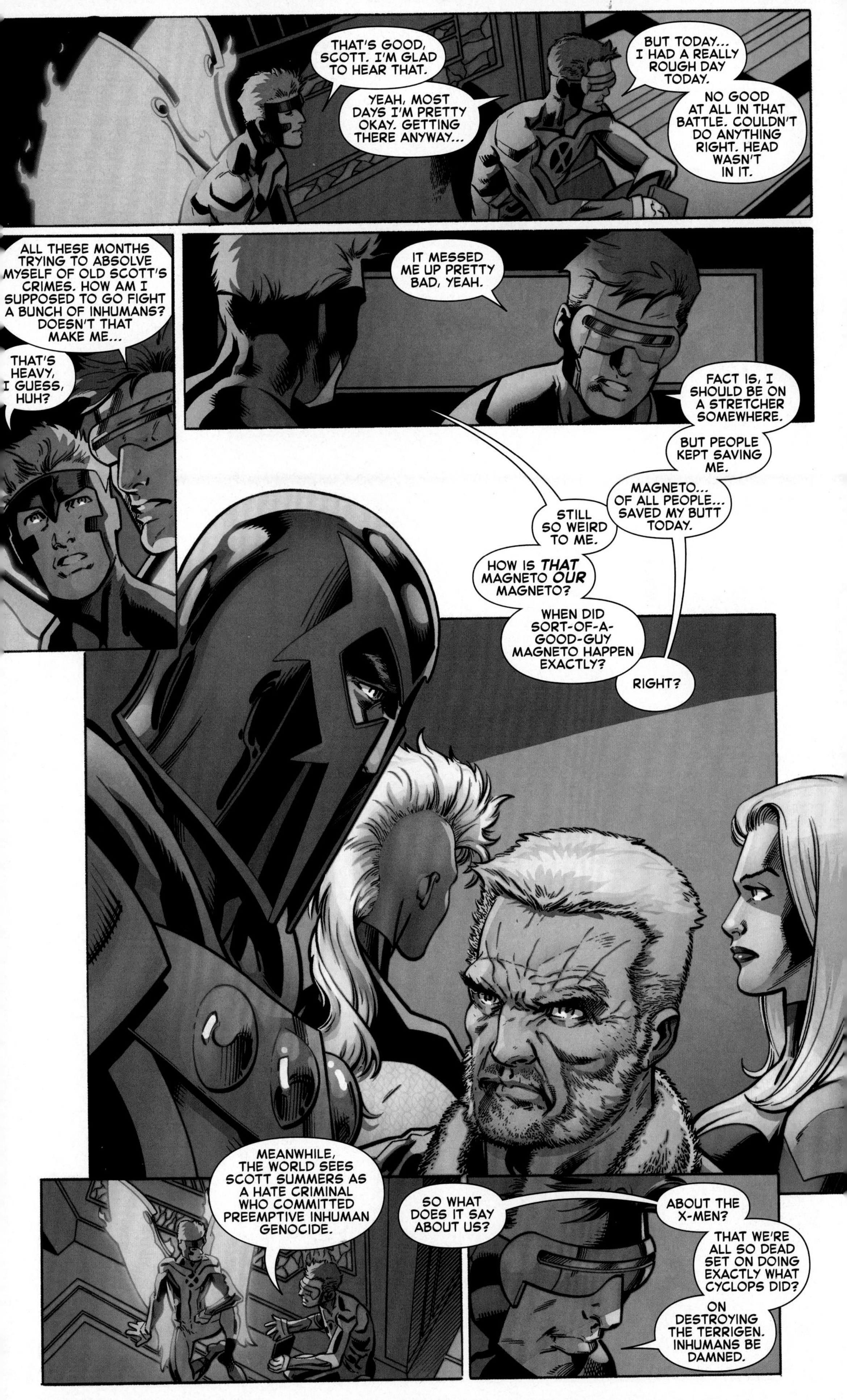
THAT'S GOOD, SCOTT. I'M GLAD TO HEAR THAT.
YEAH, MOST DAYS I'M PRETTY OKAY. GETTING THERE ANYWAY...
BUT TODAY... I HAD A REALLY ROUGH DAY TODAY.
NO GOOD AT ALL IN THAT BATTLE. COULDN'T DO ANYTHING RIGHT. HEAD WASN'T IN IT.
ALL THESE MONTHS TRYING TO ABSOLVE MYSELF OF OLD SCOTT'S CRIMES. HOW AM I SUPPOSED TO GO FIGHT A BUNCH OF INHUMANS? DOESN'T THAT MAKE ME...
THAT'S HEAVY, I GUESS, HUH?
IT MESSED ME UP PRETTY BAD, YEAH.
FACT IS, I SHOULD BE ON A STRETCHER SOMEWHERE.
BUT PEOPLE KEPT SAVING ME.
MAGNETO... OF ALL PEOPLE... SAVED MY BUTT TODAY.
STILL SO WEIRD TO ME.
HOW IS THAT MAGNETO OUR MAGNETO?
WHEN DID SORT-OF-A-GOOD-GUY MAGNETO HAPPEN EXACTLY?
RIGHT?
MEANWHILE, THE WORLD SEES SCOTT SUMMERS AS A HATE CRIMINAL WHO COMMITTED PREEMPTIVE INHUMAN GENOCIDE.
SO WHAT DOES IT SAY ABOUT US?
ABOUT THE X-MEN?
THAT WE'RE ALL SO DEAD SET ON DOING EXACTLY WHAT CYCLOPS DID?
ON DESTROYING THE TERRIGEN. INHUMANS BE DAMNED.

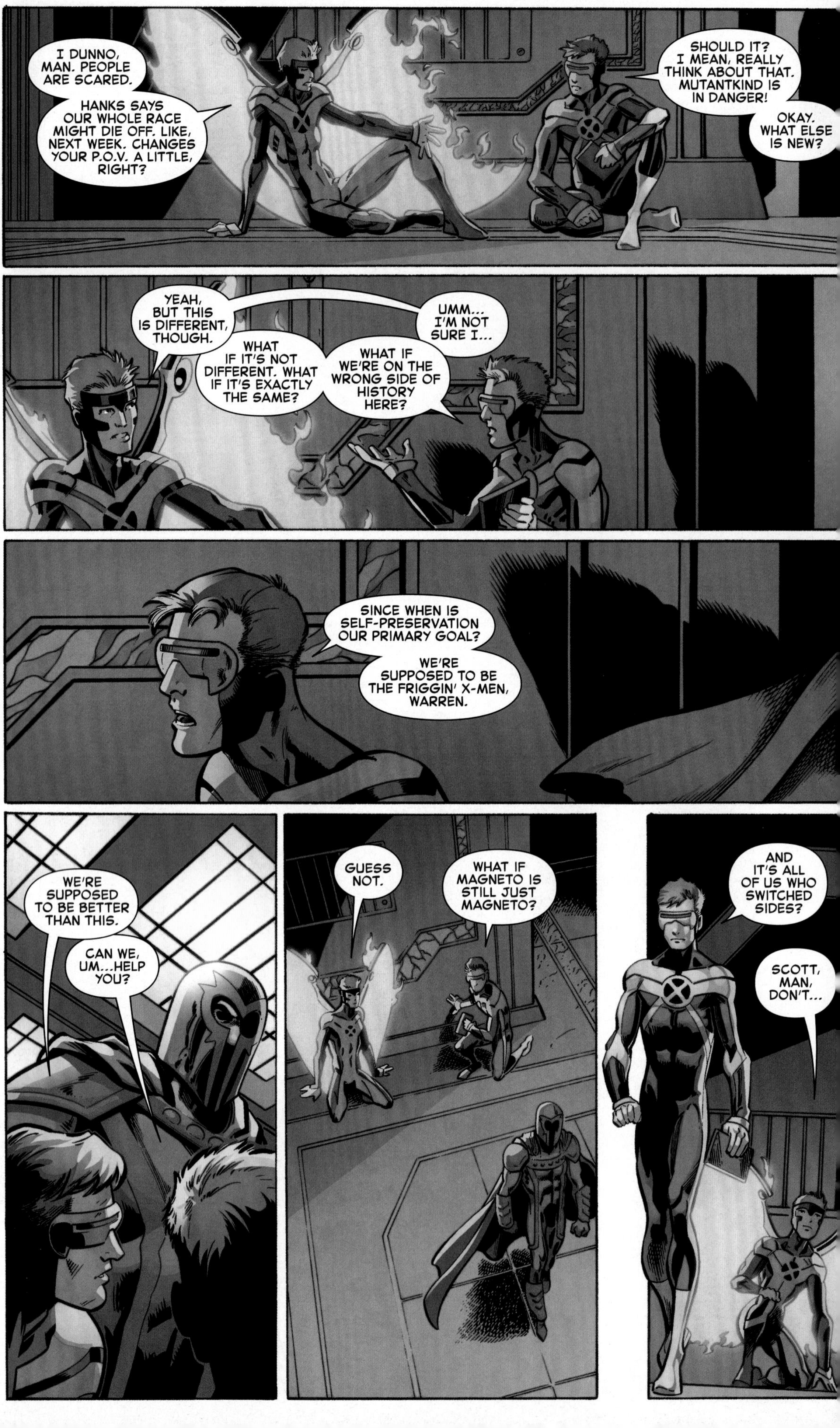

I DUNNO, MAN. PEOPLE ARE SCARED.
HANKS SAYS OUR WHOLE RACE MIGHT DIE OFF. LIKE, NEXT WEEK. CHANGES YOUR P.O.V. A LITTLE, RIGHT?
SHOULD IT? I MEAN, REALLY THINK ABOUT THAT. MUTANTKIND IS IN DANGER!
OKAY. WHAT ELSE IS NEW?
YEAH, BUT THIS IS DIFFERENT, THOUGH.
UMM... I'M NOT SURE I...
WHAT IF IT'S NOT DIFFERENT. WHAT IF IT'S EXACTLY THE SAME?
WHAT IF WE'RE ON THE WRONG SIDE OF HISTORY HERE?
SINCE WHEN IS SELF-PRESERVATION OUR PRIMARY GOAL?
WE'RE SUPPOSED TO BE THE FRIGGIN' X-MEN, WARREN.
WE'RE SUPPOSED TO BE BETTER THAN THIS.
CAN WE, UM...HELP YOU?
GUESS NOT.
WHAT IF MAGNETO IS STILL JUST MAGNETO?
AND IT'S ALL OF US WHO SWITCHED SIDES?
SCOTT, MAN, DON'T...

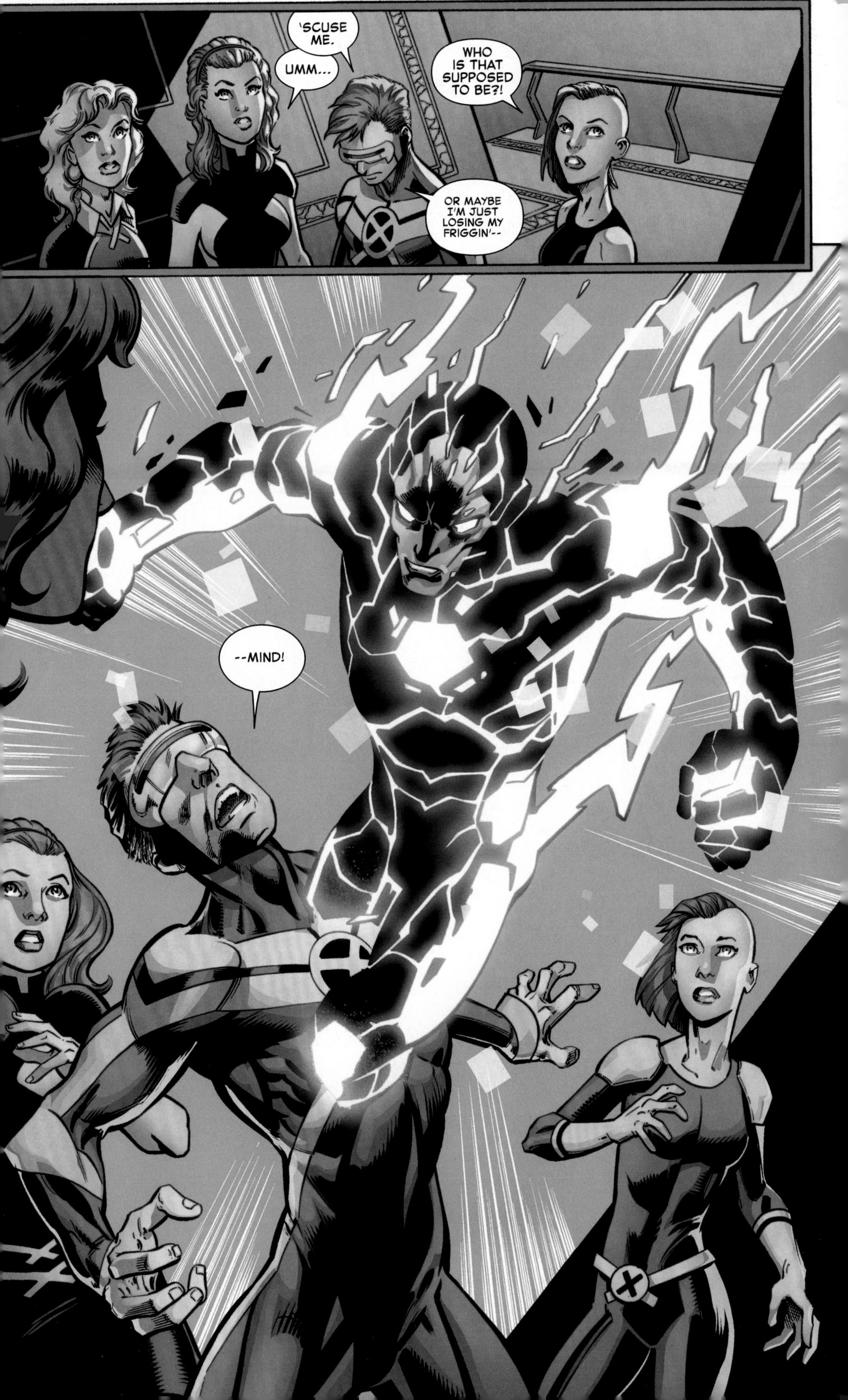
'SCUSE ME.
UMM...
WHO IS THAT SUPPOSED TO BE?!
OR MAYBE I'M JUST LOSING MY FRIGGIN'--
--MIND!

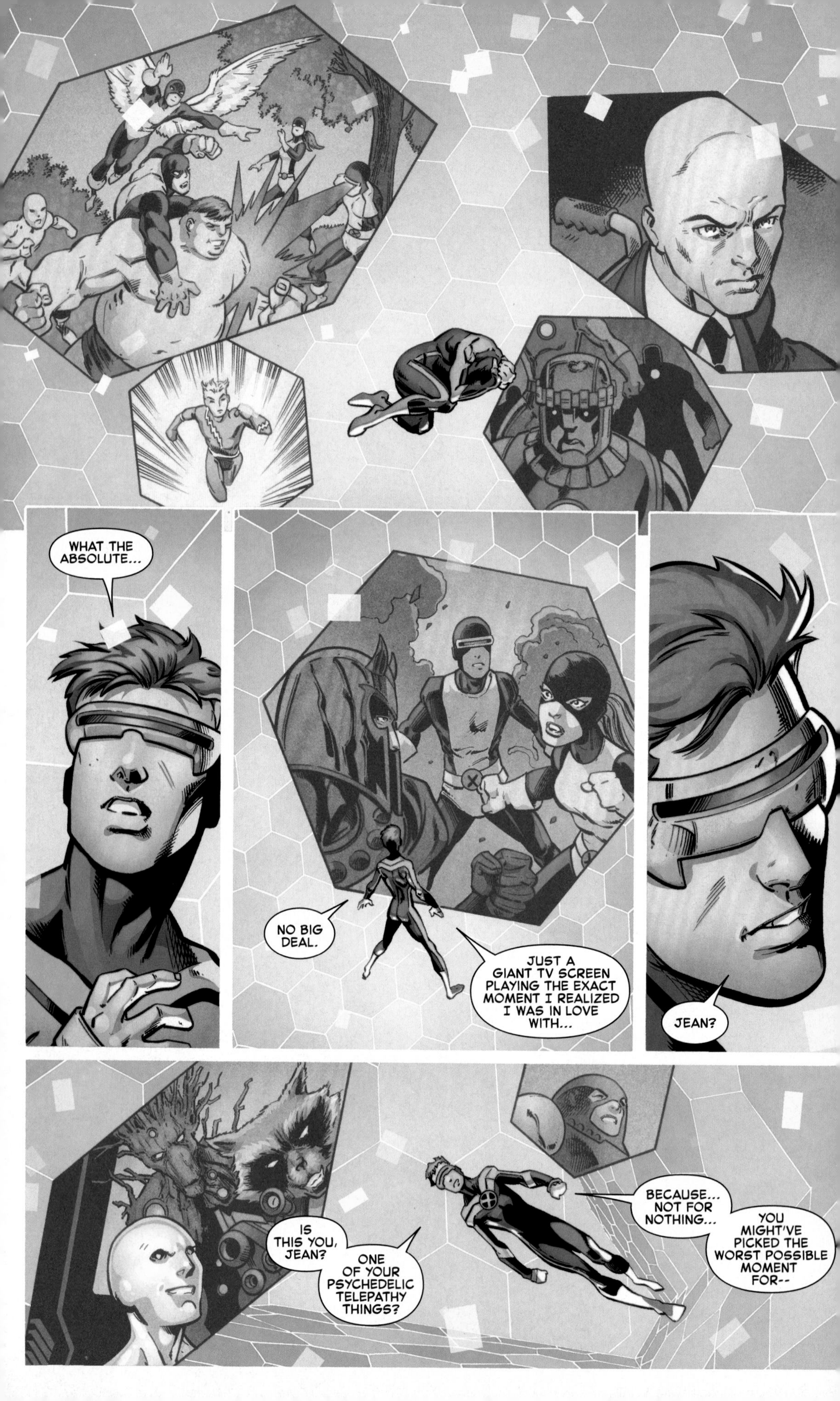

WHAT THE ABSOLUTE...
NO BIG DEAL.
JUST A GIANT TV SCREEN PLAYING THE EXACT MOMENT I REALIZED I WAS IN LOVE WITH...
JEAN?
IS THIS YOU, JEAN?
ONE OF YOUR PSYCHEDELIC TELEPATHY THINGS?
BECAUSE... NOT FOR NOTHING...
YOU MIGHT'VE PICKED THE WORST POSSIBLE MOMENT FOR--

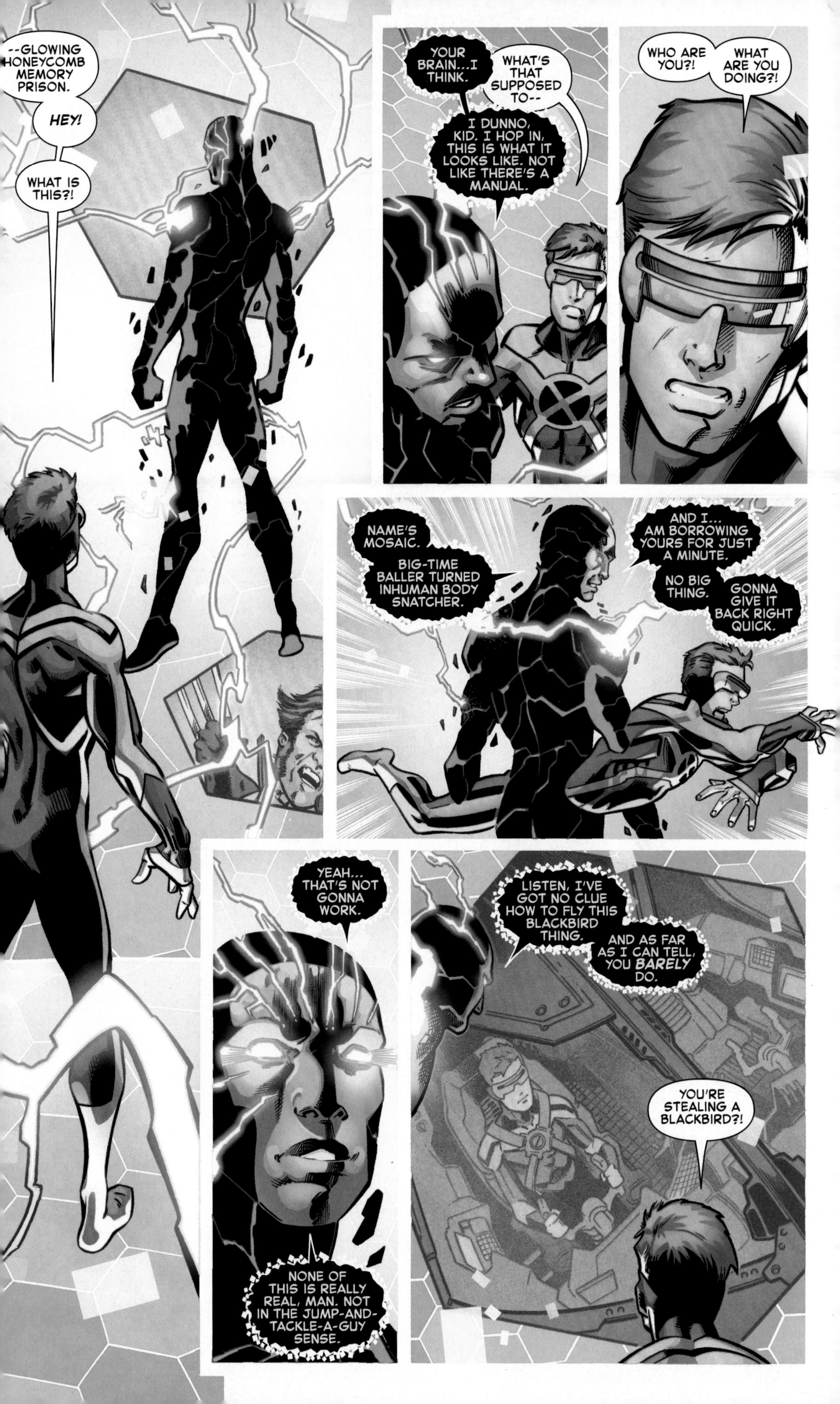
--GLOWING HONEYCOMB MEMORY PRISON.
HEY!
WHAT IS THIS?!
YOUR BRAIN...I THINK.
WHAT'S THAT SUPPOSED TO--
I DUNNO, KID. I HOP IN, THIS IS WHAT IT LOOKS LIKE. NOT LIKE THERE'S A MANUAL.
WHO ARE YOU?!
WHAT ARE YOU DOING?!
NAME'S MOSAIC.
BIG-TIME BALLER TURNED INHUMAN BODY SNATCHER.
AND I... AM BORROWING YOURS FOR JUST A MINUTE.
NO BIG THING.
GONNA GIVE IT BACK RIGHT QUICK.
YEAH... THAT'S NOT GONNA WORK.
NONE OF THIS IS REALLY REAL, MAN. NOT IN THE JUMP-AND-TACKLE-A-GUY SENSE.
LISTEN, I'VE GOT NO CLUE HOW TO FLY THIS BLACKBIRD THING.
AND AS FAR AS I CAN TELL, YOU BARELY DO.
YOU'RE STEALING A BLACKBIRD?!

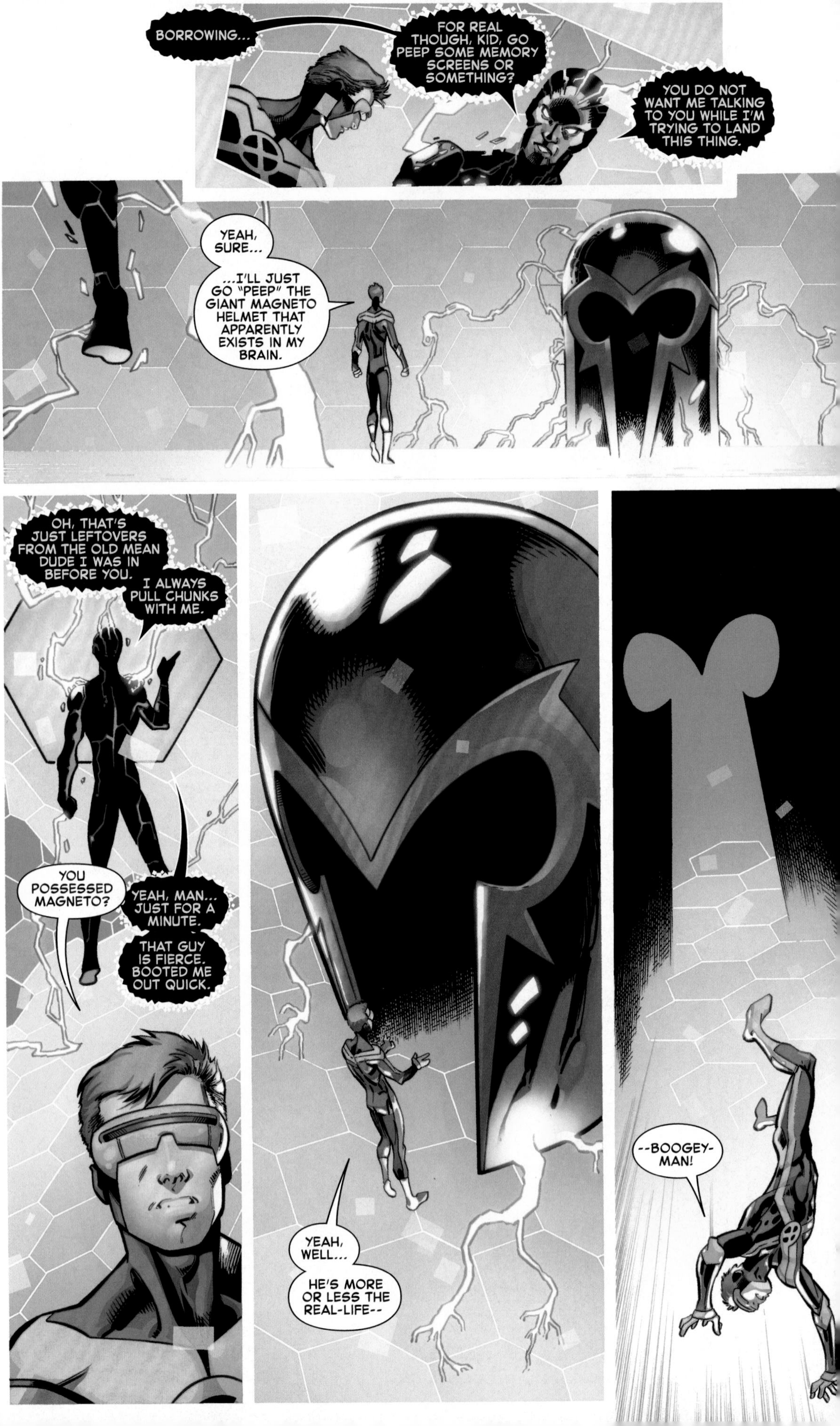

BORROWING...
FOR REAL THOUGH, KID, GO PEEP SOME MEMORY SCREENS OR SOMETHING?
YOU DO NOT WANT ME TALKING TO YOU WHILE I'M TRYING TO LAND THIS THING.
YEAH, SURE...
...I'LL JUST GO "PEEP" THE GIANT MAGNETO HELMET THAT APPARENTLY EXISTS IN MY BRAIN.
OH, THAT'S JUST LEFTOVERS FROM THE OLD MEAN DUDE I WAS IN BEFORE YOU.
I ALWAYS PULL CHUNKS WITH ME.
YOU POSSESSED MAGNETO?
YEAH, MAN... JUST FOR A MINUTE.
THAT GUY IS FIERCE. BOOTED ME OUT QUICK.
YEAH, WELL...
HE'S MORE OR LESS THE REAL-LIFE--
--BOOGEY-MAN!

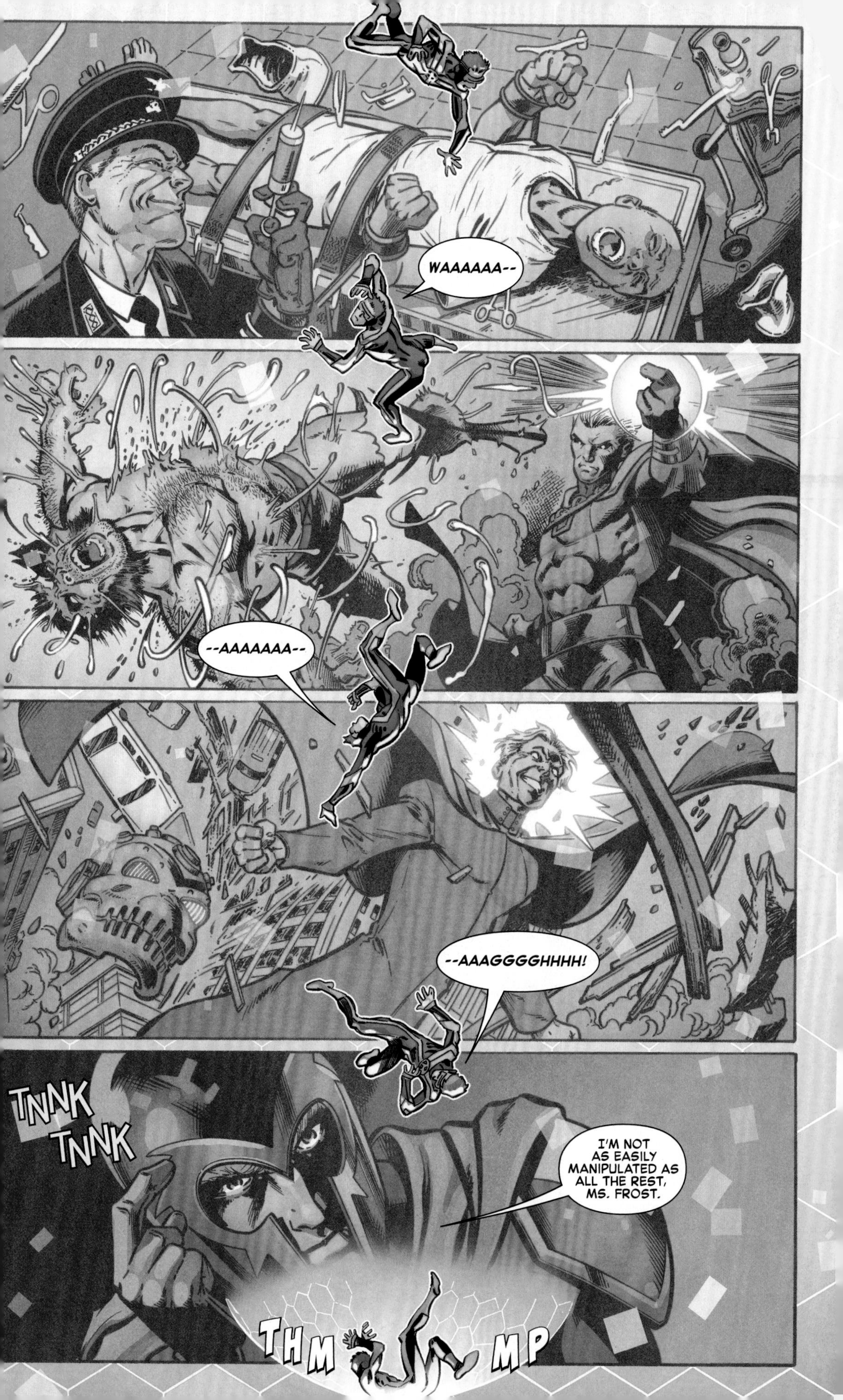
WAAAAAA--
--AAAAAAA--
--AAAGGGGHHHH!
TNNK TNNK
I'M NOT AS EASILY MANIPULATED AS ALL THE REST, MS. FROST.
THMMP

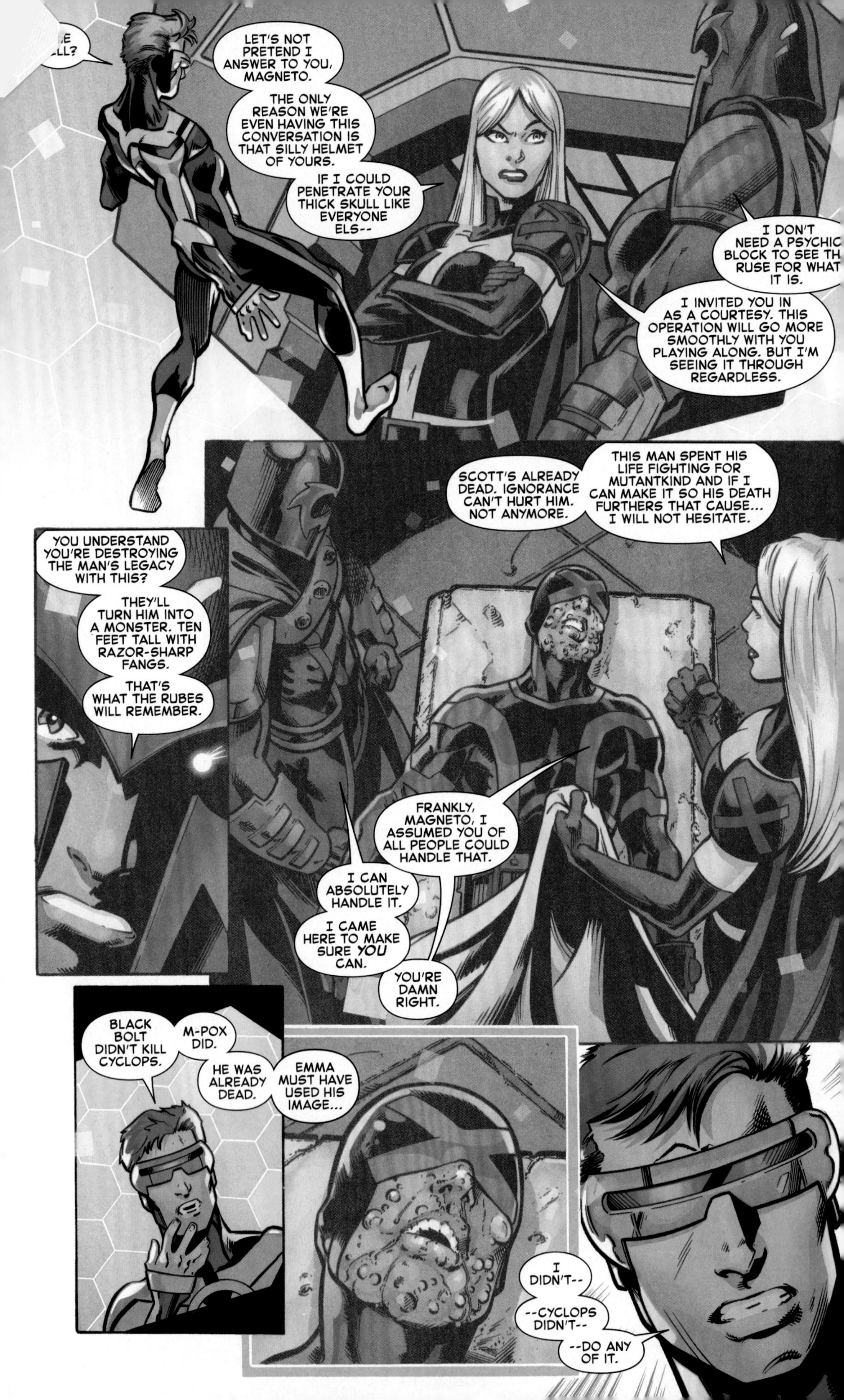

LET'S NOT PRETEND I ANSWER TO YOU, MAGNETO.
THE ONLY REASON WE'RE EVEN HAVING THIS CONVERSATION IS THAT SILLY HELMET OF YOURS.
IF I COULD PENETRATE YOUR THICK SKULL LIKE EVERYONE ELS--
I DON'T NEED A PSYCHIC BLOCK TO SEE TH RUSE FOR WHAT IT IS.
I INVITED YOU IN AS A COURTESY. THIS OPERATION WILL GO MORE SMOOTHLY WITH YOU PLAYING ALONG. BUT I'M SEEING IT THROUGH REGARDLESS.
YOU UNDERSTAND YOU'RE DESTROYING THE MAN'S LEGACY WITH THIS?
THEY'LL TURN HIM INTO A MONSTER. TEN FEET TALL WITH RAZOR-SHARP FANGS.
THAT'S WHAT THE RUBES WILL REMEMBER.
SCOTT'S ALREADY DEAD. IGNORANCE CAN'T HURT HIM. NOT ANYMORE.
THIS MAN SPENT HIS LIFE FIGHTING FOR MUTANTKIND AND IF I CAN MAKE IT SO HIS DEATH FURTHERS THAT CAUSE... I WILL NOT HESITATE.
FRANKLY, MAGNETO, I ASSUMED YOU OF ALL PEOPLE COULD HANDLE THAT.
I CAN ABSOLUTELY HANDLE IT.
I CAME HERE TO MAKE SURE *YOU* CAN.
YOU'RE DAMN RIGHT.
BLACK BOLT DIDN'T KILL CYCLOPS.
M-POX DID.
HE WAS ALREADY DEAD.
EMMA MUST HAVE USED HIS IMAGE...
I DIDN'T--
--CYCLOPS DIDN'T--
--DO ANY OF IT.

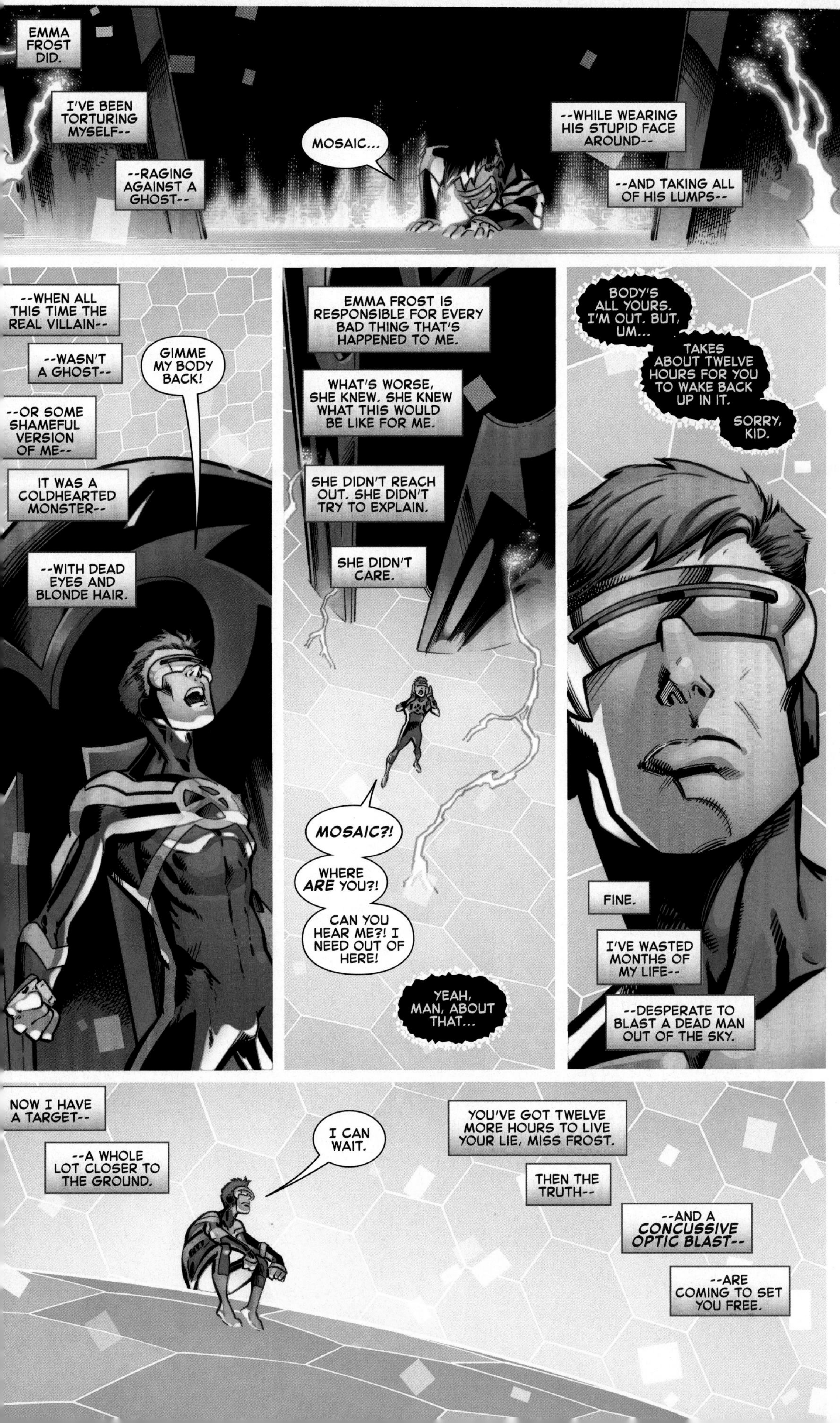
EMMA FROST DID.
I'VE BEEN TORTURING MYSELF--
--RAGING AGAINST A GHOST--
MOSAIC...
--WHILE WEARING HIS STUPID FACE AROUND--
--AND TAKING ALL OF HIS LUMPS--
--WHEN ALL THIS TIME THE REAL VILLAIN--
--WASN'T A GHOST--
--OR SOME SHAMEFUL VERSION OF ME--
IT WAS A COLDHEARTED MONSTER--
--WITH DEAD EYES AND BLONDE HAIR.
GIMME MY BODY BACK!
EMMA FROST IS RESPONSIBLE FOR EVERY BAD THING THAT'S HAPPENED TO ME.
WHAT'S WORSE, SHE KNEW. SHE KNEW WHAT THIS WOULD BE LIKE FOR ME.
SHE DIDN'T REACH OUT. SHE DIDN'T TRY TO EXPLAIN.
SHE DIDN'T CARE.
MOSAIC?!
WHERE ARE YOU?!
CAN YOU HEAR ME?! I NEED OUT OF HERE!
YEAH, MAN, ABOUT THAT...
BODY'S ALL YOURS. I'M OUT. BUT, UM...
TAKES ABOUT TWELVE HOURS FOR YOU TO WAKE BACK UP IN IT.
SORRY, KID.
FINE.
I'VE WASTED MONTHS OF MY LIFE--
--DESPERATE TO BLAST A DEAD MAN OUT OF THE SKY.
NOW I HAVE A TARGET--
--A WHOLE LOT CLOSER TO THE GROUND.
I CAN WAIT.
YOU'VE GOT TWELVE MORE HOURS TO LIVE YOUR LIE, MISS FROST.
THEN THE TRUTH--
--AND A CONCUSSIVE OPTIC BLAST--
--ARE COMING TO SET YOU FREE.

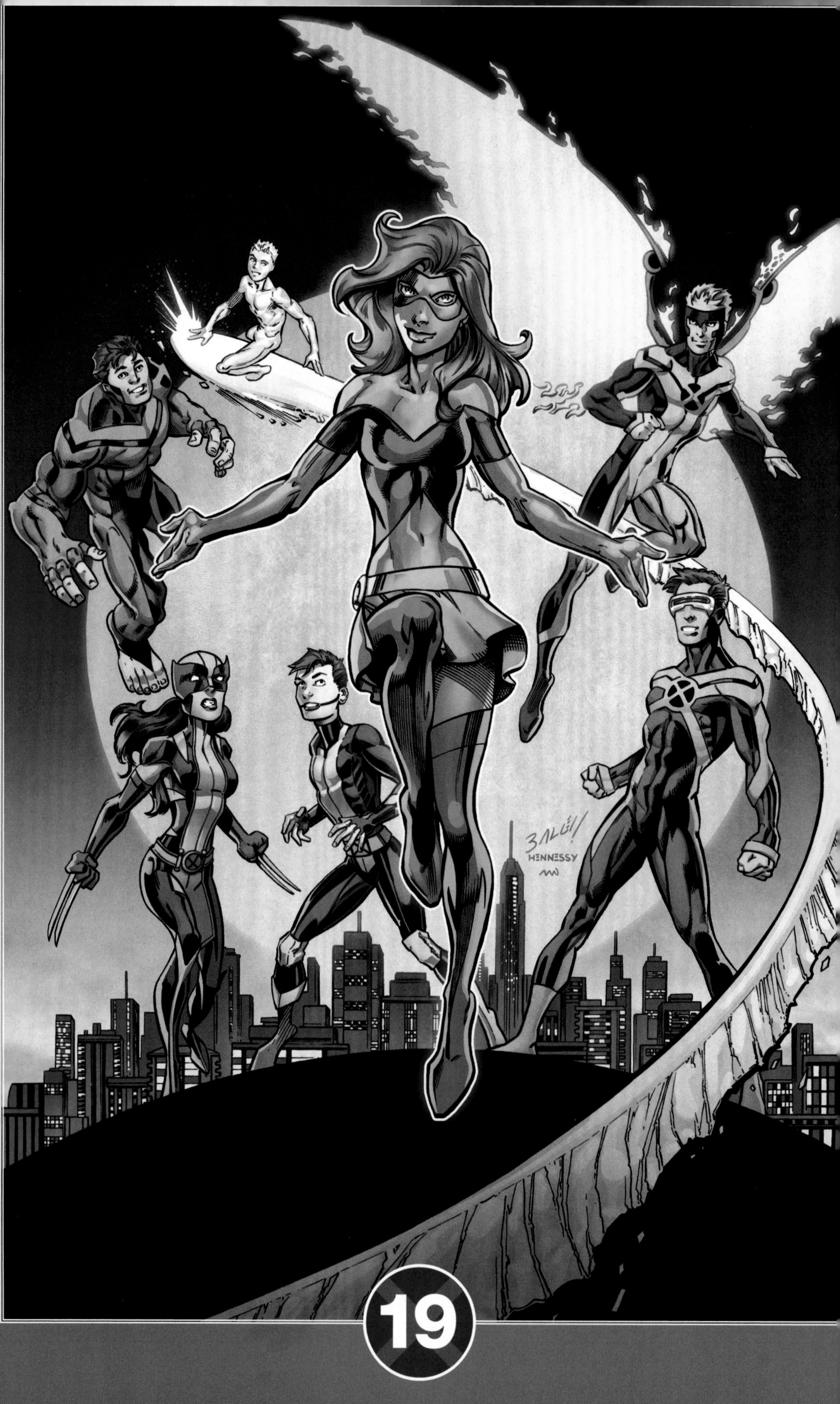
HENNESSY
19

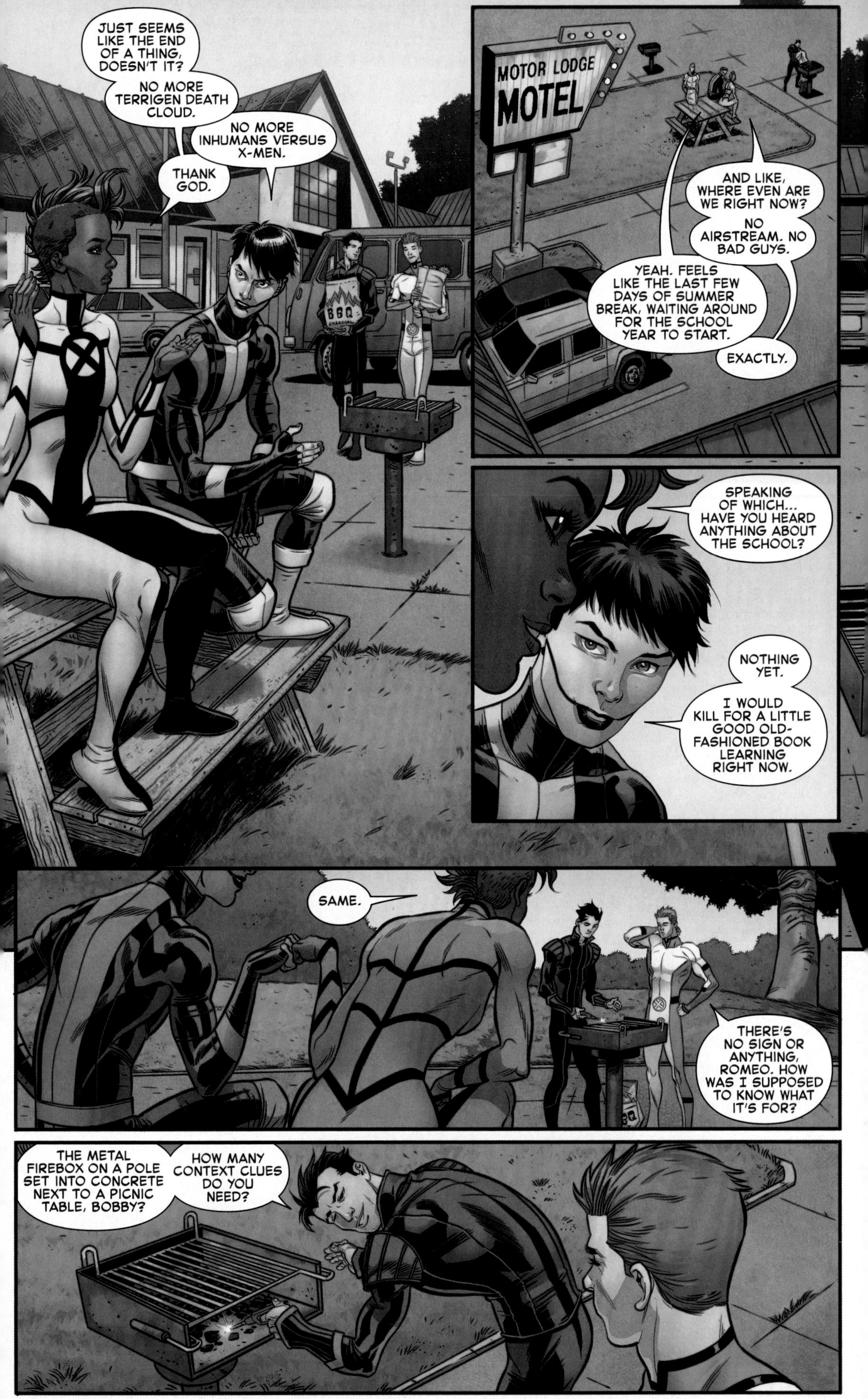
JUST SEEMS LIKE THE END OF A THING, DOESN'T IT?
NO MORE TERRIGEN DEATH CLOUD.
NO MORE INHUMANS VERSUS X-MEN.
THANK GOD.
MOTOR LODGE
MOTEL
AND LIKE, WHERE EVEN ARE WE RIGHT NOW?
NO AIRSTREAM. NO BAD GUYS.
YEAH. FEELS LIKE THE LAST FEW DAYS OF SUMMER BREAK, WAITING AROUND FOR THE SCHOOL YEAR TO START.
EXACTLY.
SPEAKING OF WHICH... HAVE YOU HEARD ANYTHING ABOUT THE SCHOOL?
NOTHING YET.
I WOULD KILL FOR A LITTLE GOOD OLD-FASHIONED BOOK LEARNING RIGHT NOW.
SAME.
THERE'S NO SIGN OR ANYTHING, ROMEO. HOW WAS I SUPPOSED TO KNOW WHAT IT'S FOR?
THE METAL FIREBOX ON A POLE SET INTO CONCRETE NEXT TO A PICNIC TABLE, BOBBY?
HOW MANY CONTEXT CLUES DO YOU NEED?

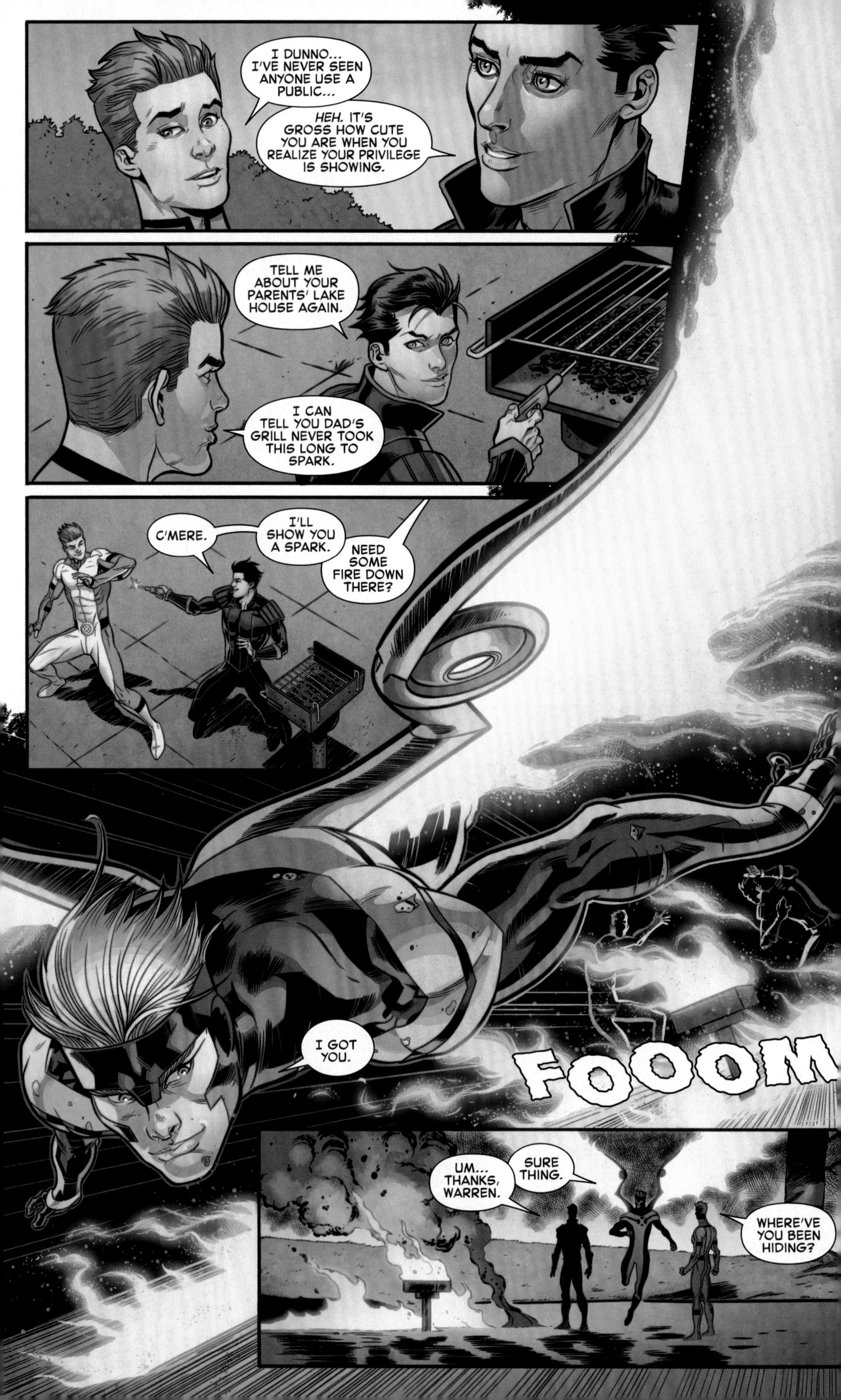
I DUNNO... I'VE NEVER SEEN ANYONE USE A PUBLIC...
HEH. IT'S GROSS HOW CUTE YOU ARE WHEN YOU REALIZE YOUR PRIVILEGE IS SHOWING.
TELL ME ABOUT YOUR PARENTS' LAKE HOUSE AGAIN.
I CAN TELL YOU DAD'S GRILL NEVER TOOK THIS LONG TO SPARK.
C'MERE.
I'LL SHOW YOU A SPARK.
NEED SOME FIRE DOWN THERE?
I GOT YOU.
FOOOM
UM... THANKS, WARREN.
SURE THING.
WHERE'VE YOU BEEN HIDING?

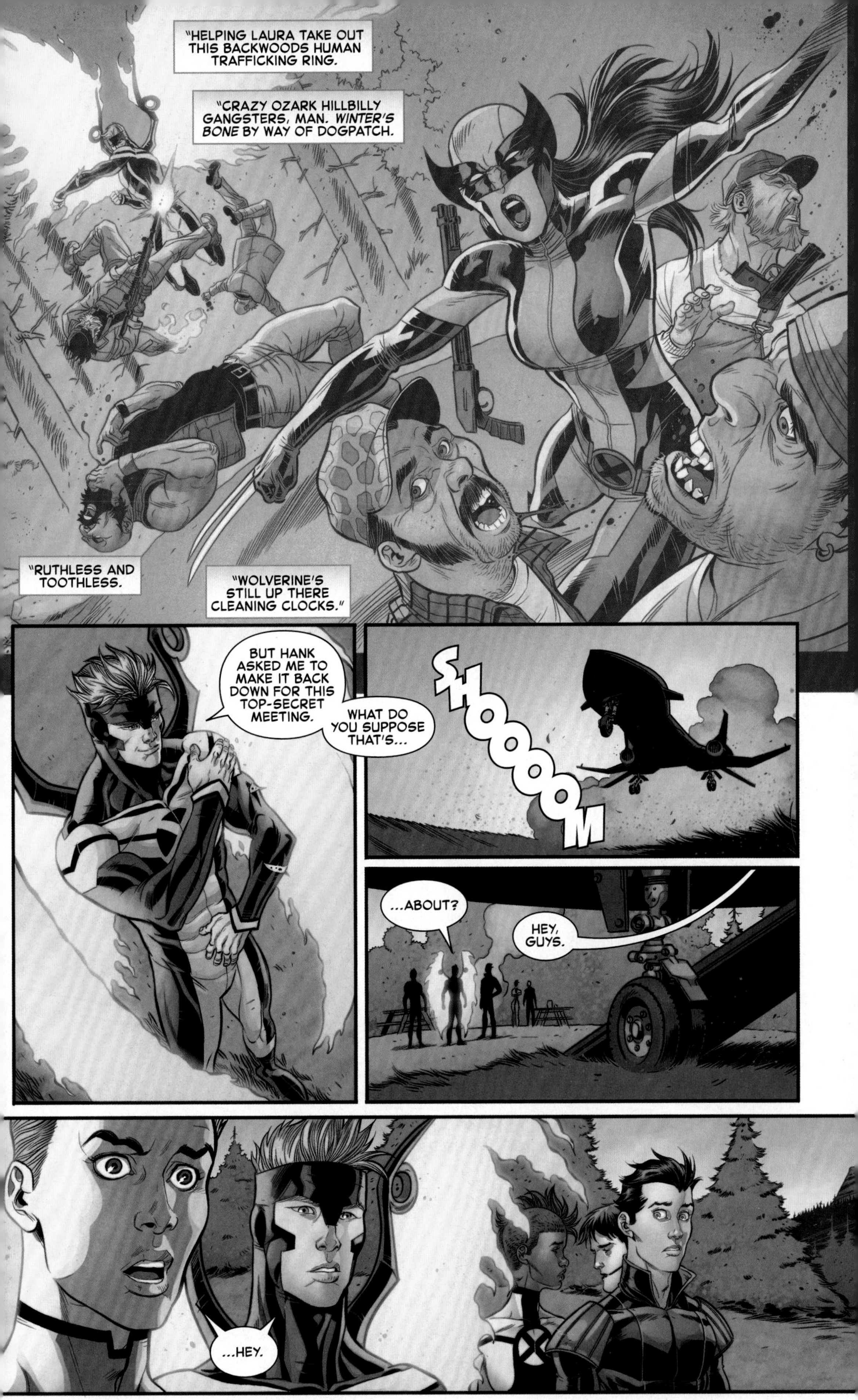
"HELPING LAURA TAKE OUT THIS BACKWOODS HUMAN TRAFFICKING RING.
"CRAZY OZARK HILLBILLY GANGSTERS, MAN. *WINTER'S BONE* BY WAY OF DOGPATCH.
"RUTHLESS AND TOOTHLESS.
"WOLVERINE'S STILL UP THERE CLEANING CLOCKS."
BUT HANK ASKED ME TO MAKE IT BACK DOWN FOR THIS TOP-SECRET MEETING.
WHAT DO YOU SUPPOSE THAT'S...
SHOOOOOM
...ABOUT?
HEY, GUYS.
...HEY.

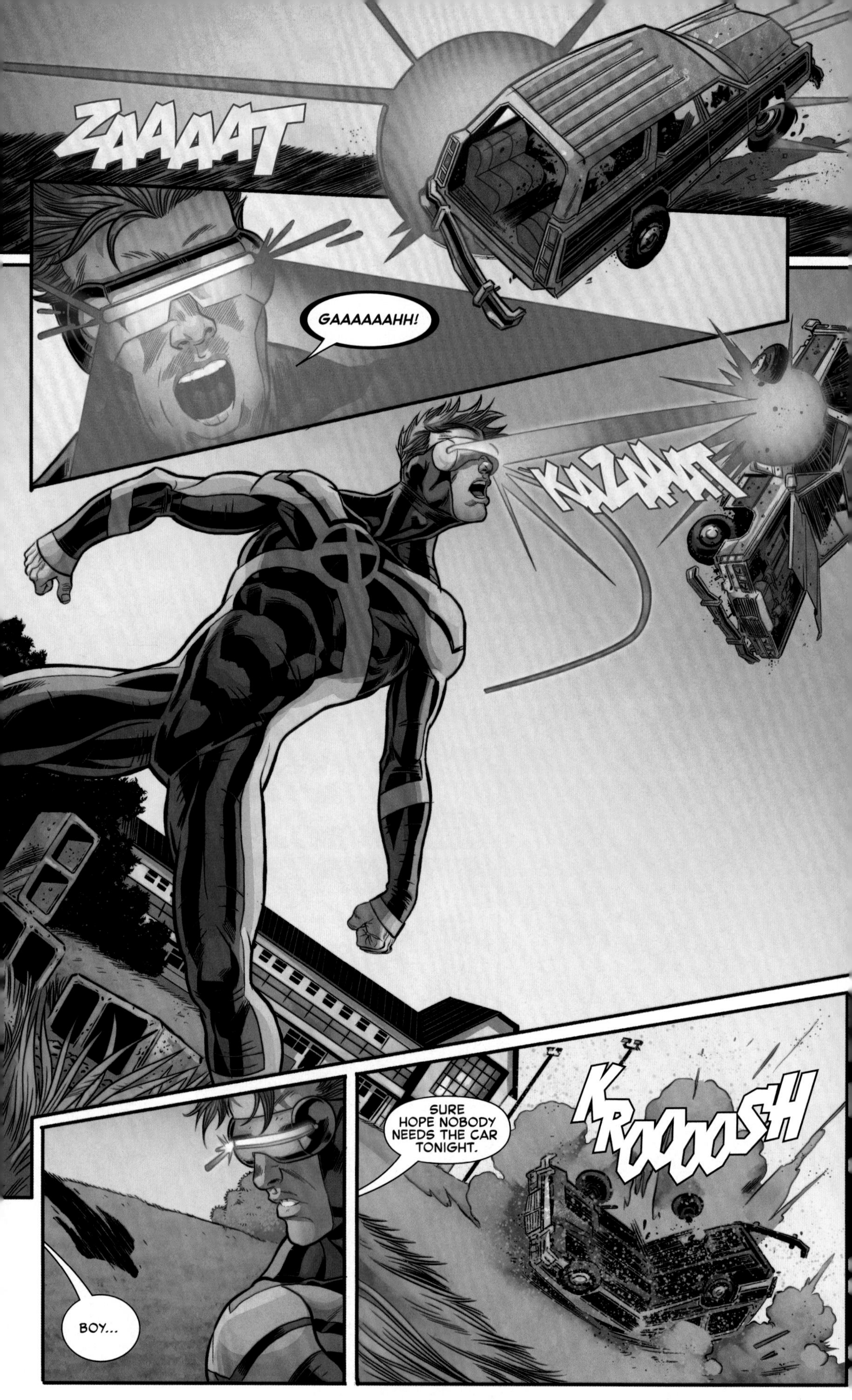

ZAAAAT
GAAAAAAHH!
KAZAAAT
KROOOOSH
SURE HOPE NOBODY NEEDS THE CAR TONIGHT.
BOY...

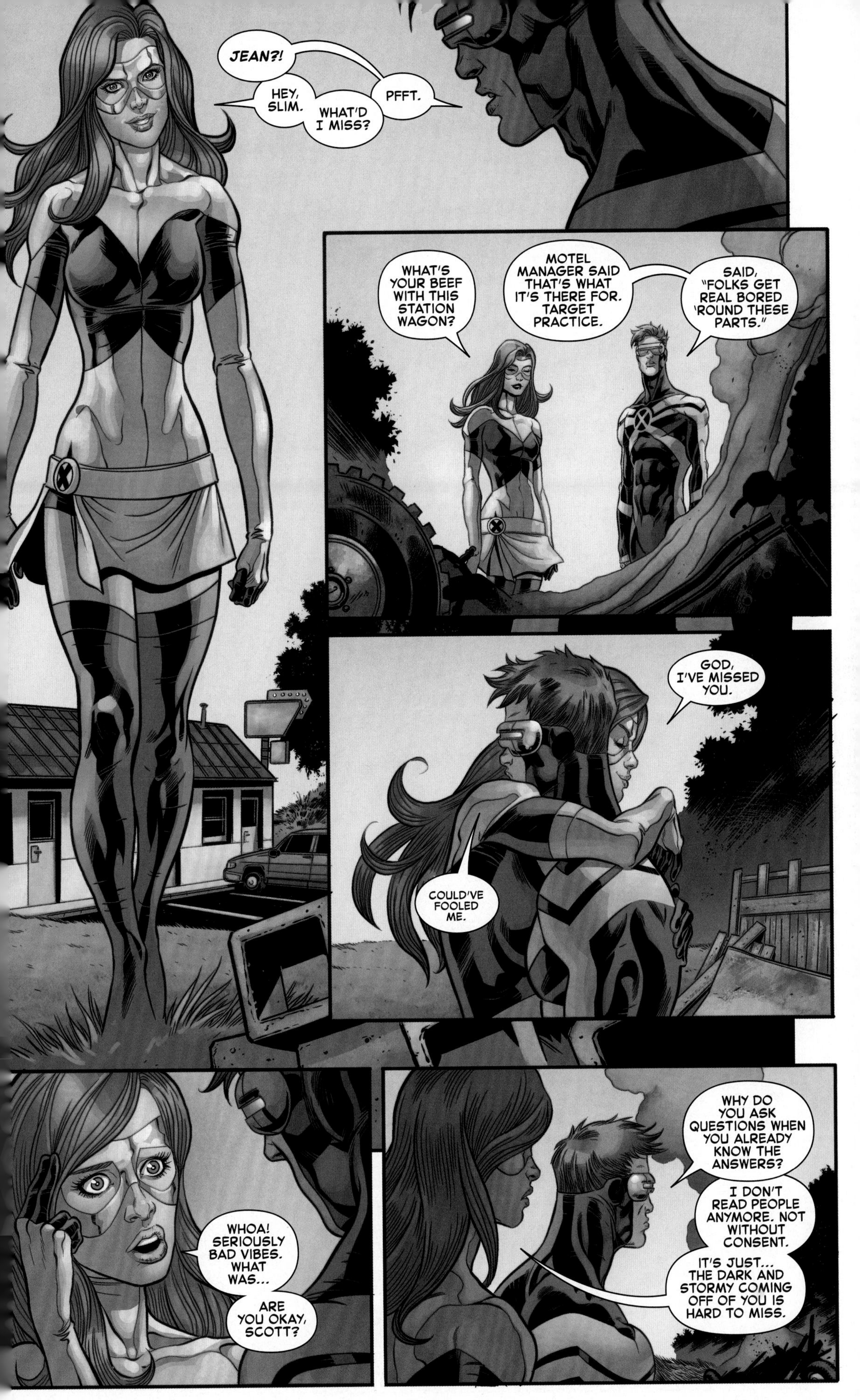
JEAN?!
HEY, SLIM.
WHAT'D I MISS?
PFFT.
WHAT'S YOUR BEEF WITH THIS STATION WAGON?
MOTEL MANAGER SAID THAT'S WHAT IT'S THERE FOR. TARGET PRACTICE.
SAID, "FOLKS GET REAL BORED 'ROUND THESE PARTS."
GOD, I'VE MISSED YOU.
COULD'VE FOOLED ME.
WHOA! SERIOUSLY BAD VIBES. WHAT WAS...
ARE YOU OKAY, SCOTT?
WHY DO YOU ASK QUESTIONS WHEN YOU ALREADY KNOW THE ANSWERS?
I DON'T READ PEOPLE ANYMORE. NOT WITHOUT CONSENT.
IT'S JUST... THE DARK AND STORMY COMING OFF OF YOU IS HARD TO MISS.

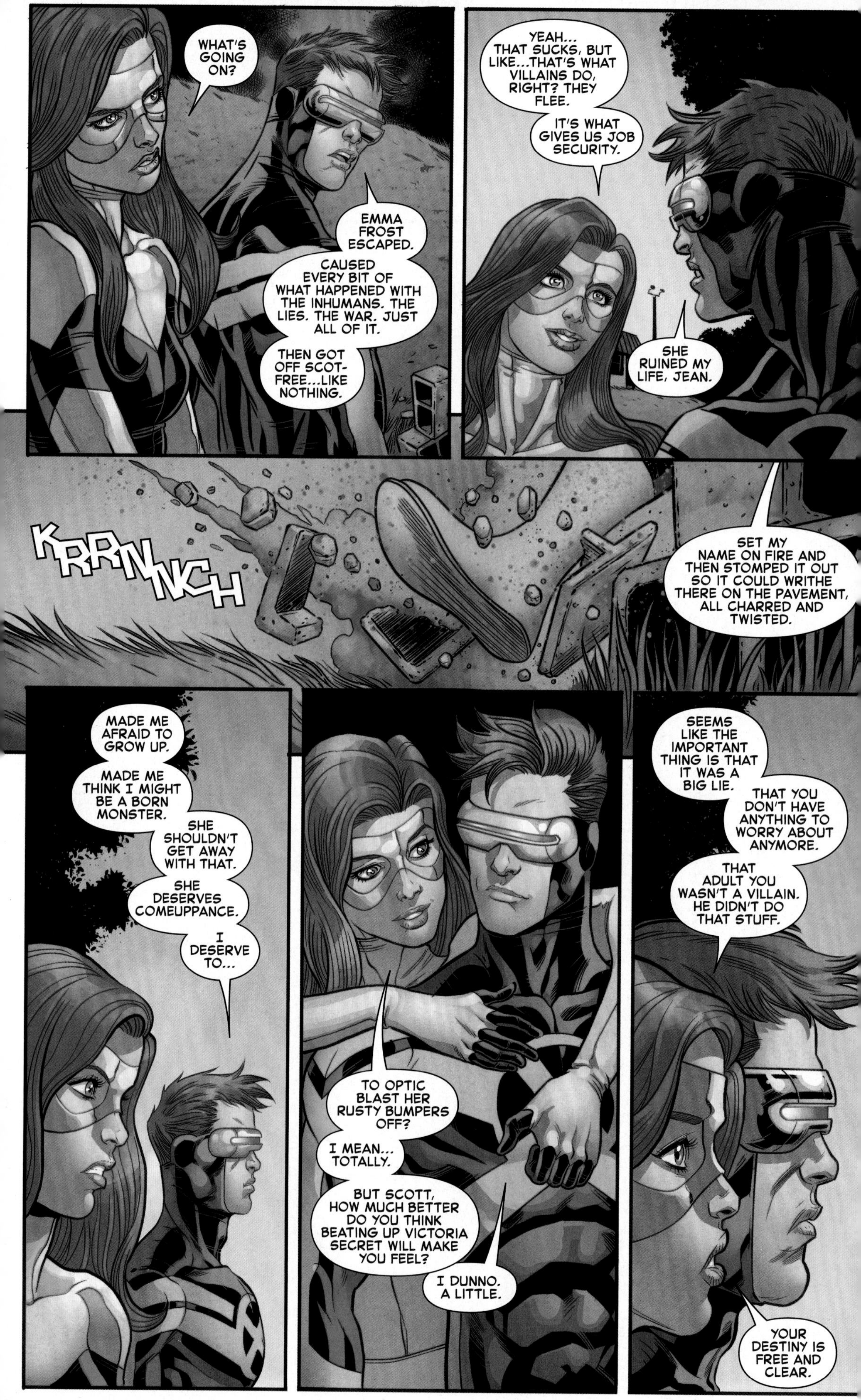
WHAT'S GOING ON?
EMMA FROST ESCAPED.
CAUSED EVERY BIT OF WHAT HAPPENED WITH THE INHUMANS. THE LIES. THE WAR. JUST ALL OF IT.
THEN GOT OFF SCOT-FREE...LIKE NOTHING.
YEAH... THAT SUCKS, BUT LIKE...THAT'S WHAT VILLAINS DO, RIGHT? THEY FLEE.
IT'S WHAT GIVES US JOB SECURITY.
SHE RUINED MY LIFE, JEAN.
KRRNNCH
SET MY NAME ON FIRE AND THEN STOMPED IT OUT SO IT COULD WRITHE THERE ON THE PAVEMENT, ALL CHARRED AND TWISTED.
MADE ME AFRAID TO GROW UP.
MADE ME THINK I MIGHT BE A BORN MONSTER.
SHE SHOULDN'T GET AWAY WITH THAT.
SHE DESERVES COMEUPPANCE.
I DESERVE TO...
TO OPTIC BLAST HER RUSTY BUMPERS OFF?
I MEAN... TOTALLY.
BUT SCOTT, HOW MUCH BETTER DO YOU THINK BEATING UP VICTORIA SECRET WILL MAKE YOU FEEL?
I DUNNO. A LITTLE.
SEEMS LIKE THE IMPORTANT THING IS THAT IT WAS A BIG LIE.
THAT YOU DON'T HAVE ANYTHING TO WORRY ABOUT ANYMORE.
THAT ADULT YOU WASN'T A VILLAIN. HE DIDN'T DO THAT STUFF.
YOUR DESTINY IS FREE AND CLEAR.

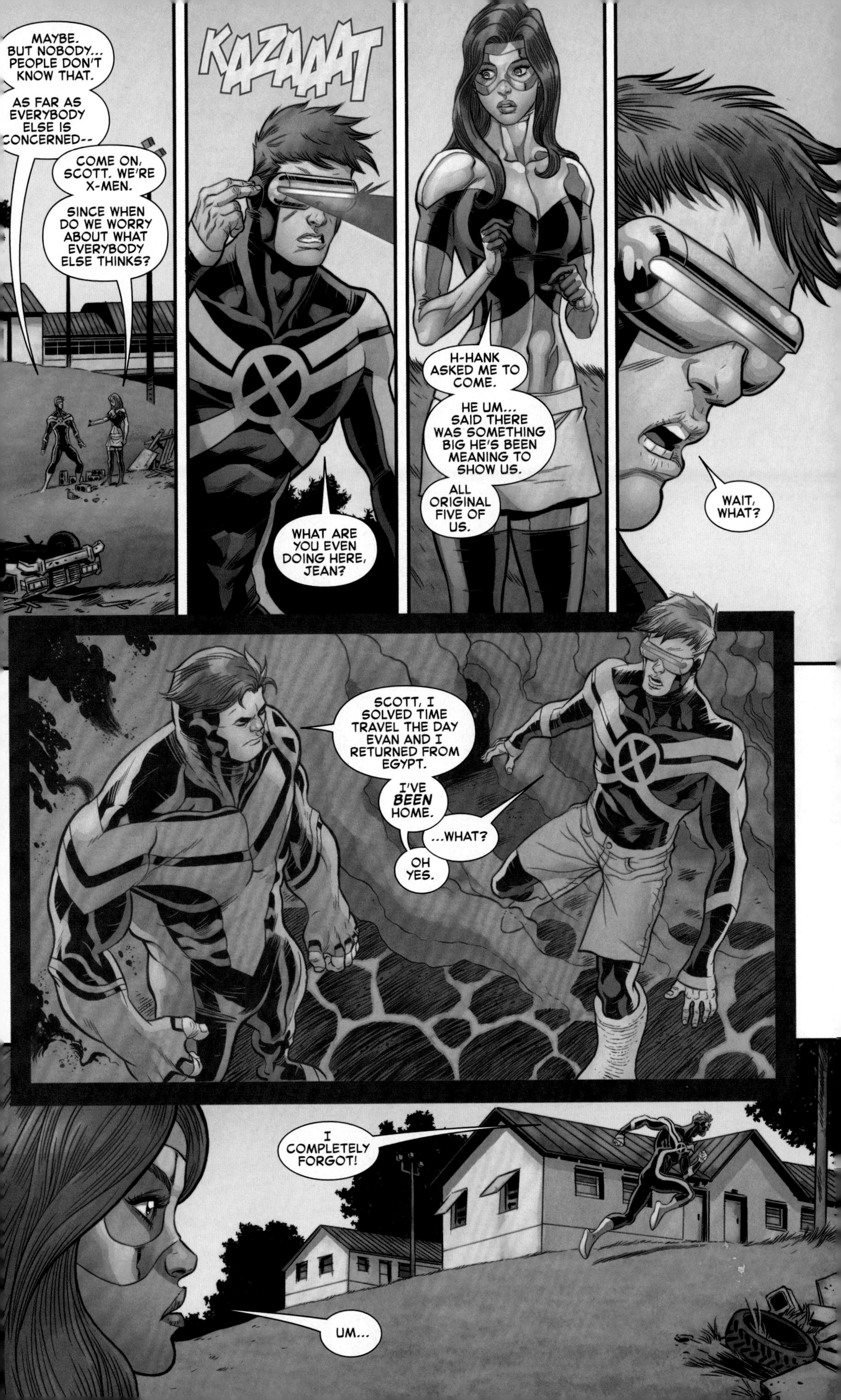
MAYBE. BUT NOBODY... PEOPLE DON'T KNOW THAT.
AS FAR AS EVERYBODY ELSE IS CONCERNED--
COME ON, SCOTT. WE'RE X-MEN.
SINCE WHEN DO WE WORRY ABOUT WHAT EVERYBODY ELSE THINKS?
KAZAAAT
WHAT ARE YOU EVEN DOING HERE, JEAN?
H-HANK ASKED ME TO COME.
HE UM... SAID THERE WAS SOMETHING BIG HE'S BEEN MEANING TO SHOW US.
ALL ORIGINAL FIVE OF US.
WAIT, WHAT?
SCOTT, I SOLVED TIME TRAVEL THE DAY EVAN AND I RETURNED FROM EGYPT.
I'VE BEEN HOME.
...WHAT?
OH YES.
I COMPLETELY FORGOT!
UM...

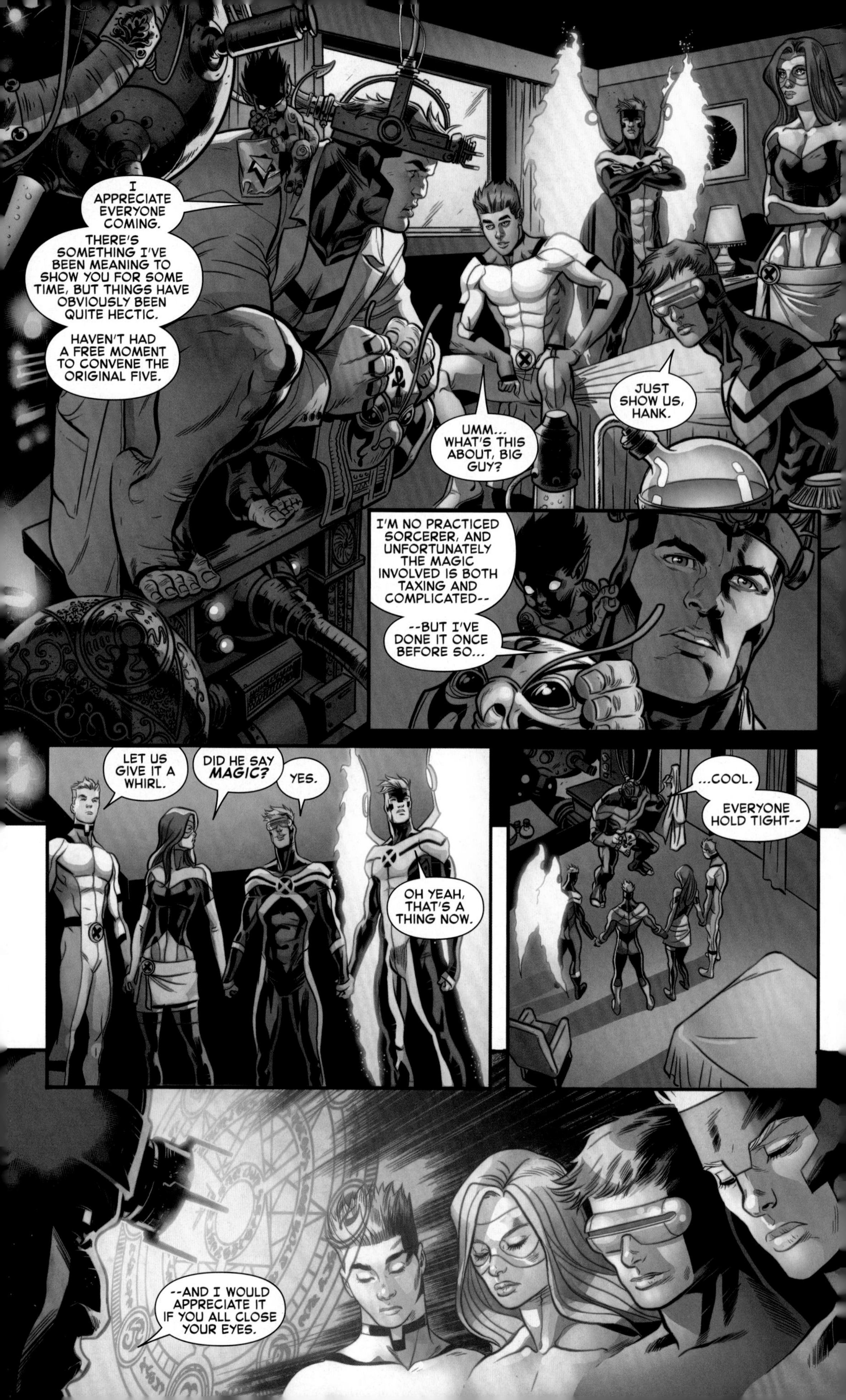
I APPRECIATE EVERYONE COMING.
THERE'S SOMETHING I'VE BEEN MEANING TO SHOW YOU FOR SOME TIME, BUT THINGS HAVE OBVIOUSLY BEEN QUITE HECTIC.
HAVEN'T HAD A FREE MOMENT TO CONVENE THE ORIGINAL FIVE.
UMM... WHAT'S THIS ABOUT, BIG GUY?
JUST SHOW US, HANK.
I'M NO PRACTICED SORCERER, AND UNFORTUNATELY THE MAGIC INVOLVED IS BOTH TAXING AND COMPLICATED--
--BUT I'VE DONE IT ONCE BEFORE SO...
LET US GIVE IT A WHIRL.
DID HE SAY *MAGIC?*
YES.
OH YEAH, THAT'S A THING NOW.
...COOL.
EVERYONE HOLD TIGHT--
--AND I WOULD APPRECIATE IT IF YOU ALL CLOSE YOUR EYES.

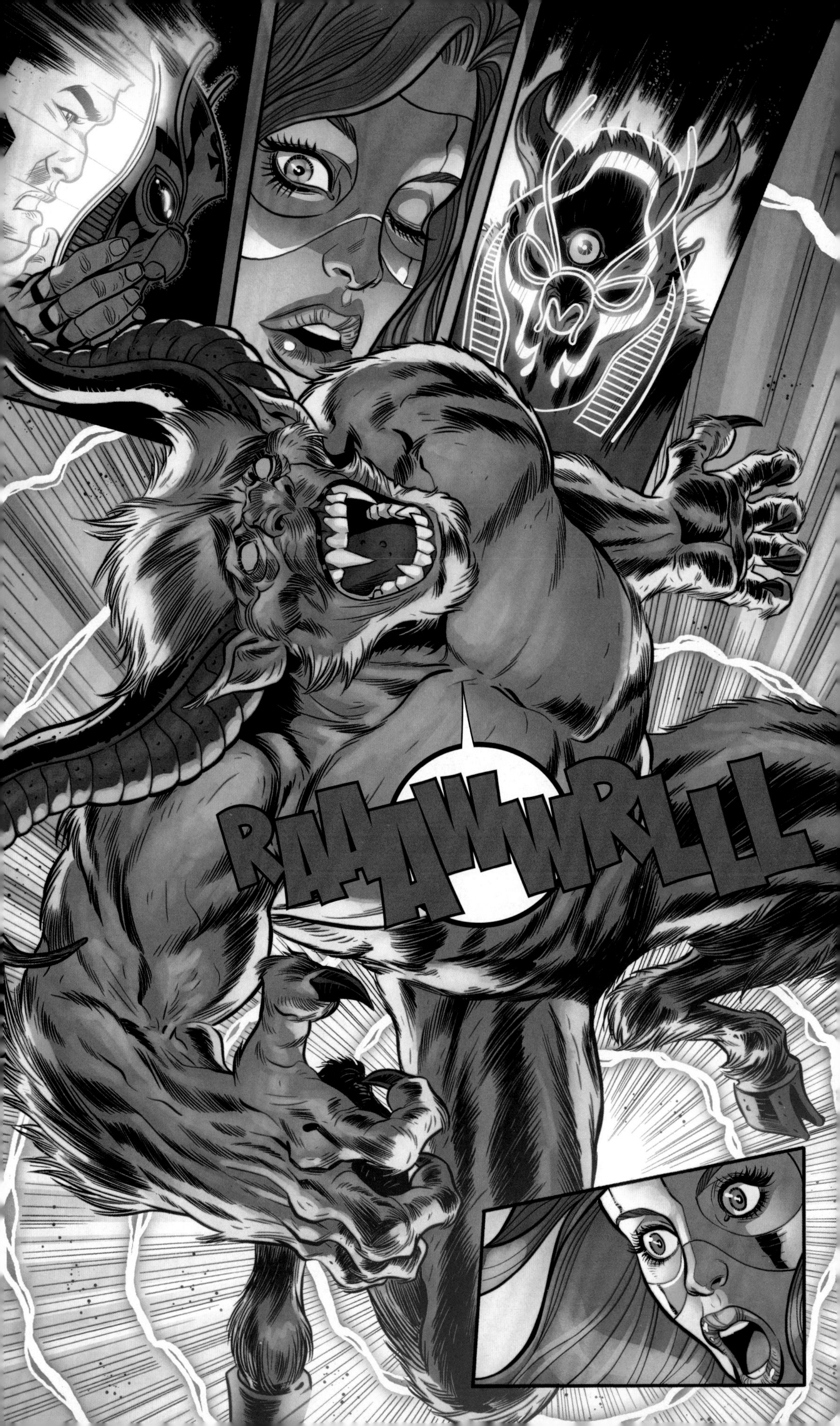
RAAAWWRLLL

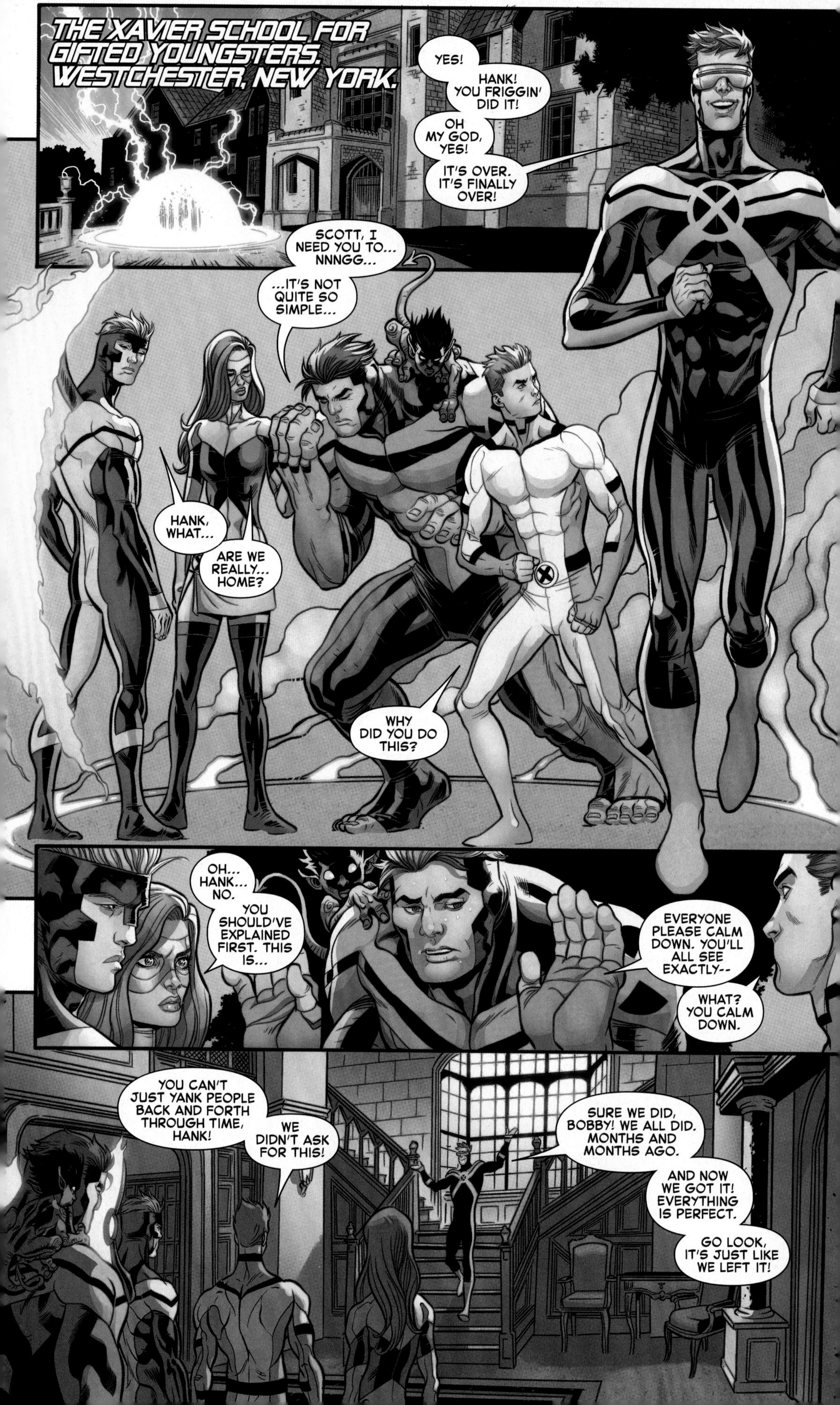
THE XAVIER SCHOOL FOR GIFTED YOUNGSTERS. WESTCHESTER, NEW YORK.
YES!
HANK! YOU FRIGGIN' DID IT!
OH MY GOD, YES!
IT'S OVER. IT'S FINALLY OVER!
SCOTT, I NEED YOU TO... NNNGG...
...IT'S NOT QUITE SO SIMPLE...
HANK, WHAT...
ARE WE REALLY... HOME?
WHY DID YOU DO THIS?
OH... HANK... NO.
YOU SHOULD'VE EXPLAINED FIRST. THIS IS...
EVERYONE PLEASE CALM DOWN. YOU'LL ALL SEE EXACTLY--
WHAT? YOU CALM DOWN.
YOU CAN'T JUST YANK PEOPLE BACK AND FORTH THROUGH TIME, HANK!
WE DIDN'T ASK FOR THIS!
SURE WE DID, BOBBY! WE ALL DID. MONTHS AND MONTHS AGO.
AND NOW WE GOT IT! EVERYTHING IS PERFECT.
GO LOOK, IT'S JUST LIKE WE LEFT IT!

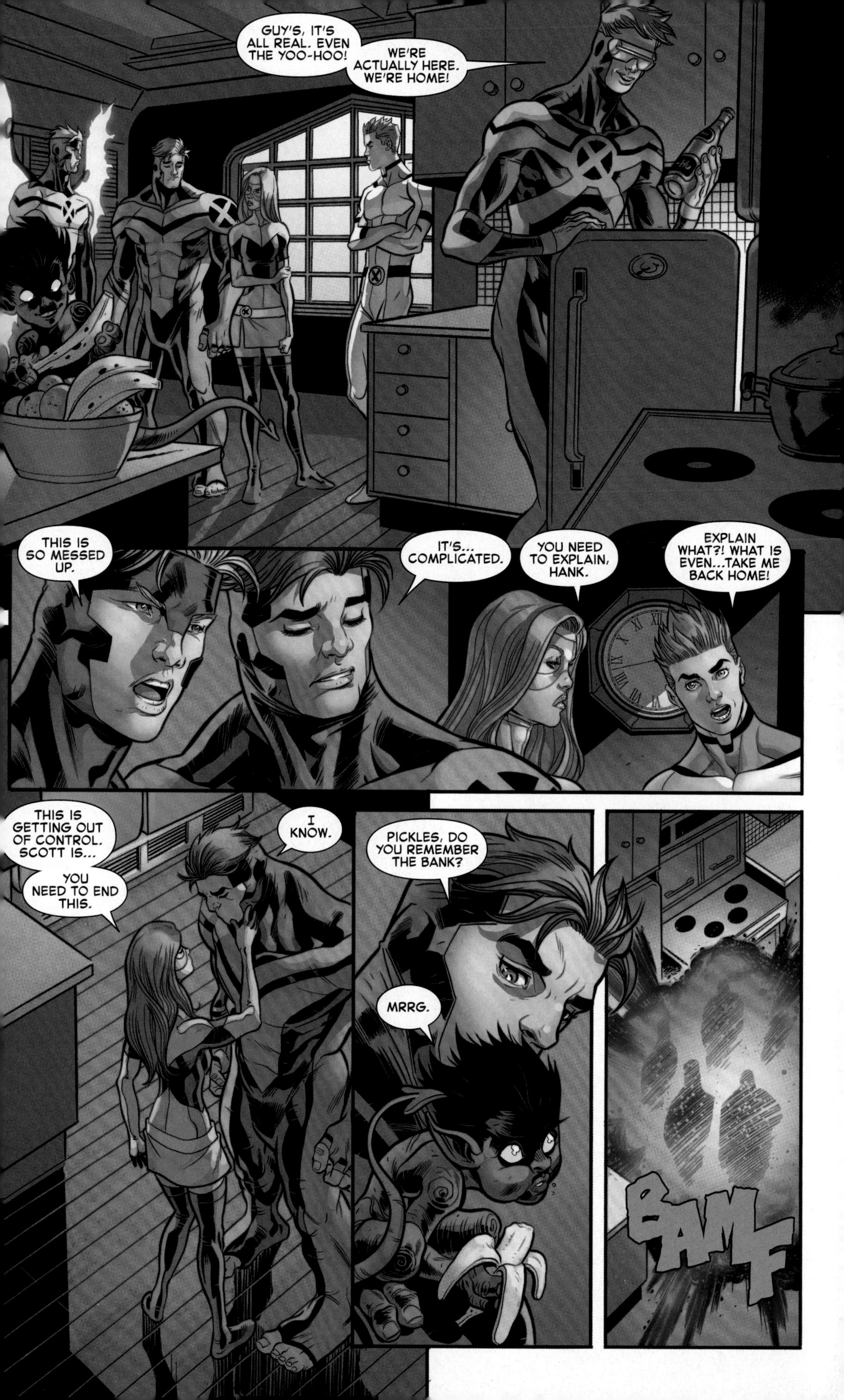
GUY'S, IT'S ALL REAL. EVEN THE YOO-HOO!
WE'RE ACTUALLY HERE. WE'RE HOME!
THIS IS SO MESSED UP.
IT'S... COMPLICATED.
YOU NEED TO EXPLAIN, HANK.
EXPLAIN WHAT?! WHAT IS EVEN...TAKE ME BACK HOME!
THIS IS GETTING OUT OF CONTROL. SCOTT IS...
YOU NEED TO END THIS.
I KNOW.
PICKLES, DO YOU REMEMBER THE BANK?
MRRG.
BAMF

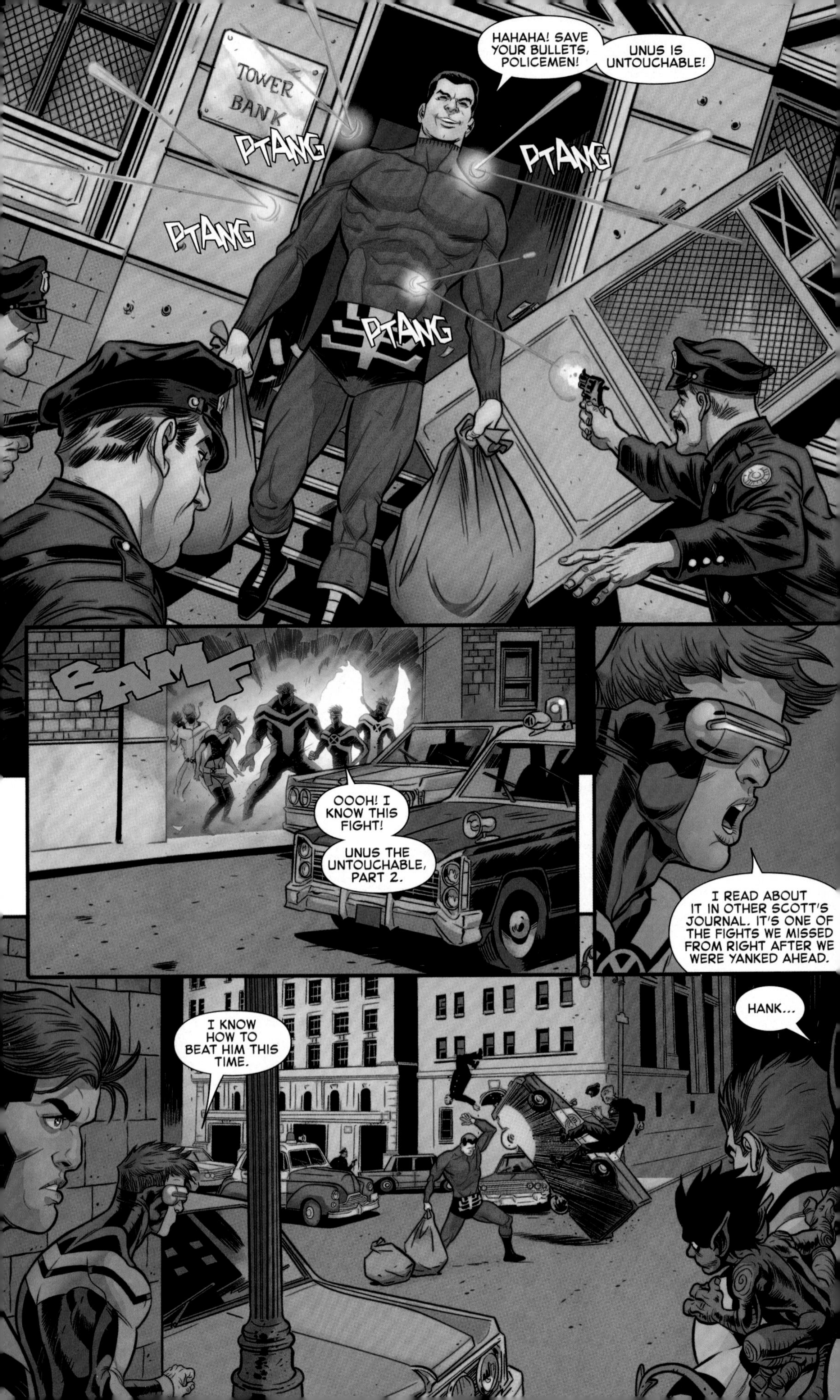
TOWER BANK
HAHAHA! SAVE YOUR BULLETS, POLICEMEN!
UNUS IS UNTOUCHABLE!
PTANG
PTANG
PTANG
PTANG
BAMF
OOOH! I KNOW THIS FIGHT!
UNUS THE UNTOUCHABLE, PART 2.
I READ ABOUT IT IN OTHER SCOTT'S JOURNAL. IT'S ONE OF THE FIGHTS WE MISSED FROM RIGHT AFTER WE WERE YANKED AHEAD.
I KNOW HOW TO BEAT HIM THIS TIME.
HANK...

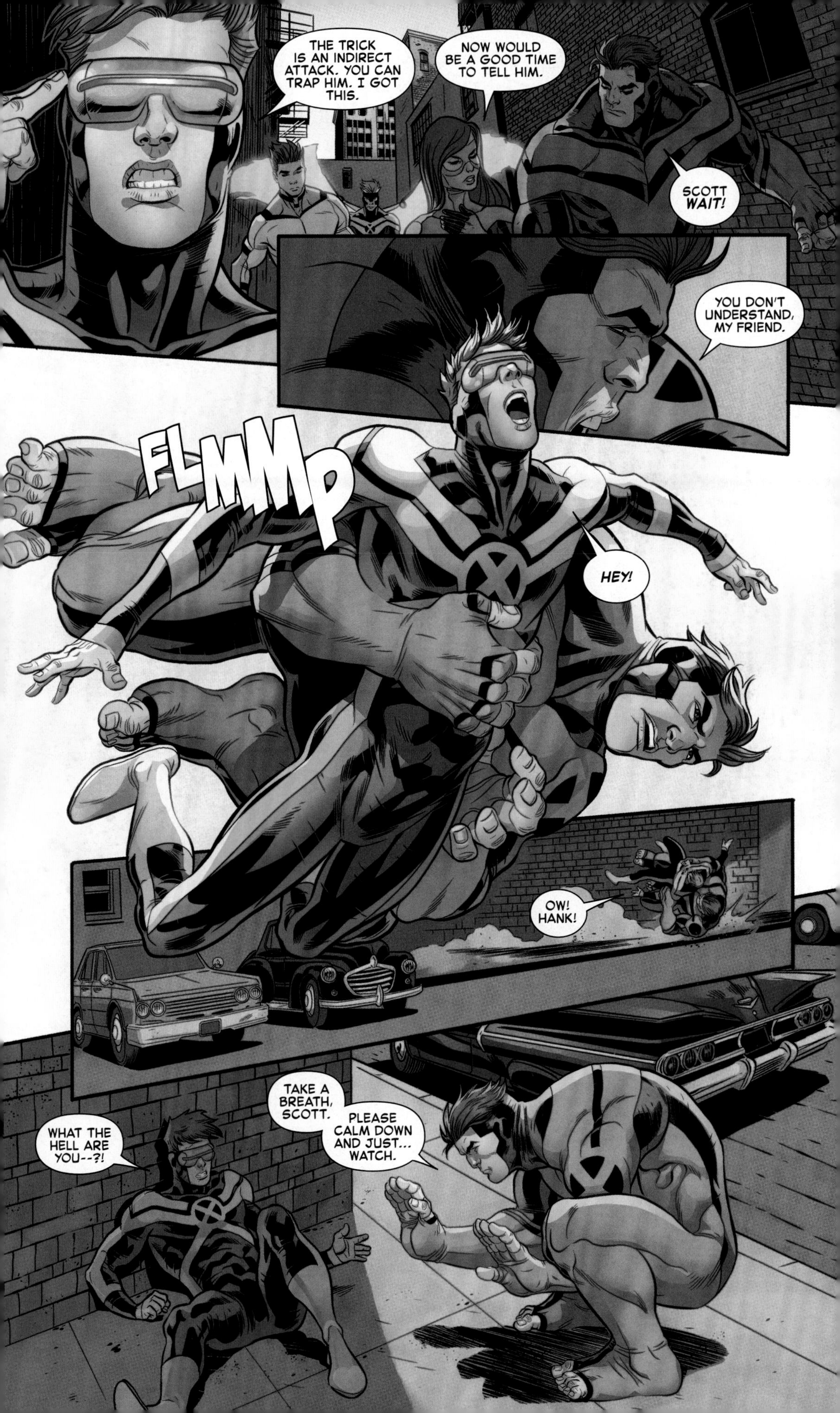
THE TRICK IS AN INDIRECT ATTACK. YOU CAN TRAP HIM. I GOT THIS.
NOW WOULD BE A GOOD TIME TO TELL HIM.
SCOTT WAIT!
YOU DON'T UNDERSTAND, MY FRIEND.
FLMMP
HEY!
OW! HANK!
WHAT THE HELL ARE YOU--?!
TAKE A BREATH, SCOTT.
PLEASE CALM DOWN AND JUST... WATCH.

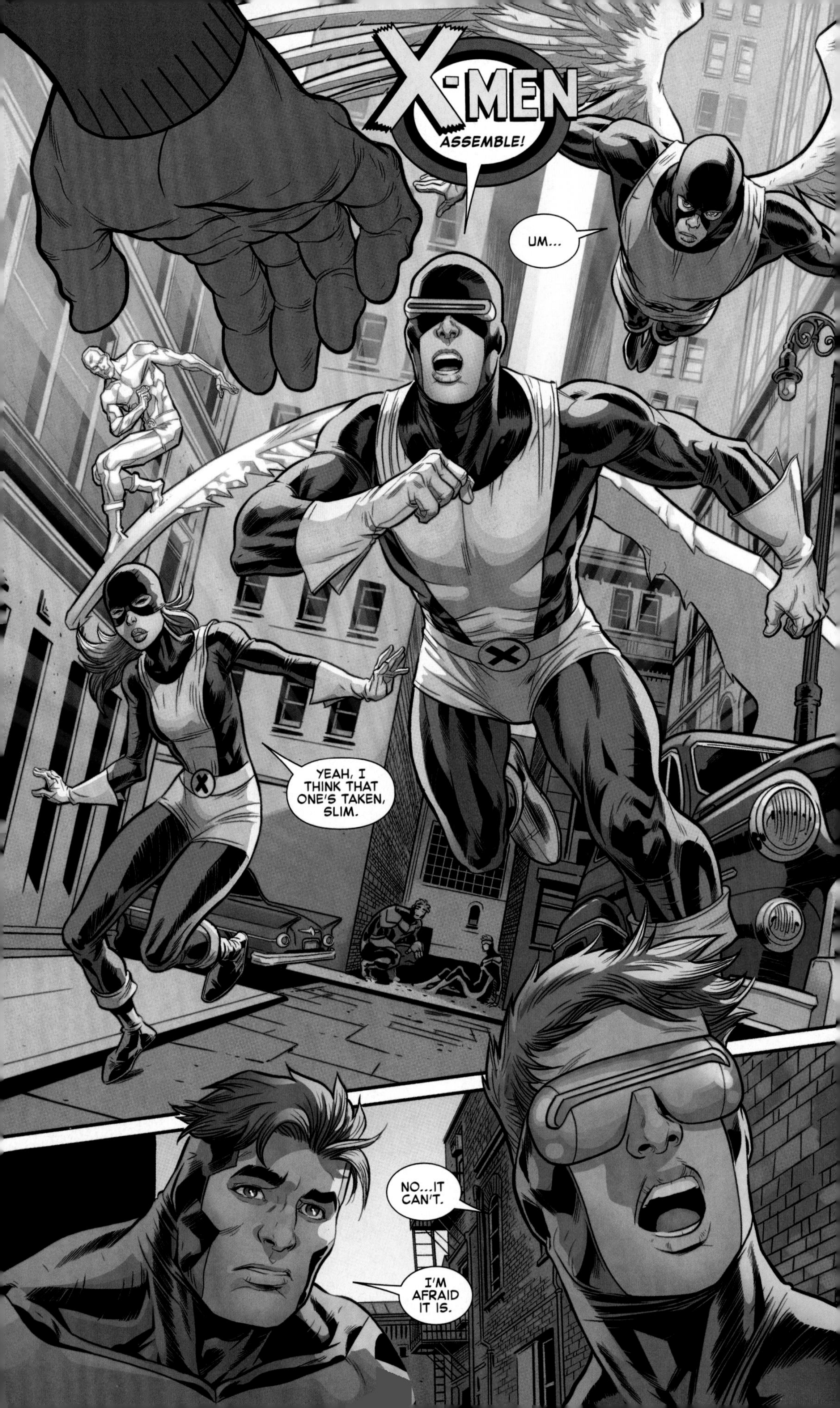
X-MEN ASSEMBLE!
UM...
YEAH, I THINK THAT ONE'S TAKEN, SLIM.
NO...IT CAN'T.
I'M AFRAID IT IS.

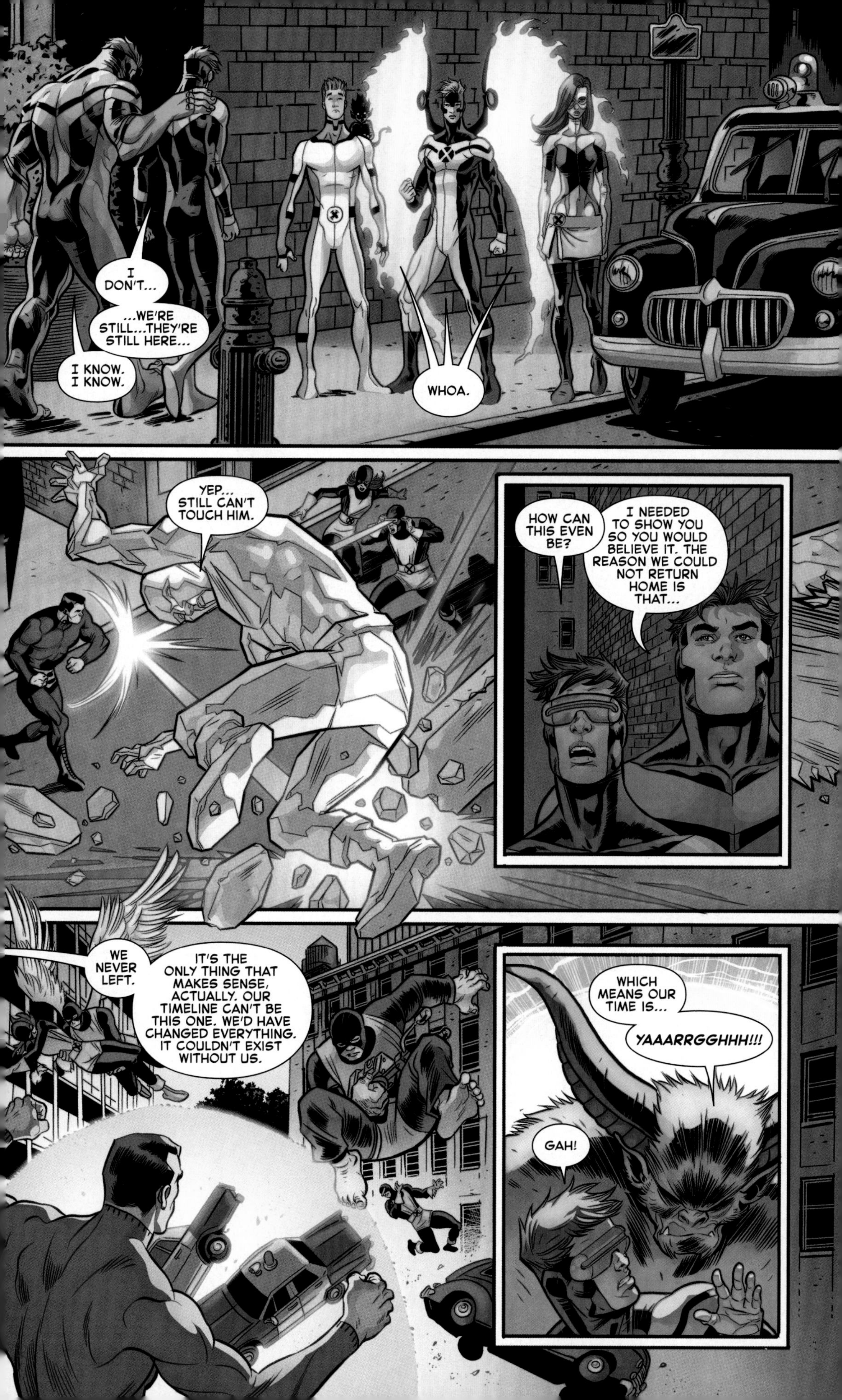

I DON'T...
...WE'RE STILL...THEY'RE STILL HERE...
I KNOW. I KNOW.
WHOA.
YEP... STILL CAN'T TOUCH HIM.
HOW CAN THIS EVEN BE?
I NEEDED TO SHOW YOU SO YOU WOULD BELIEVE IT. THE REASON WE COULD NOT RETURN HOME IS THAT...
WE NEVER LEFT.
IT'S THE ONLY THING THAT MAKES SENSE, ACTUALLY. OUR TIMELINE CAN'T BE THIS ONE. WE'D HAVE CHANGED EVERYTHING. IT COULDN'T EXIST WITHOUT US.
WHICH MEANS OUR TIME IS...
YAAARRGGHHH!!!
GAH!

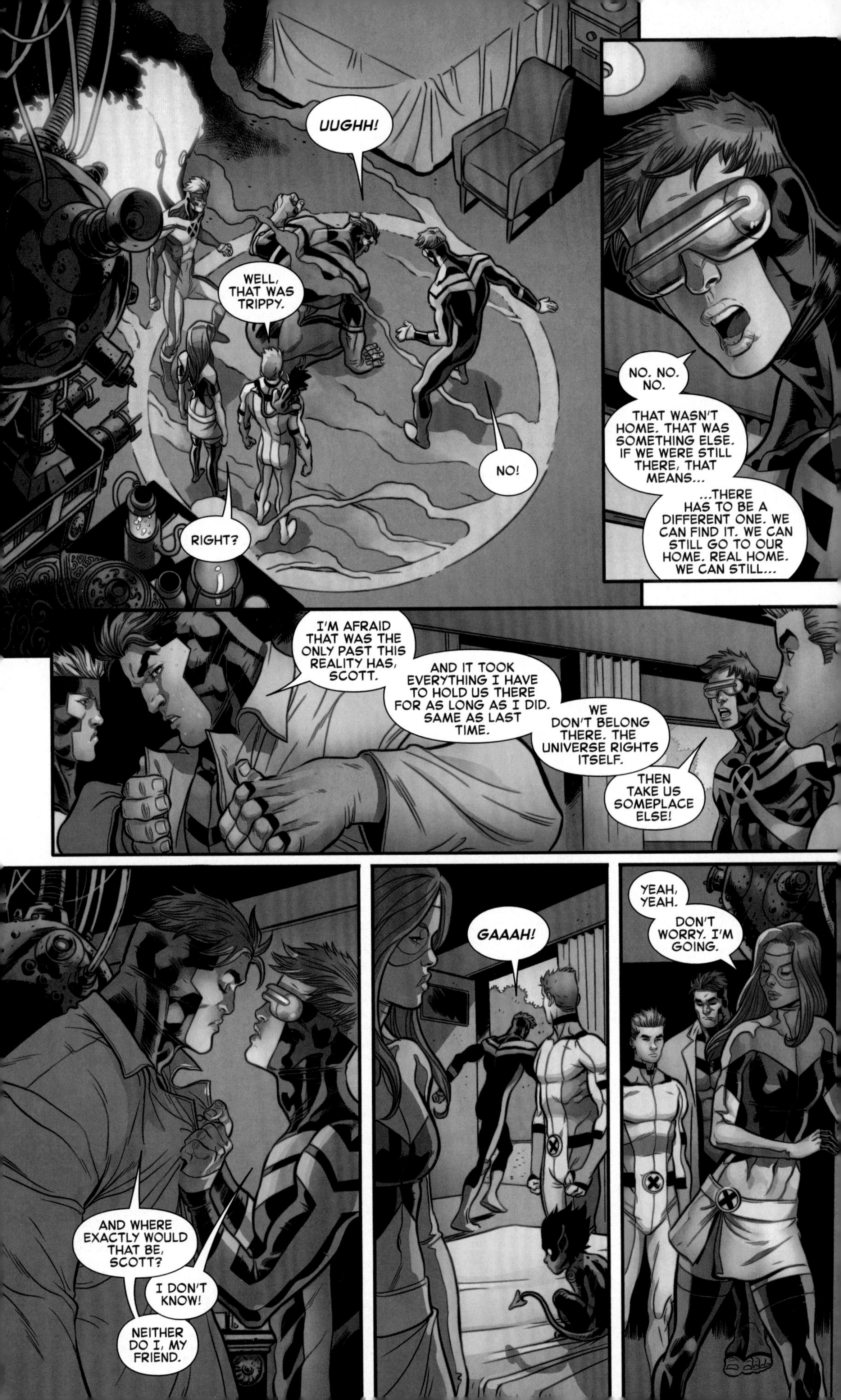
UUGHH!
WELL, THAT WAS TRIPPY.
NO!
RIGHT?
NO. NO. NO.
THAT WASN'T HOME. THAT WAS SOMETHING ELSE. IF WE WERE STILL THERE, THAT MEANS...
...THERE HAS TO BE A DIFFERENT ONE. WE CAN FIND IT. WE CAN STILL GO TO OUR HOME. REAL HOME. WE CAN STILL...
I'M AFRAID THAT WAS THE ONLY PAST THIS REALITY HAS, SCOTT.
AND IT TOOK EVERYTHING I HAVE TO HOLD US THERE FOR AS LONG AS I DID. SAME AS LAST TIME.
WE DON'T BELONG THERE. THE UNIVERSE RIGHTS ITSELF.
THEN TAKE US SOMEPLACE ELSE!
AND WHERE EXACTLY WOULD THAT BE, SCOTT?
I DON'T KNOW!
NEITHER DO I, MY FRIEND.
GAAAH!
YEAH, YEAH.
DON'T WORRY. I'M GOING.

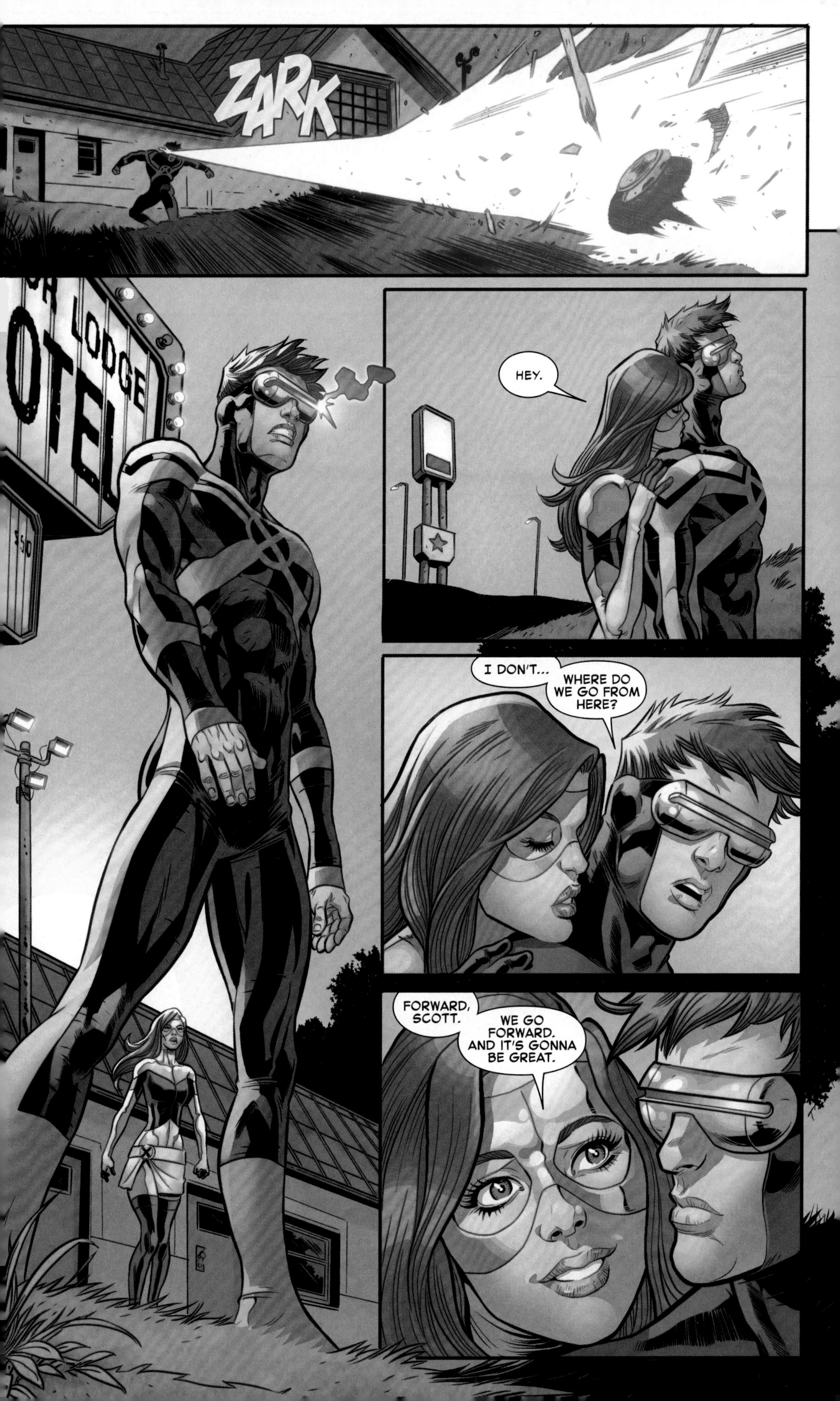
ZARK
HEY.
I DON'T...
WHERE DO WE GO FROM HERE?
FORWARD, SCOTT.
WE GO FORWARD. AND IT'S GONNA BE GREAT.

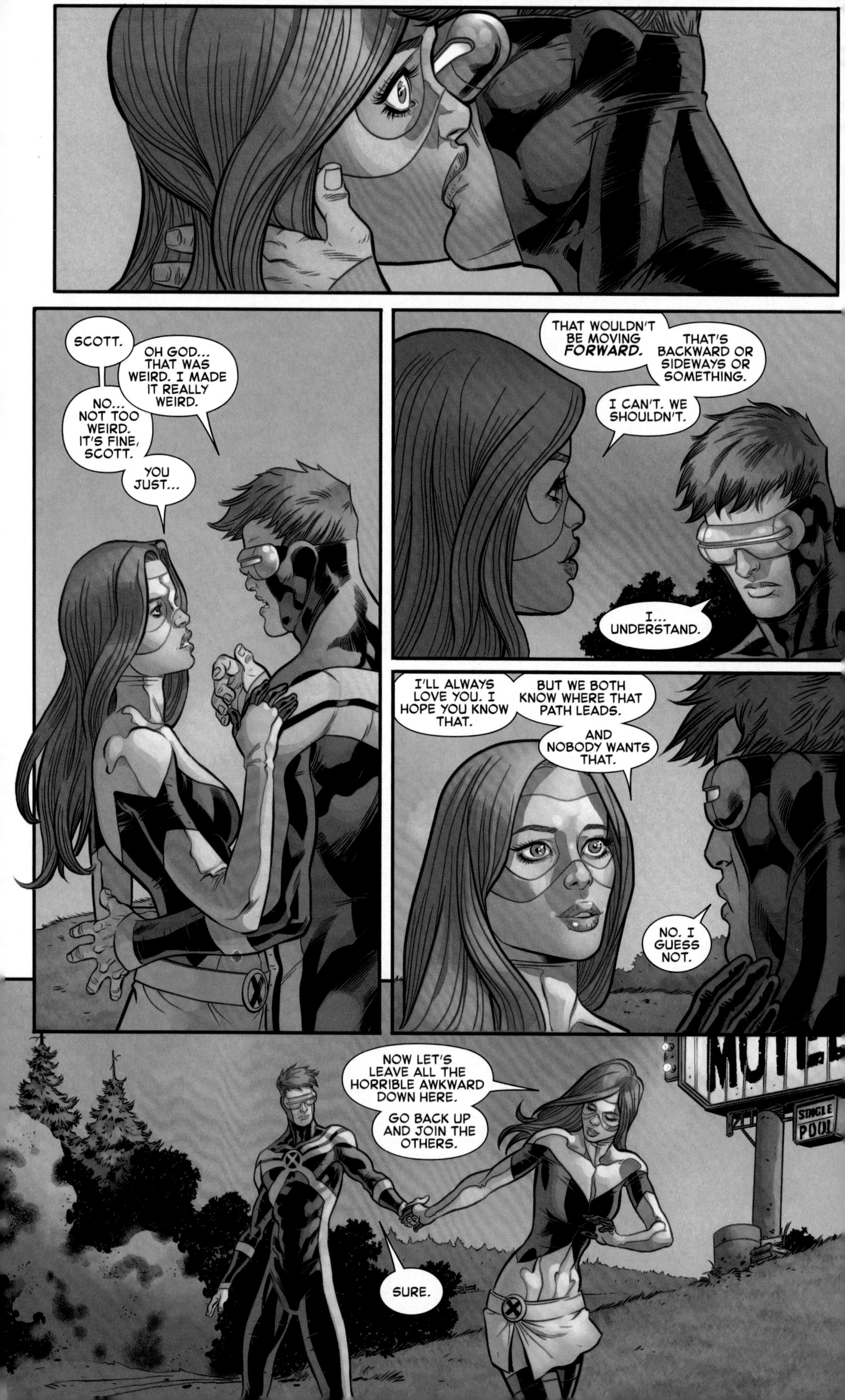
SCOTT.
OH GOD... THAT WAS WEIRD. I MADE IT REALLY WEIRD.
NO... NOT TOO WEIRD. IT'S FINE, SCOTT.
YOU JUST...
THAT WOULDN'T BE MOVING FORWARD.
THAT'S BACKWARD OR SIDEWAYS OR SOMETHING.
I CAN'T. WE SHOULDN'T.
I... UNDERSTAND.
I'LL ALWAYS LOVE YOU. I HOPE YOU KNOW THAT.
BUT WE BOTH KNOW WHERE THAT PATH LEADS.
AND NOBODY WANTS THAT.
NO. I GUESS NOT.
NOW LET'S LEAVE ALL THE HORRIBLE AWKWARD DOWN HERE.
GO BACK UP AND JOIN THE OTHERS.
SURE.
MOTE
SINGLE
POOL

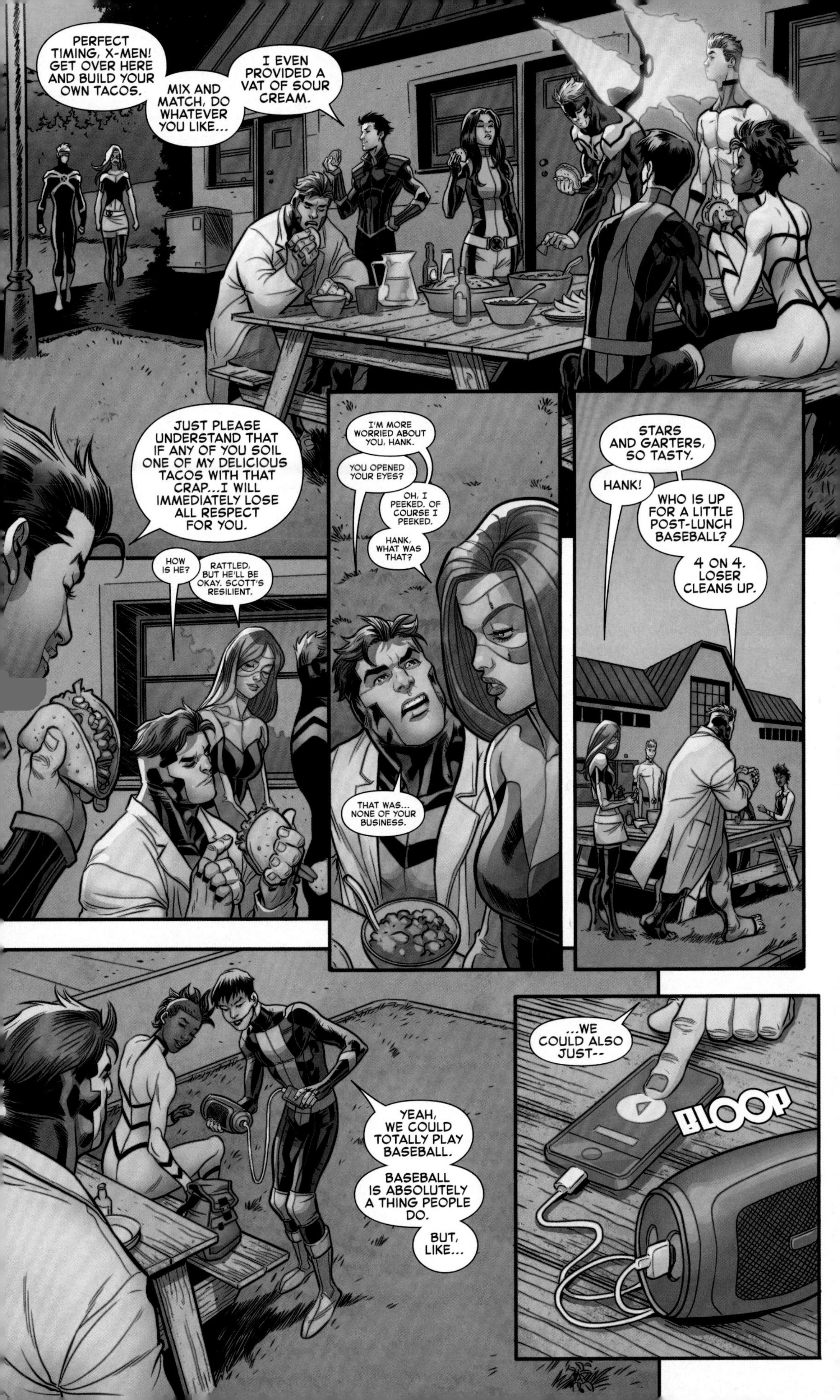
PERFECT TIMING, X-MEN! GET OVER HERE AND BUILD YOUR OWN TACOS.
MIX AND MATCH, DO WHATEVER YOU LIKE...
I EVEN PROVIDED A VAT OF SOUR CREAM.
JUST PLEASE UNDERSTAND THAT IF ANY OF YOU SOIL ONE OF MY DELICIOUS TACOS WITH THAT CRAP...I WILL IMMEDIATELY LOSE ALL RESPECT FOR YOU.
HOW IS HE?
RATTLED, BUT HE'LL BE OKAY. SCOTT'S RESILIENT.
I'M MORE WORRIED ABOUT YOU, HANK.
YOU OPENED YOUR EYES?
OH, I PEEKED. OF COURSE I PEEKED.
HANK, WHAT WAS THAT?
THAT WAS... NONE OF YOUR BUSINESS.
STARS AND GARTERS, SO TASTY.
HANK!
WHO IS UP FOR A LITTLE POST-LUNCH BASEBALL?
4 ON 4. LOSER CLEANS UP.
YEAH, WE COULD TOTALLY PLAY BASEBALL.
BASEBALL IS ABSOLUTELY A THING PEOPLE DO.
BUT, LIKE...
...WE COULD ALSO JUST--
BLOOP

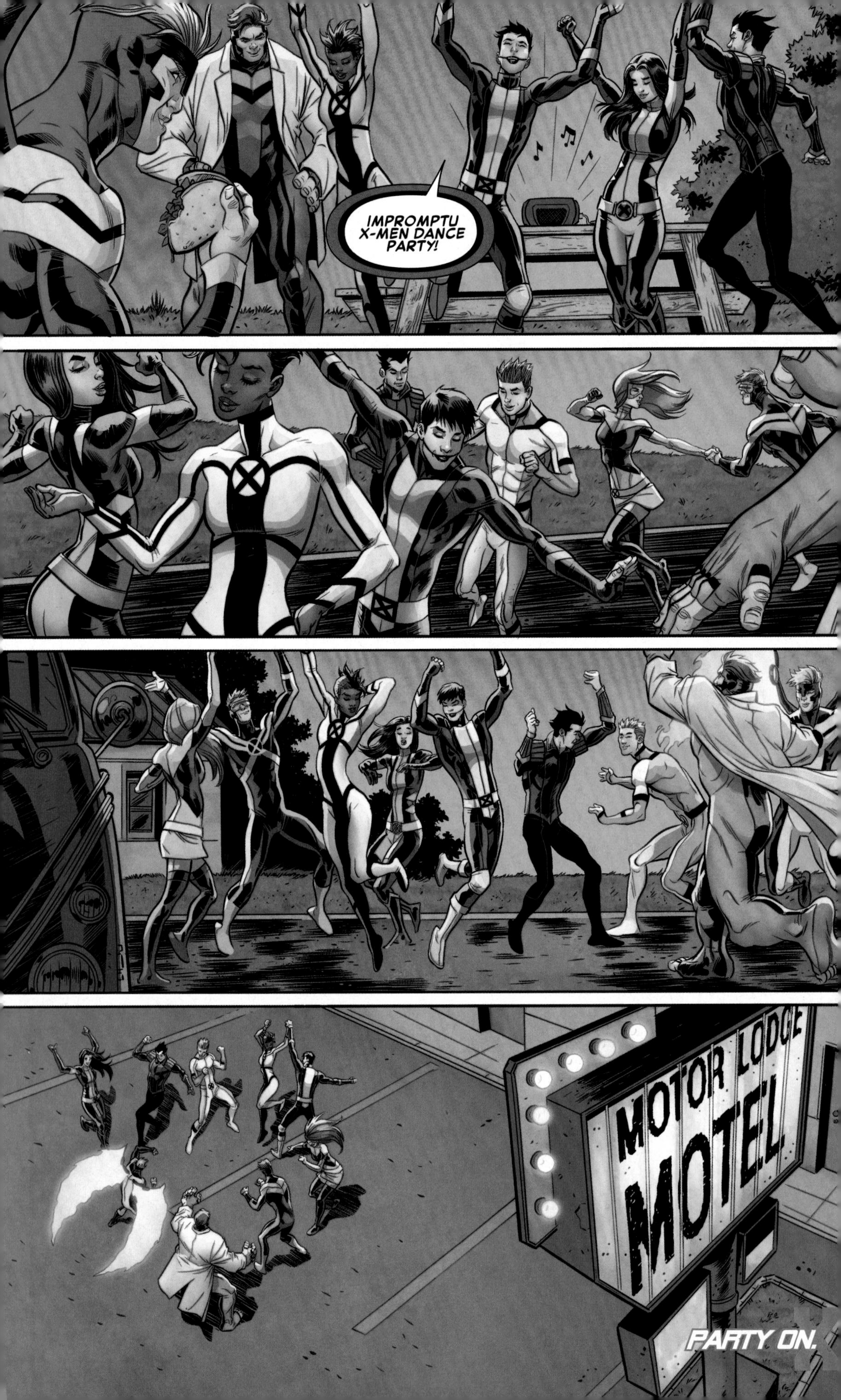

IMPROMPTU X-MEN DANCE PARTY!
MOTOR LODGE
MOTEL
PARTY ON.

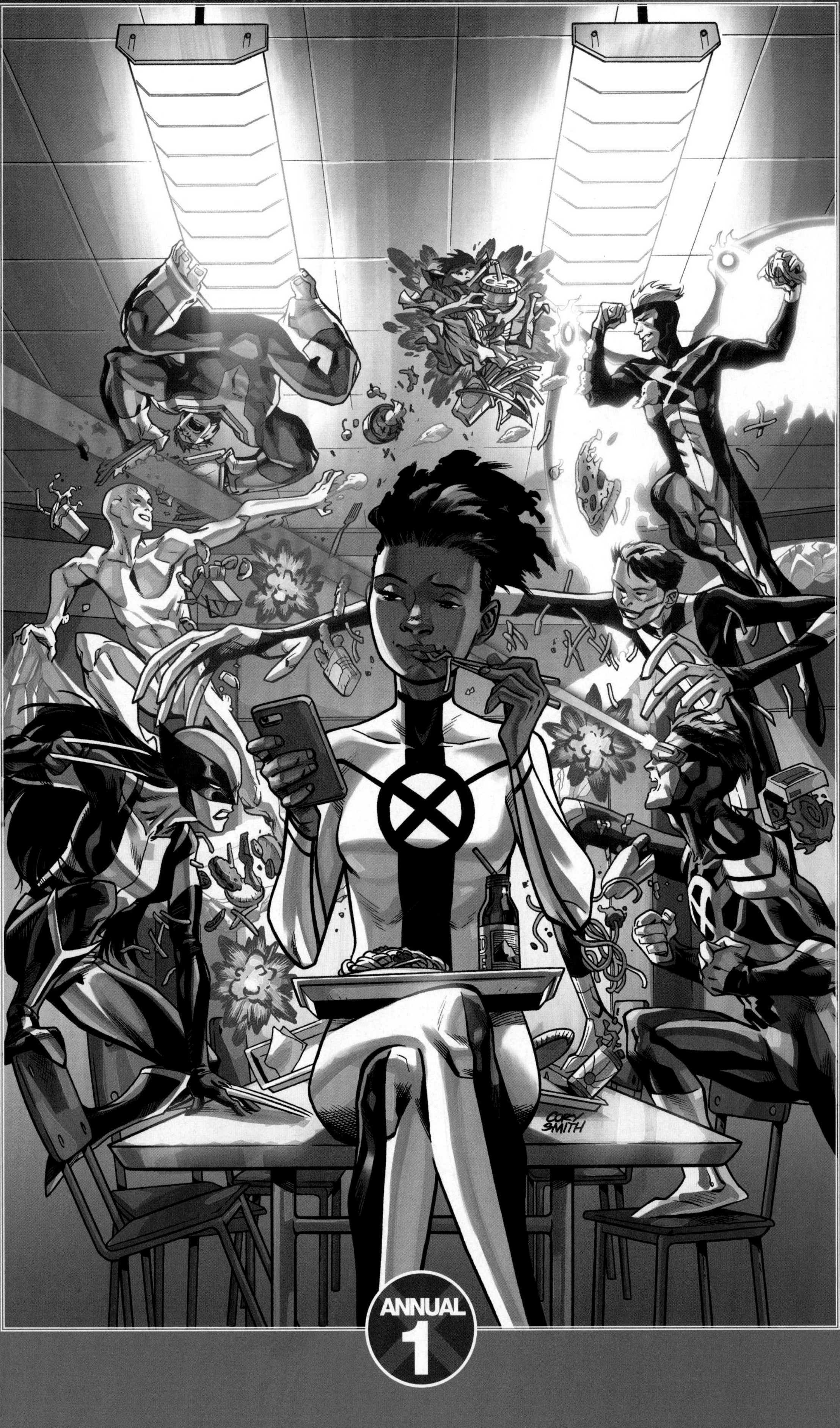
CORY SMITH
ANNUAL
1

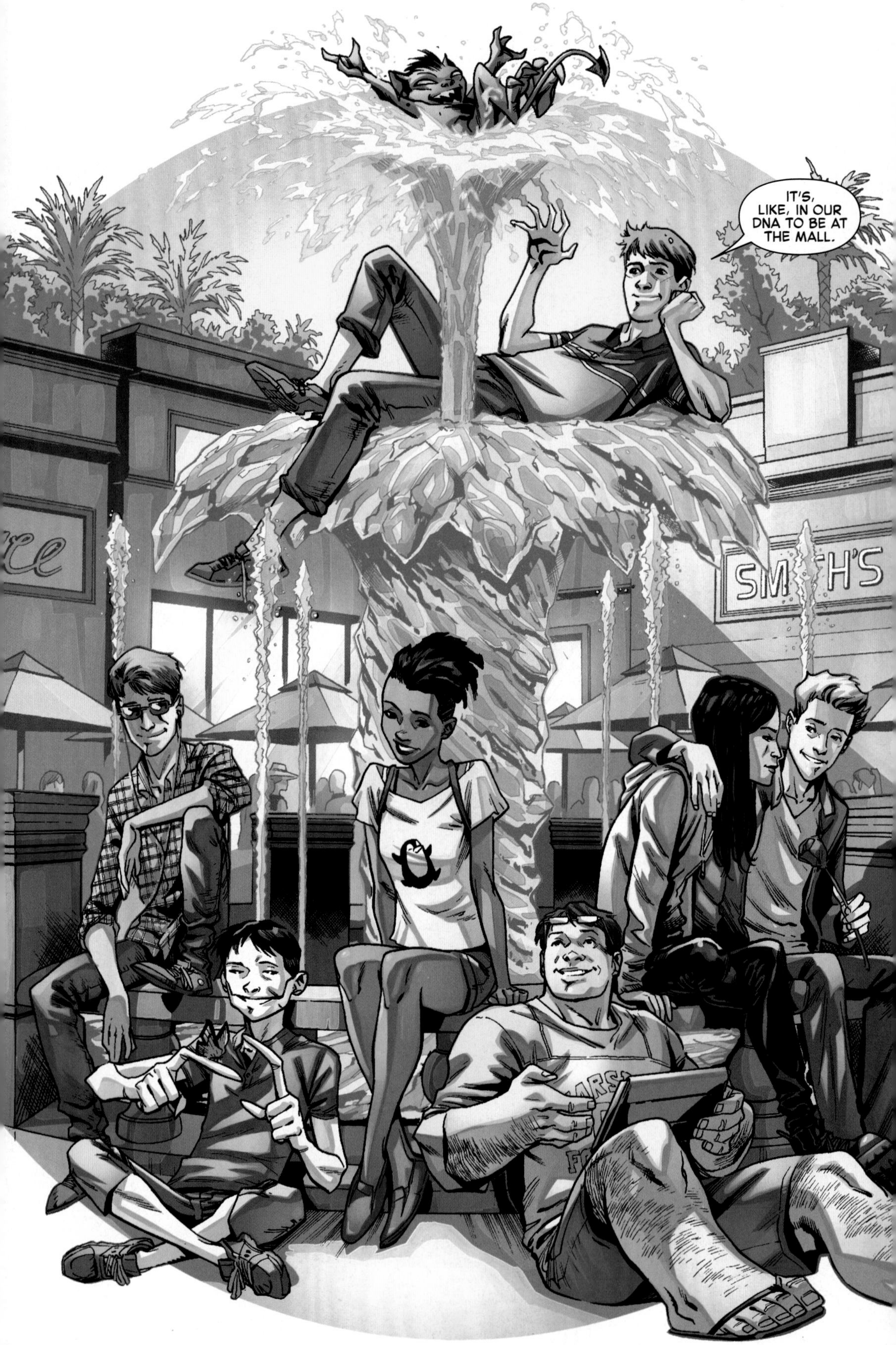
IT'S, LIKE, IN OUR DNA TO BE AT THE MALL.
SMITH'S

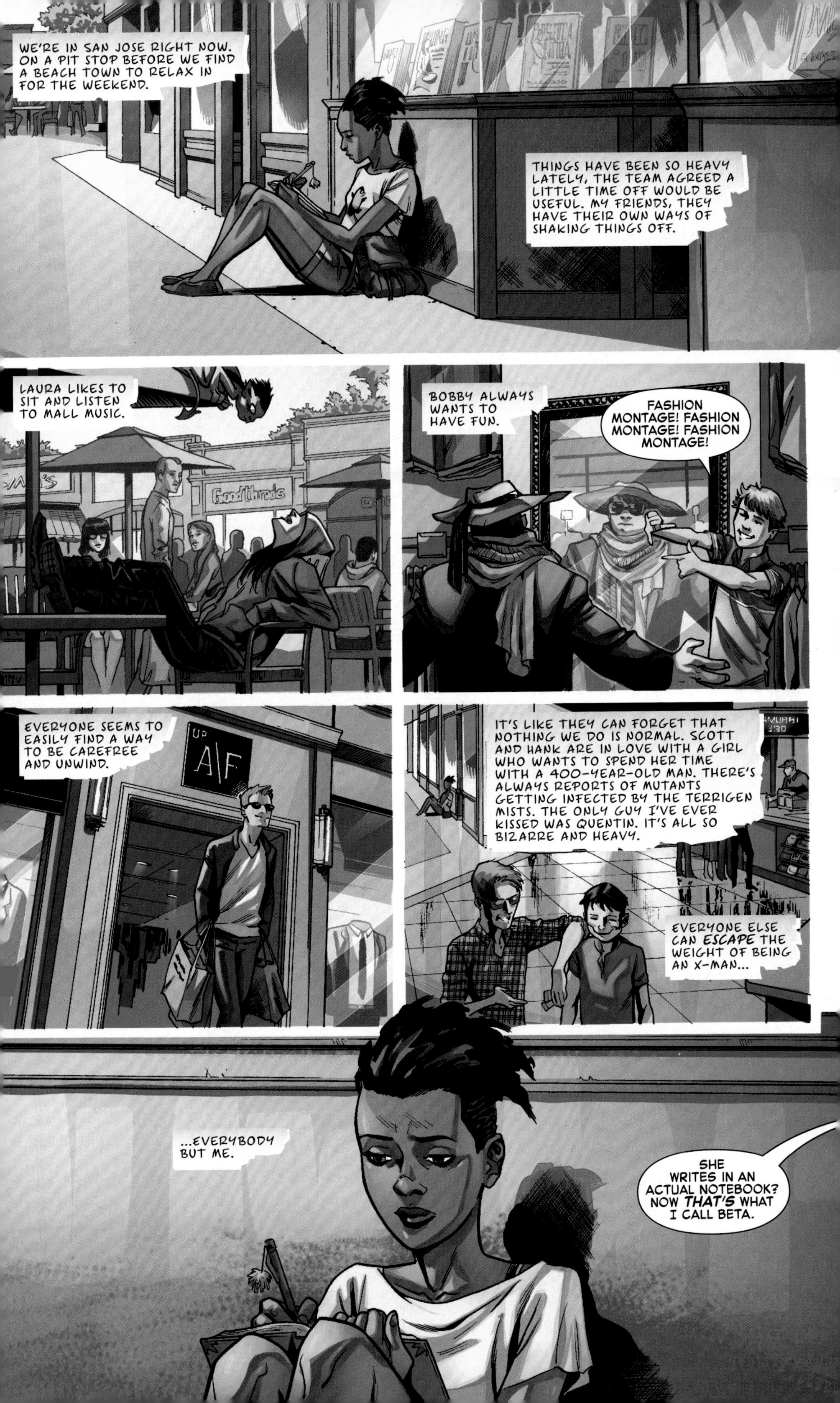
WE'RE IN SAN JOSE RIGHT NOW. ON A PIT STOP BEFORE WE FIND A BEACH TOWN TO RELAX IN FOR THE WEEKEND.
THINGS HAVE BEEN SO HEAVY LATELY, THE TEAM AGREED A LITTLE TIME OFF WOULD BE USEFUL. MY FRIENDS, THEY HAVE THEIR OWN WAYS OF SHAKING THINGS OFF.
LAURA LIKES TO SIT AND LISTEN TO MALL MUSIC.
GoodThreads
BOBBY ALWAYS WANTS TO HAVE FUN.
FASHION MONTAGE! FASHION MONTAGE! FASHION MONTAGE!
EVERYONE SEEMS TO EASILY FIND A WAY TO BE CAREFREE AND UNWIND.
UP
A|F
IT'S LIKE THEY CAN FORGET THAT NOTHING WE DO IS NORMAL. SCOTT AND HANK ARE IN LOVE WITH A GIRL WHO WANTS TO SPEND HER TIME WITH A 400-YEAR-OLD MAN. THERE'S ALWAYS REPORTS OF MUTANTS GETTING INFECTED BY THE TERRIGEN MISTS. THE ONLY GUY I'VE EVER KISSED WAS QUENTIN. IT'S ALL SO BIZARRE AND HEAVY.
EVERYONE ELSE CAN ESCAPE THE WEIGHT OF BEING AN X-MAN...
...EVERYBODY BUT ME.
SHE WRITES IN AN ACTUAL NOTEBOOK? NOW THAT'S WHAT I CALL BETA.

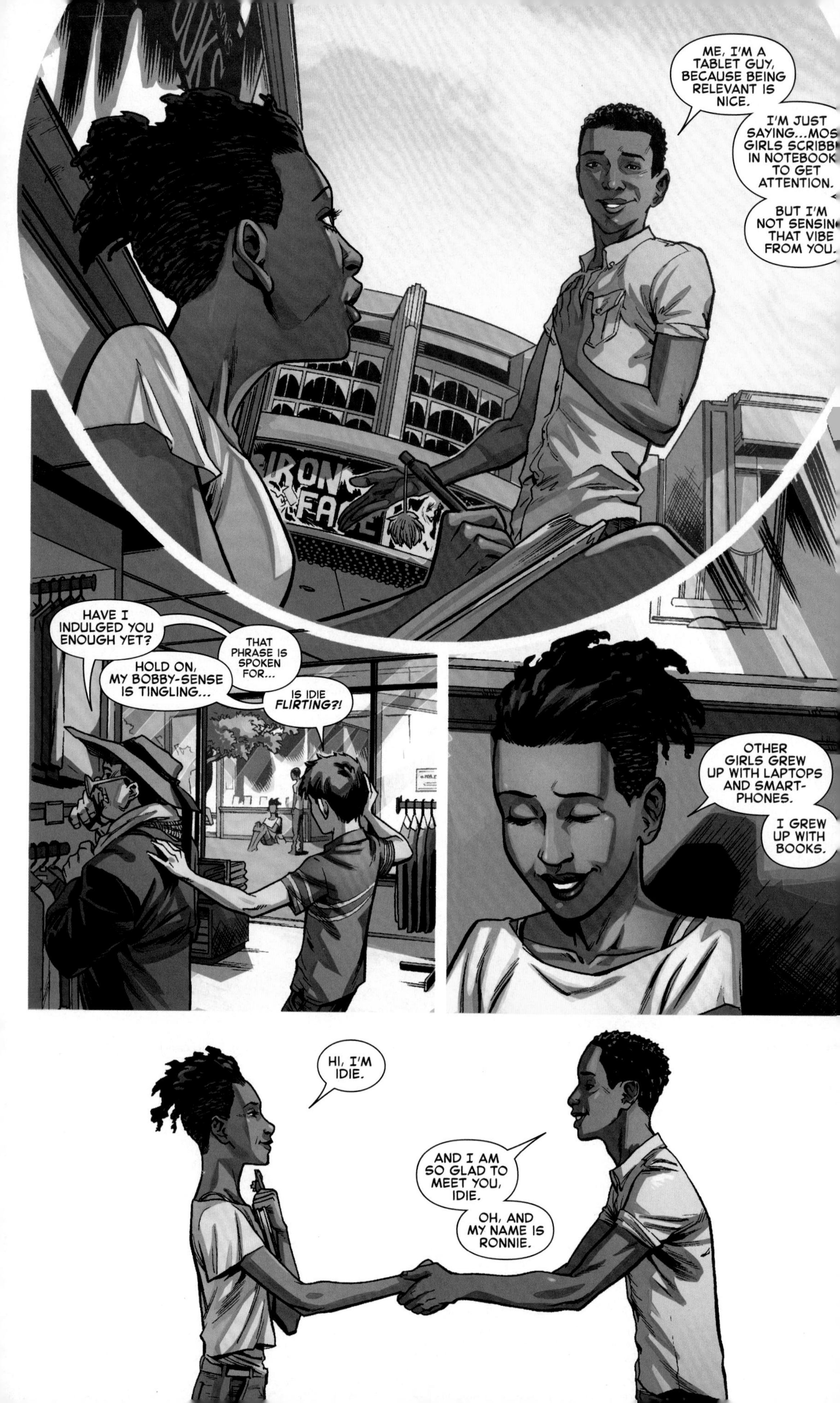
ME, I'M A TABLET GUY, BECAUSE BEING RELEVANT IS NICE.
I'M JUST SAYING...MOS GIRLS SCRIBB IN NOTEBOOK TO GET ATTENTION.
BUT I'M NOT SENSIN THAT VIBE FROM YOU.
HAVE I INDULGED YOU ENOUGH YET?
HOLD ON, MY BOBBY-SENSE IS TINGLING...
THAT PHRASE IS SPOKEN FOR...
IS IDIE *FLIRTING?!*
OTHER GIRLS GREW UP WITH LAPTOPS AND SMART-PHONES.
I GREW UP WITH BOOKS.
HI, I'M IDIE.
AND I AM SO GLAD TO MEET YOU, IDIE.
OH, AND MY NAME IS RONNIE.

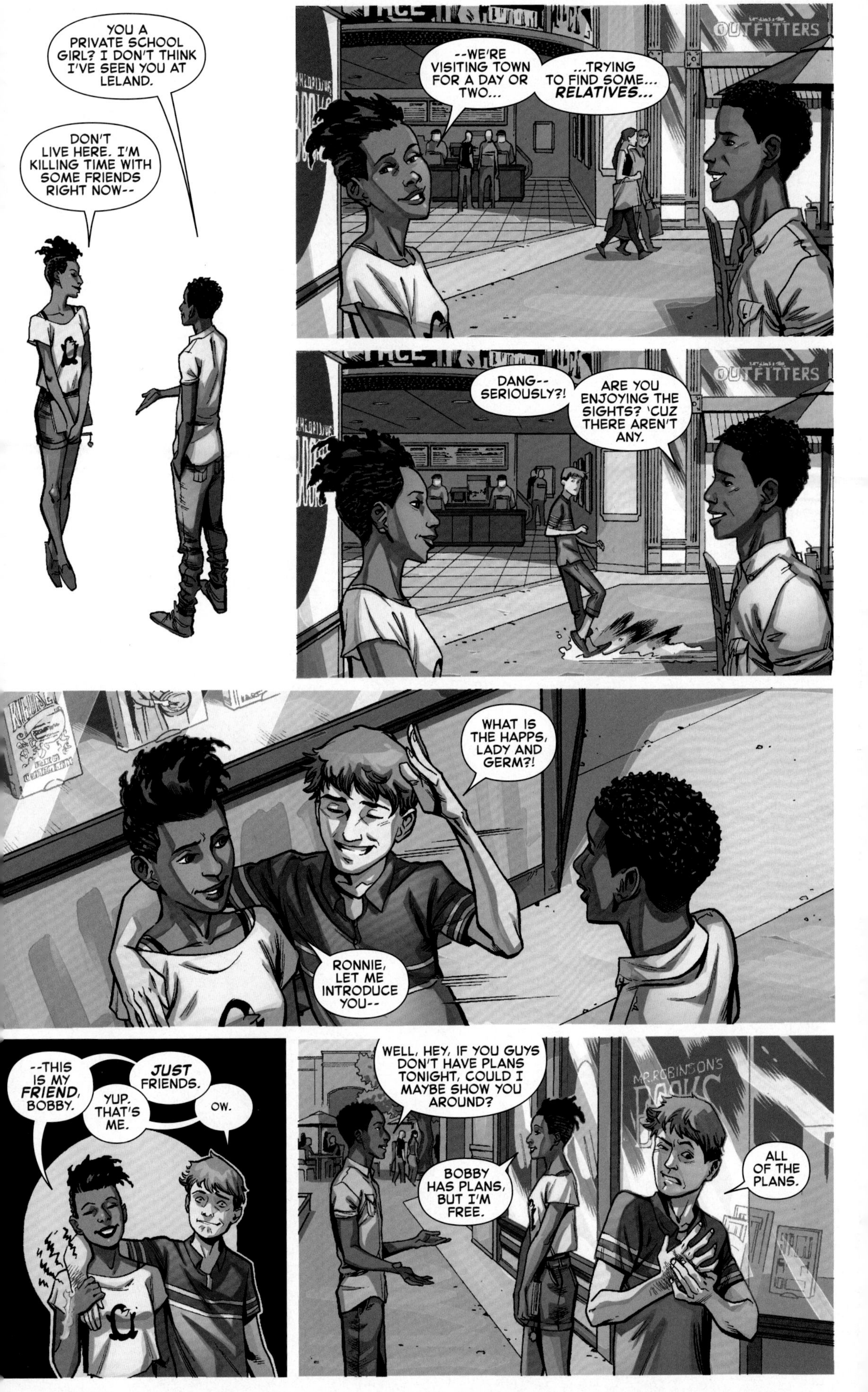
YOU A PRIVATE SCHOOL GIRL? I DON'T THINK I'VE SEEN YOU AT LELAND.
DON'T LIVE HERE. I'M KILLING TIME WITH SOME FRIENDS RIGHT NOW--
--WE'RE VISITING TOWN FOR A DAY OR TWO...
...TRYING TO FIND SOME... *RELATIVES...*
OUTFITTERS
DANG-- SERIOUSLY?!
ARE YOU ENJOYING THE SIGHTS? 'CUZ THERE AREN'T ANY.
WHAT IS THE HAPPS, LADY AND GERM?!
RONNIE, LET ME INTRODUCE YOU--
--THIS IS MY *FRIEND*, BOBBY.
JUST FRIENDS.
YUP. THAT'S ME.
OW.
WELL, HEY, IF YOU GUYS DON'T HAVE PLANS TONIGHT, COULD I MAYBE SHOW YOU AROUND?
BOBBY HAS PLANS, BUT I'M FREE.
ALL OF THE PLANS.
MR. ROBINSON'S BOOKS

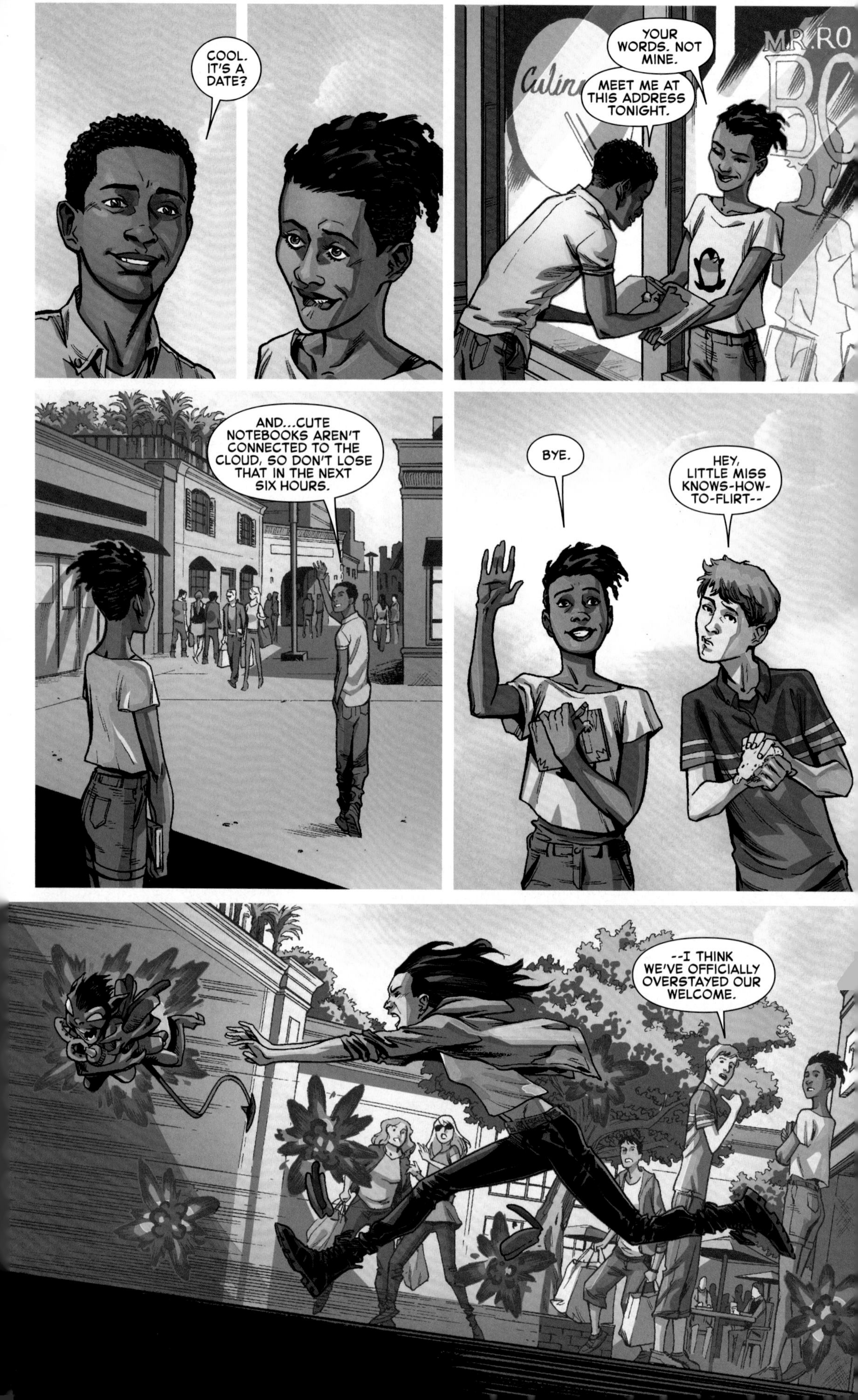
COOL. IT'S A DATE?
YOUR WORDS. NOT MINE.
MEET ME AT THIS ADDRESS TONIGHT.
MR.RO
AND...CUTE NOTEBOOKS AREN'T CONNECTED TO THE CLOUD, SO DON'T LOSE THAT IN THE NEXT SIX HOURS.
BYE.
HEY, LITTLE MISS KNOWS-HOW-TO-FLIRT--
--I THINK WE'VE OFFICIALLY OVERSTAYED OUR WELCOME.

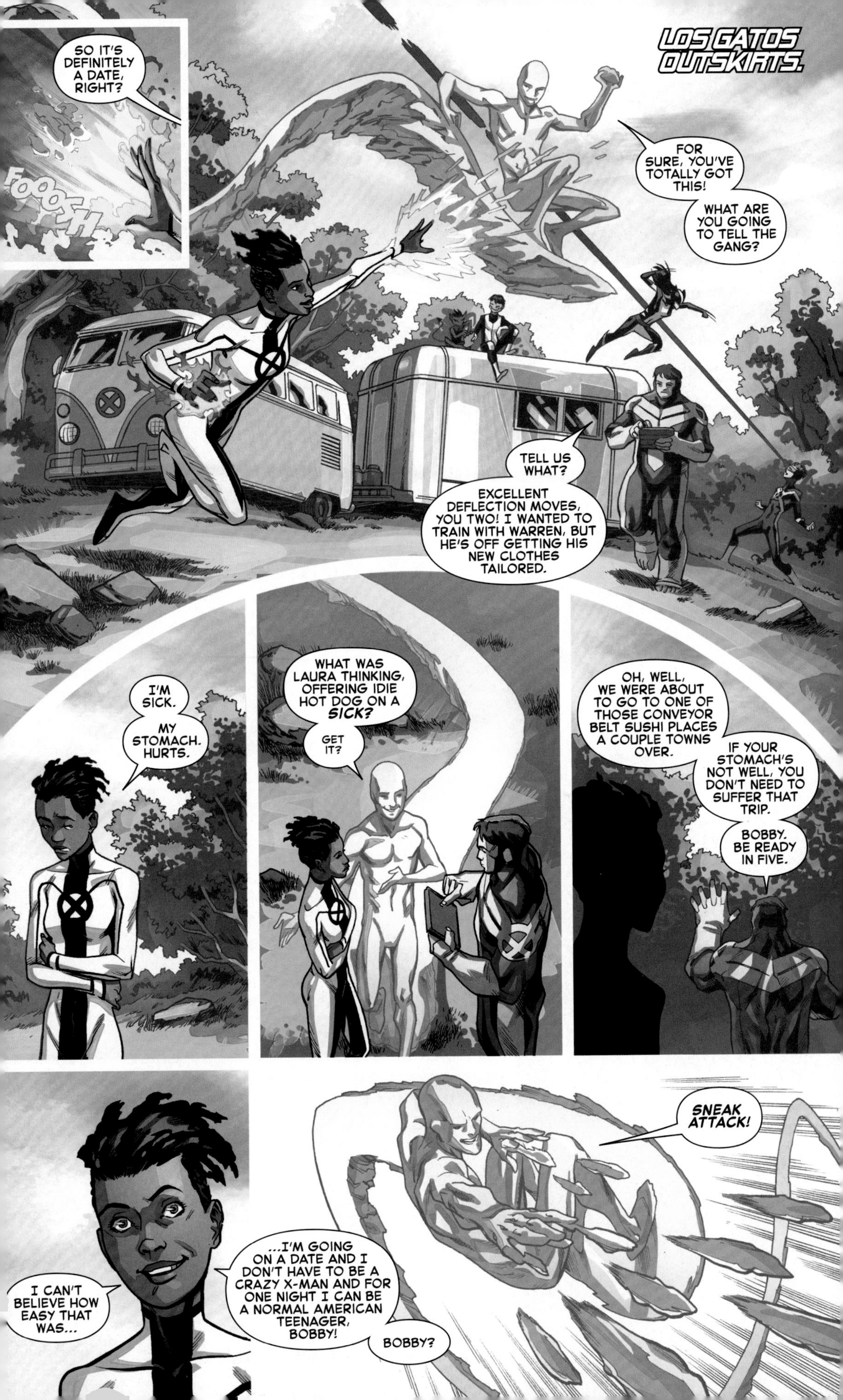

LOS GATOS OUTSKIRTS.
SO IT'S DEFINITELY A DATE, RIGHT?
FOOOSH
FOR SURE, YOU'VE TOTALLY GOT THIS!
WHAT ARE YOU GOING TO TELL THE GANG?
TELL US WHAT?
EXCELLENT DEFLECTION MOVES, YOU TWO! I WANTED TO TRAIN WITH WARREN, BUT HE'S OFF GETTING HIS NEW CLOTHES TAILORED.
I'M SICK.
MY STOMACH. HURTS.
WHAT WAS LAURA THINKING, OFFERING IDIE HOT DOG ON A SICK?
GET IT?
OH, WELL, WE WERE ABOUT TO GO TO ONE OF THOSE CONVEYOR BELT SUSHI PLACES A COUPLE TOWNS OVER.
IF YOUR STOMACH'S NOT WELL, YOU DON'T NEED TO SUFFER THAT TRIP.
BOBBY. BE READY IN FIVE.
I CAN'T BELIEVE HOW EASY THAT WAS...
...I'M GOING ON A DATE AND I DON'T HAVE TO BE A CRAZY X-MAN AND FOR ONE NIGHT I CAN BE A NORMAL AMERICAN TEENAGER, BOBBY!
BOBBY?
SNEAK ATTACK!

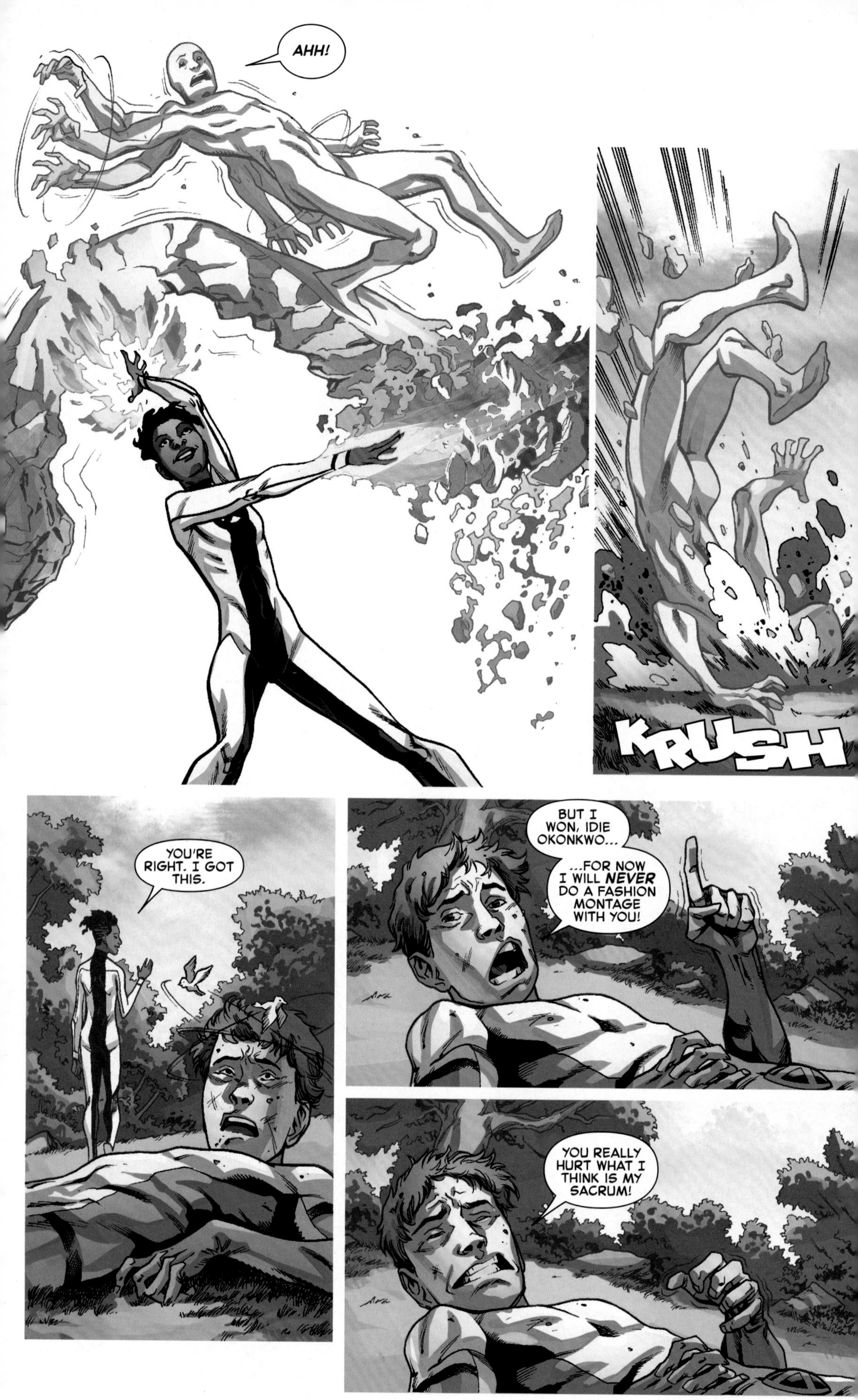
AHH!
KRUSH
YOU'RE RIGHT. I GOT THIS.
BUT I WON, IDIE OKONKWO...
...FOR NOW I WILL NEVER DO A FASHION MONTAGE WITH YOU!
YOU REALLY HURT WHAT I THINK IS MY SACRUM!

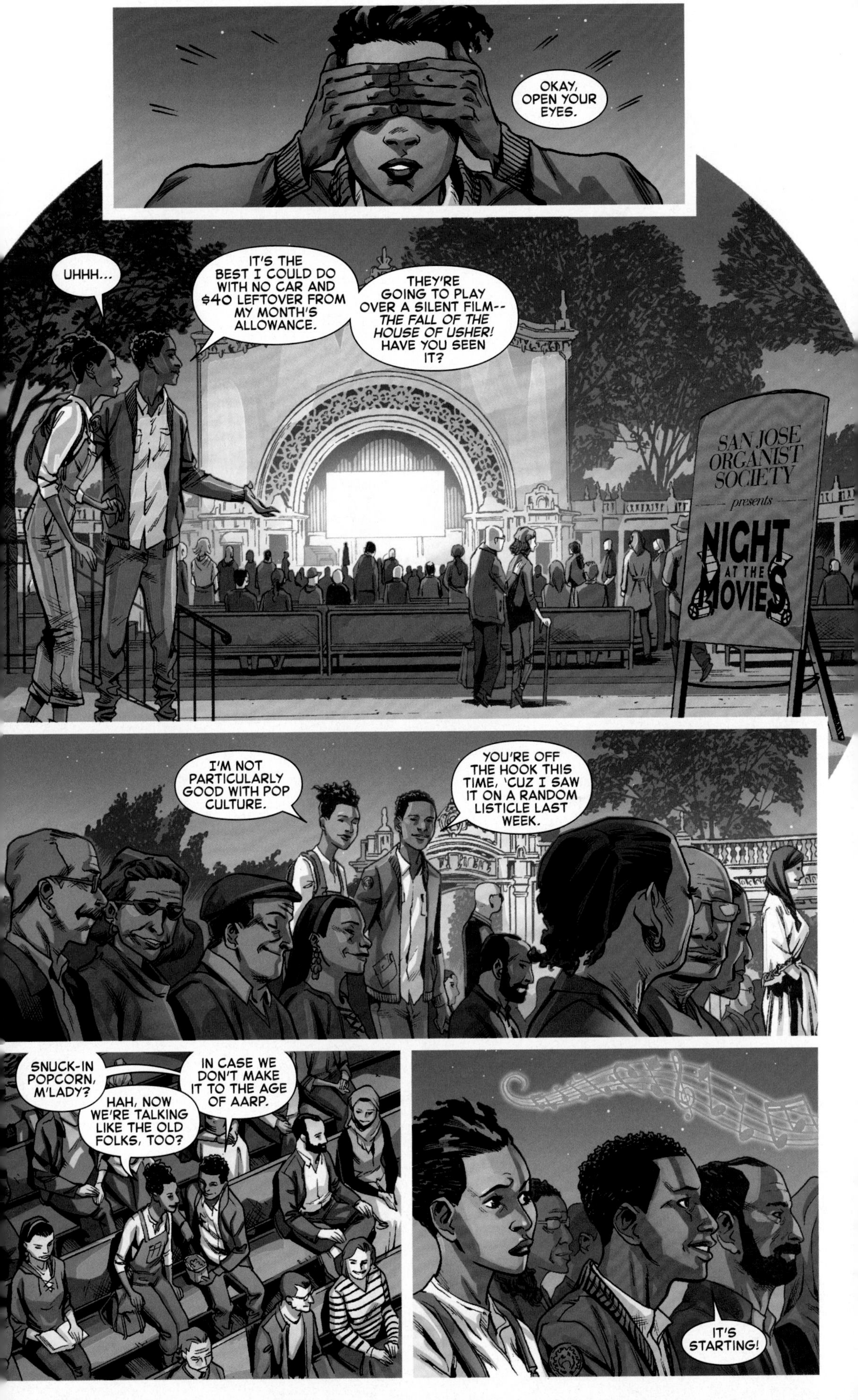

OKAY, OPEN YOUR EYES.
UHHH...
IT'S THE BEST I COULD DO WITH NO CAR AND $40 LEFTOVER FROM MY MONTH'S ALLOWANCE.
THEY'RE GOING TO PLAY OVER A SILENT FILM-- THE FALL OF THE HOUSE OF USHER! HAVE YOU SEEN IT?
SAN JOSE ORGANIST SOCIETY presents NIGHT AT THE MOVIES
I'M NOT PARTICULARLY GOOD WITH POP CULTURE.
YOU'RE OFF THE HOOK THIS TIME, 'CUZ I SAW IT ON A RANDOM LISTICLE LAST WEEK.
SNUCK-IN POPCORN, M'LADY?
IN CASE WE DON'T MAKE IT TO THE AGE OF AARP.
HAH, NOW WE'RE TALKING LIKE THE OLD FOLKS, TOO?
IT'S STARTING!

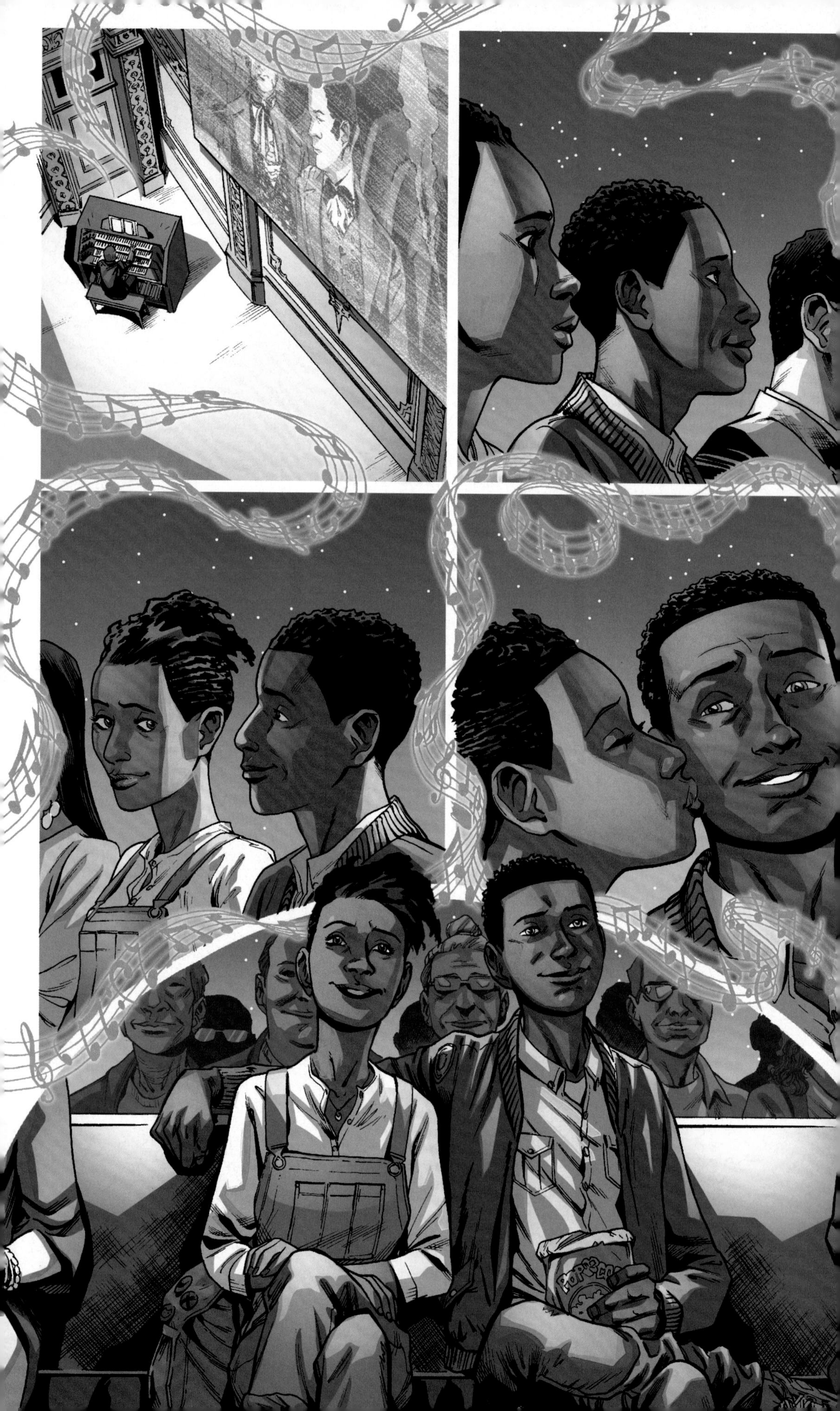

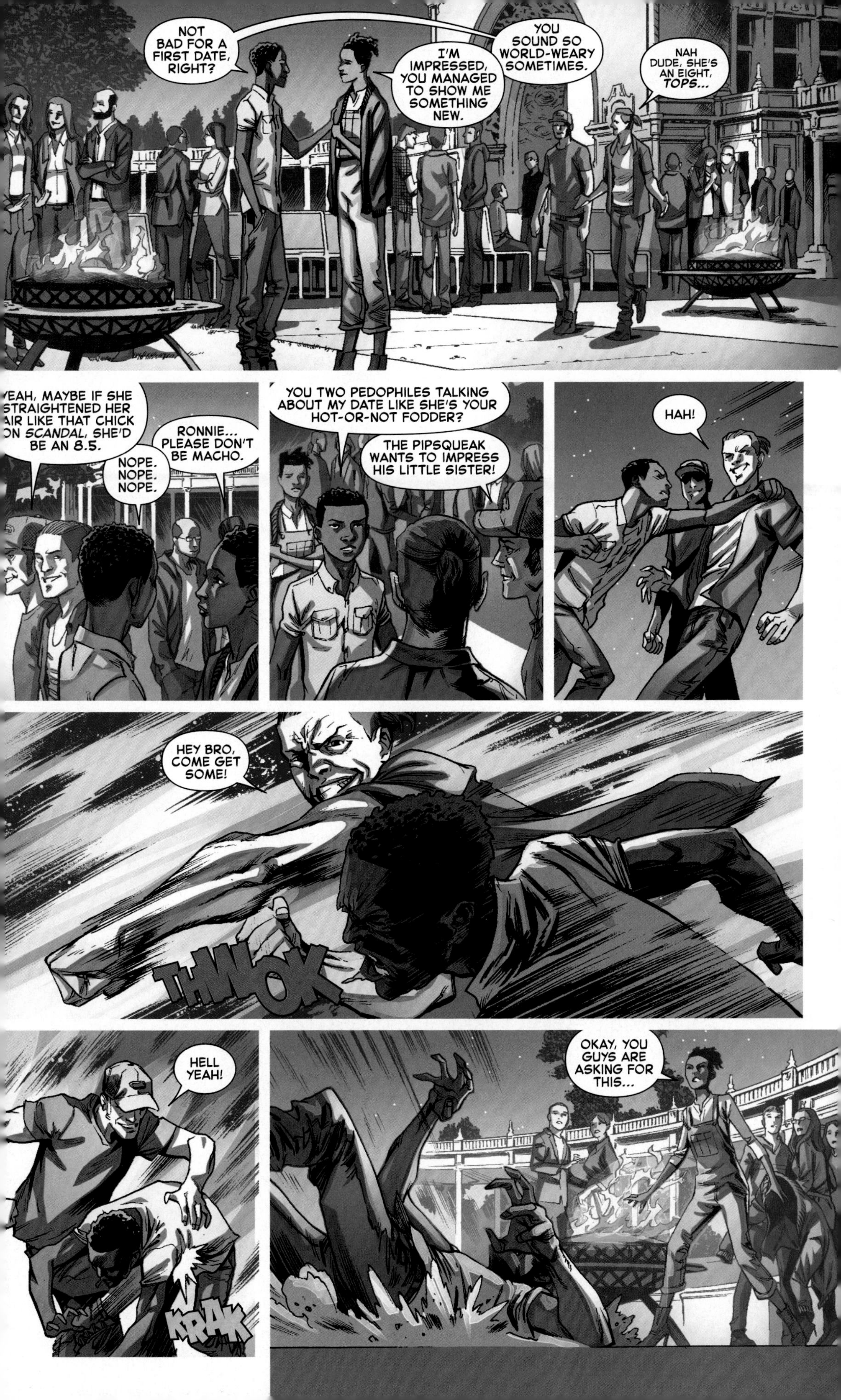
NOT BAD FOR A FIRST DATE, RIGHT?
I'M IMPRESSED, YOU MANAGED TO SHOW ME SOMETHING NEW.
YOU SOUND SO WORLD-WEARY SOMETIMES.
NAH DUDE, SHE'S AN EIGHT, *TOPS*...
YEAH, MAYBE IF SHE STRAIGHTENED HER HAIR LIKE THAT CHICK ON *SCANDAL*, SHE'D BE AN 8.5.
NOPE. NOPE. NOPE.
RONNIE... PLEASE DON'T BE MACHO.
YOU TWO PEDOPHILES TALKING ABOUT MY DATE LIKE SHE'S YOUR HOT-OR-NOT FODDER?
THE PIPSQUEAK WANTS TO IMPRESS HIS LITTLE SISTER!
HAH!
HEY BRO, COME GET SOME!
THWOK
HELL YEAH!
KRAK
OKAY, YOU GUYS ARE ASKING FOR THIS...

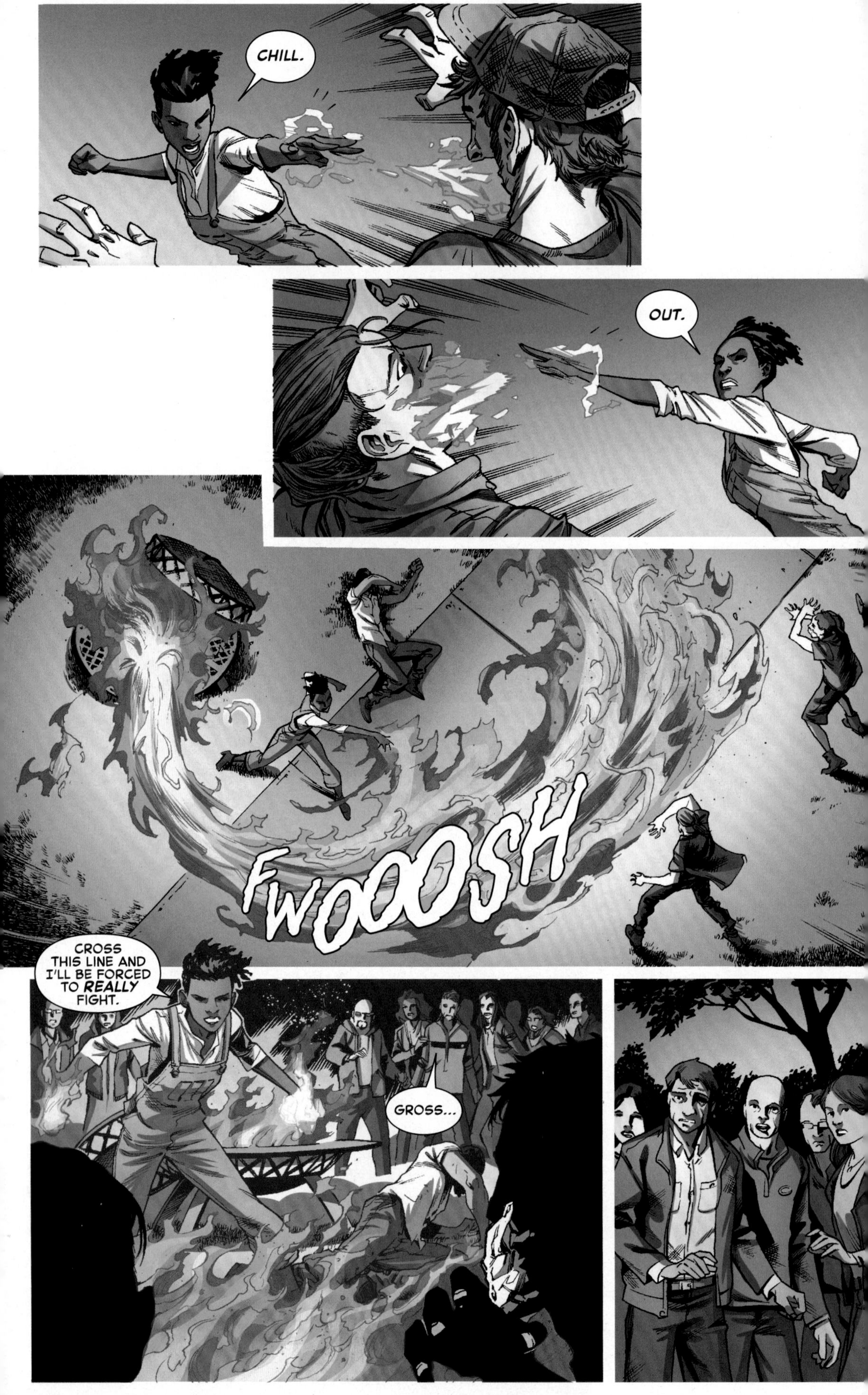
CHILL.
OUT.
FWOOOSH
CROSS THIS LINE AND I'LL BE FORCED TO REALLY FIGHT.
GROSS...

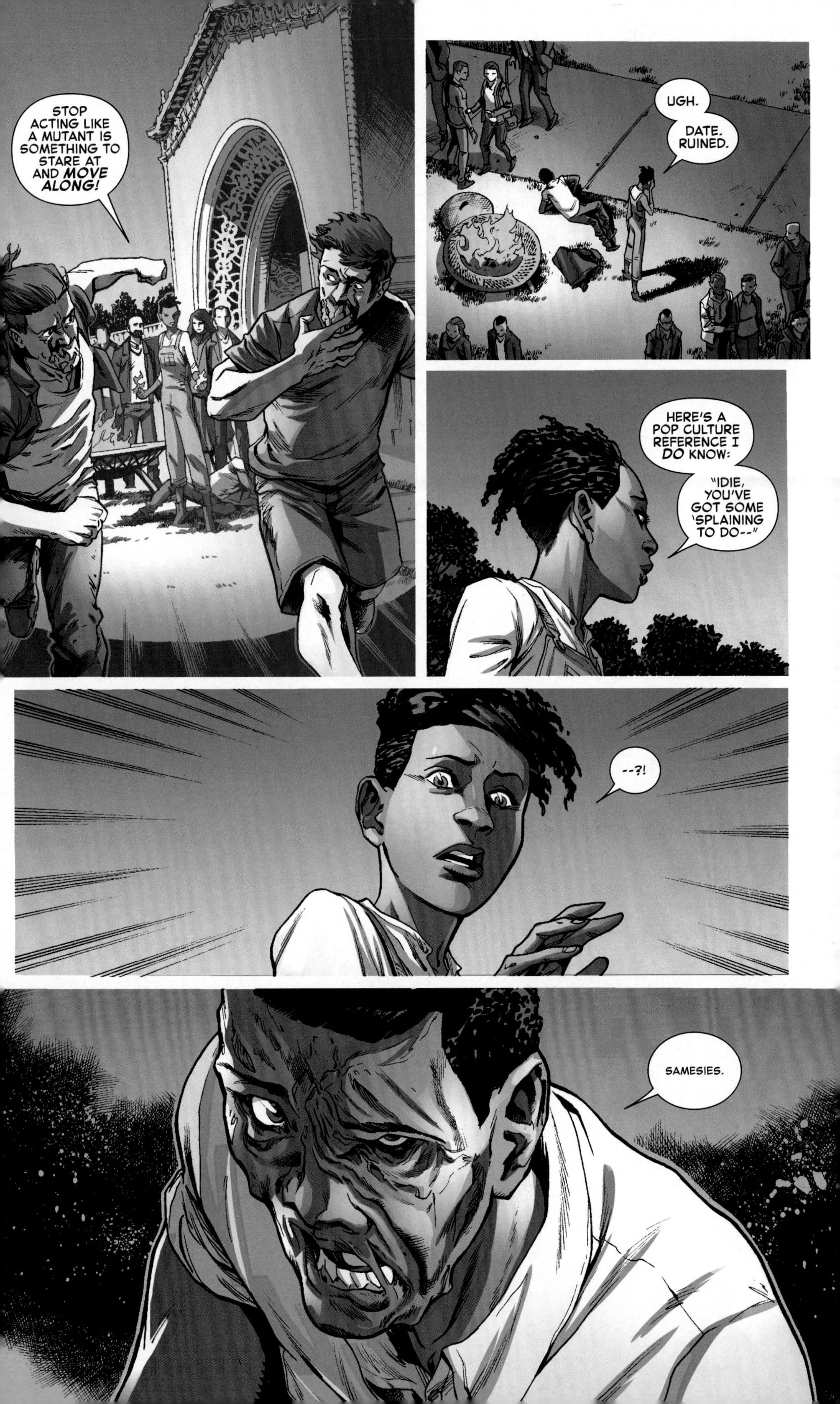
STOP ACTING LIKE A MUTANT IS SOMETHING TO STARE AT AND MOVE ALONG!
UGH.
DATE. RUINED.
HERE'S A POP CULTURE REFERENCE I DO KNOW:
"IDIE, YOU'VE GOT SOME 'SPLAINING TO DO--"
--?!
SAMESIES.

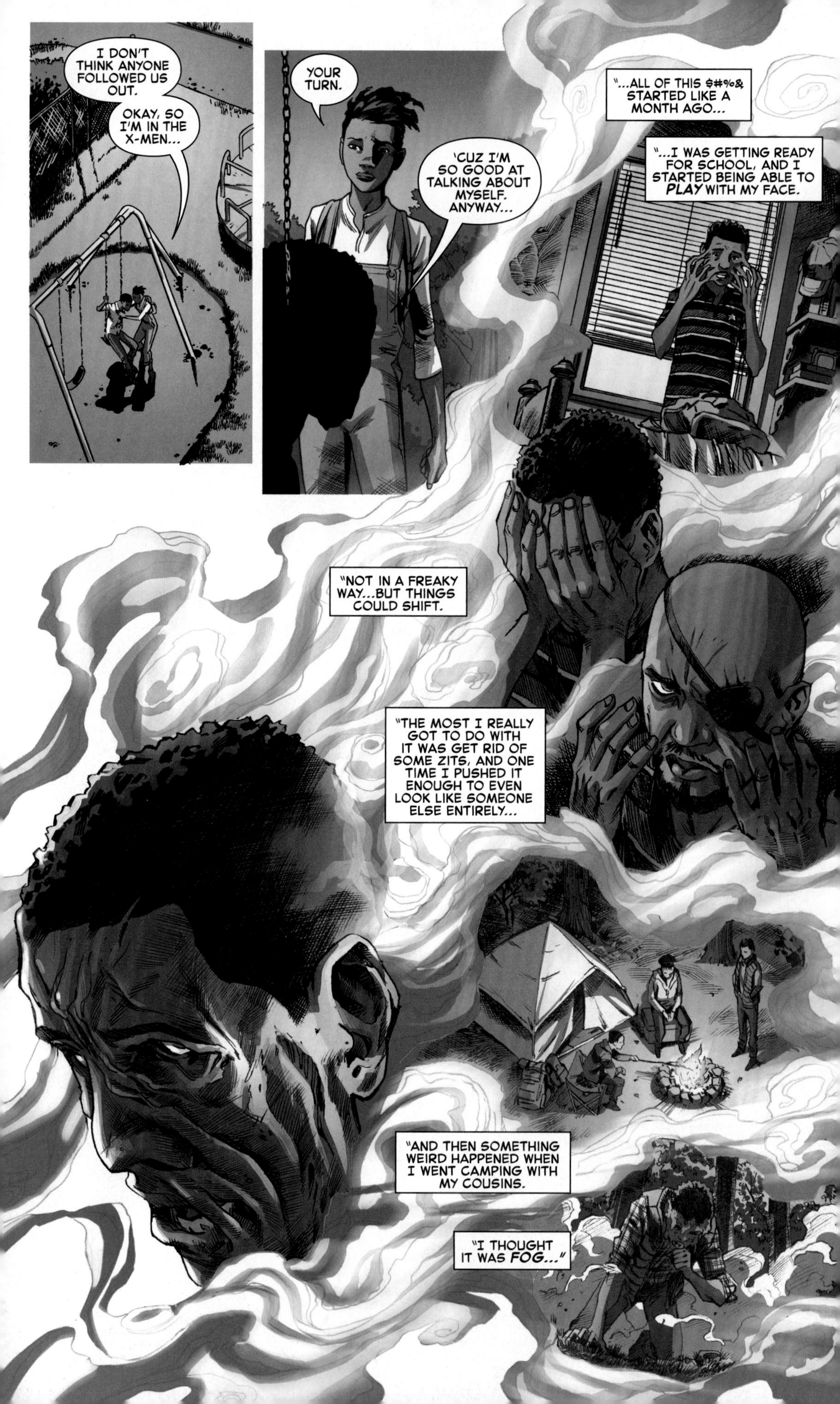

I DON'T THINK ANYONE FOLLOWED US OUT.
OKAY, SO I'M IN THE X-MEN...
YOUR TURN.
'CUZ I'M SO GOOD AT TALKING ABOUT MYSELF. ANYWAY...
"...ALL OF THIS $#%& STARTED LIKE A MONTH AGO...
"...I WAS GETTING READY FOR SCHOOL, AND I STARTED BEING ABLE TO PLAY WITH MY FACE.
"NOT IN A FREAKY WAY...BUT THINGS COULD SHIFT.
"THE MOST I REALLY GOT TO DO WITH IT WAS GET RID OF SOME ZITS, AND ONE TIME I PUSHED IT ENOUGH TO EVEN LOOK LIKE SOMEONE ELSE ENTIRELY...
"AND THEN SOMETHING WEIRD HAPPENED WHEN I WENT CAMPING WITH MY COUSINS.
"I THOUGHT IT WAS FOG..."

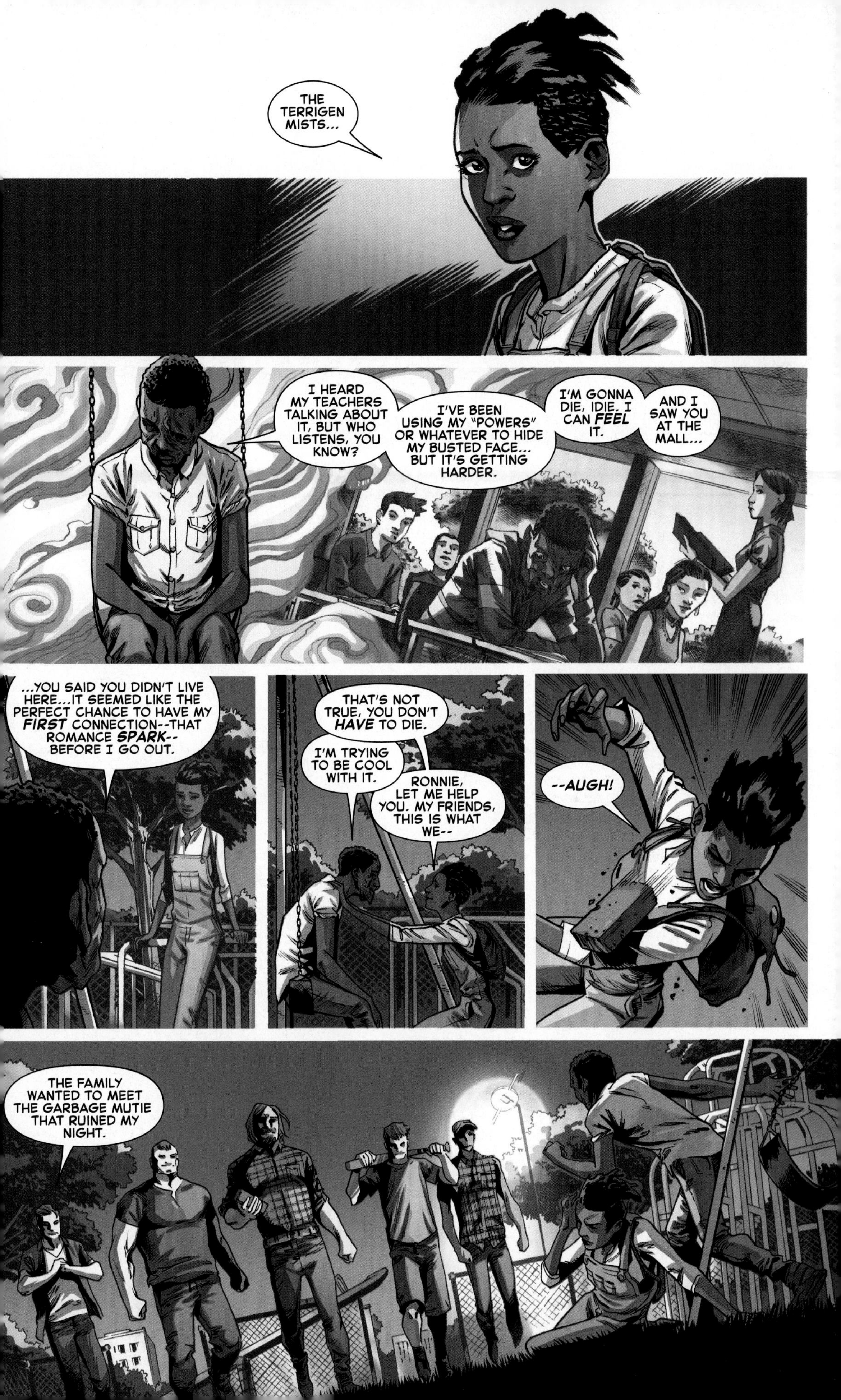

THE TERRIGEN MISTS...
I HEARD MY TEACHERS TALKING ABOUT IT, BUT WHO LISTENS, YOU KNOW?
I'VE BEEN USING MY "POWERS" OR WHATEVER TO HIDE MY BUSTED FACE... BUT IT'S GETTING HARDER.
I'M GONNA DIE, IDIE. I CAN FEEL IT.
AND I SAW YOU AT THE MALL...
...YOU SAID YOU DIDN'T LIVE HERE...IT SEEMED LIKE THE PERFECT CHANCE TO HAVE MY FIRST CONNECTION--THAT ROMANCE SPARK-- BEFORE I GO OUT.
THAT'S NOT TRUE, YOU DON'T HAVE TO DIE.
I'M TRYING TO BE COOL WITH IT.
RONNIE, LET ME HELP YOU. MY FRIENDS, THIS IS WHAT WE--
--AUGH!
THE FAMILY WANTED TO MEET THE GARBAGE MUTIE THAT RUINED MY NIGHT.

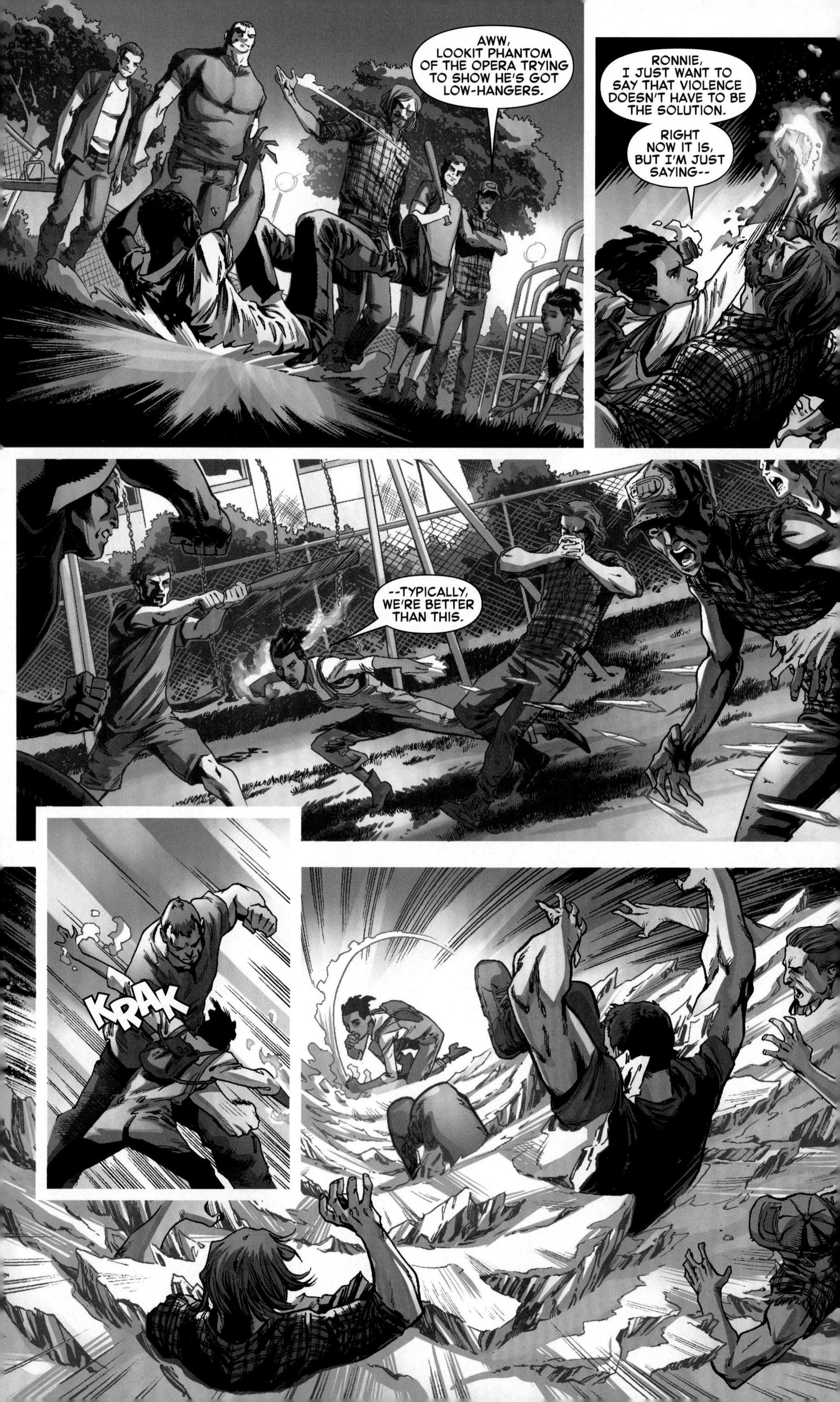
AWW, LOOKIT PHANTOM OF THE OPERA TRYING TO SHOW HE'S GOT LOW-HANGERS.
RONNIE, I JUST WANT TO SAY THAT VIOLENCE DOESN'T HAVE TO BE THE SOLUTION.
RIGHT NOW IT IS, BUT I'M JUST SAYING--
--TYPICALLY, WE'RE BETTER THAN THIS.
KRAK

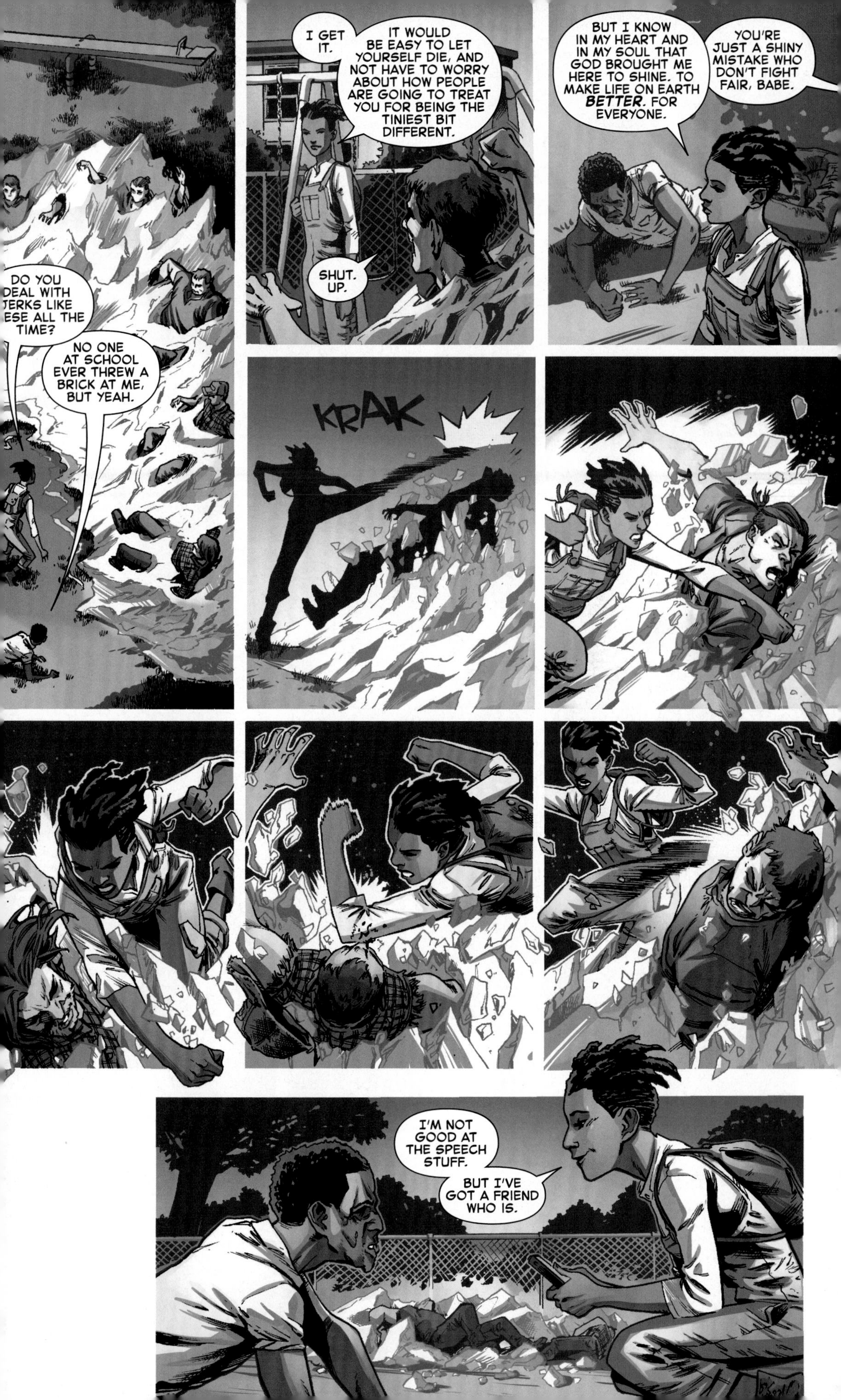
DO YOU
DEAL WITH
JERKS LIKE
ESE ALL THE
TIME?
NO ONE AT SCHOOL EVER THREW A BRICK AT ME, BUT YEAH.
I GET IT.
IT WOULD BE EASY TO LET YOURSELF DIE, AND NOT HAVE TO WORRY ABOUT HOW PEOPLE ARE GOING TO TREAT YOU FOR BEING THE TINIEST BIT DIFFERENT.
SHUT. UP.
BUT I KNOW IN MY HEART AND IN MY SOUL THAT GOD BROUGHT ME HERE TO SHINE. TO MAKE LIFE ON EARTH BETTER. FOR EVERYONE.
YOU'RE JUST A SHINY MISTAKE WHO DON'T FIGHT FAIR, BABE.
KRAK
I'M NOT GOOD AT THE SPEECH STUFF.
BUT I'VE GOT A FRIEND WHO IS.

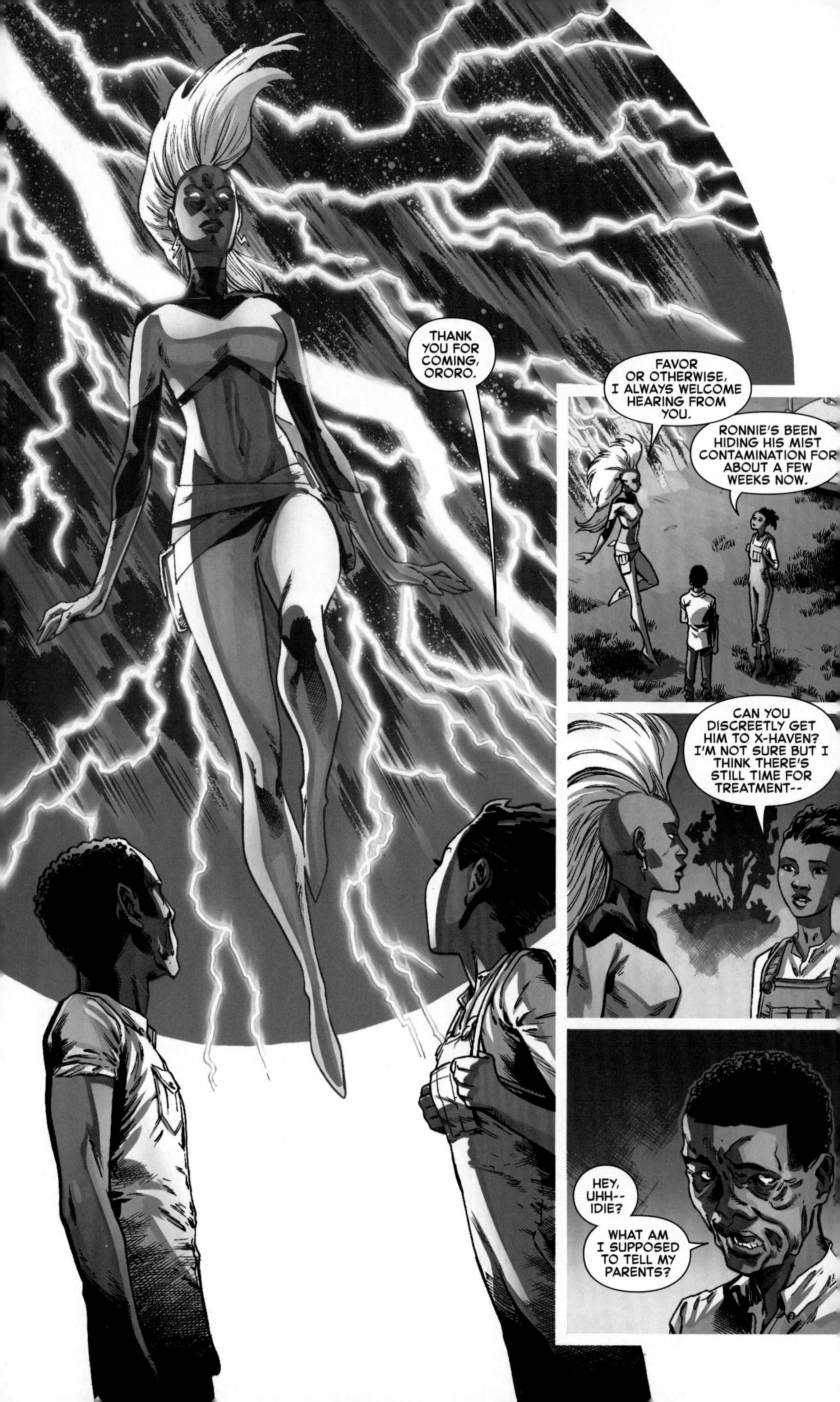
THANK YOU FOR COMING, ORORO.
FAVOR OR OTHERWISE, I ALWAYS WELCOME HEARING FROM YOU.
RONNIE'S BEEN HIDING HIS MIST CONTAMINATION FOR ABOUT A FEW WEEKS NOW.
CAN YOU DISCREETLY GET HIM TO X-HAVEN? I'M NOT SURE BUT I THINK THERE'S STILL TIME FOR TREATMENT--
HEY, UHH-- IDIE?
WHAT AM I SUPPOSED TO TELL MY PARENTS?

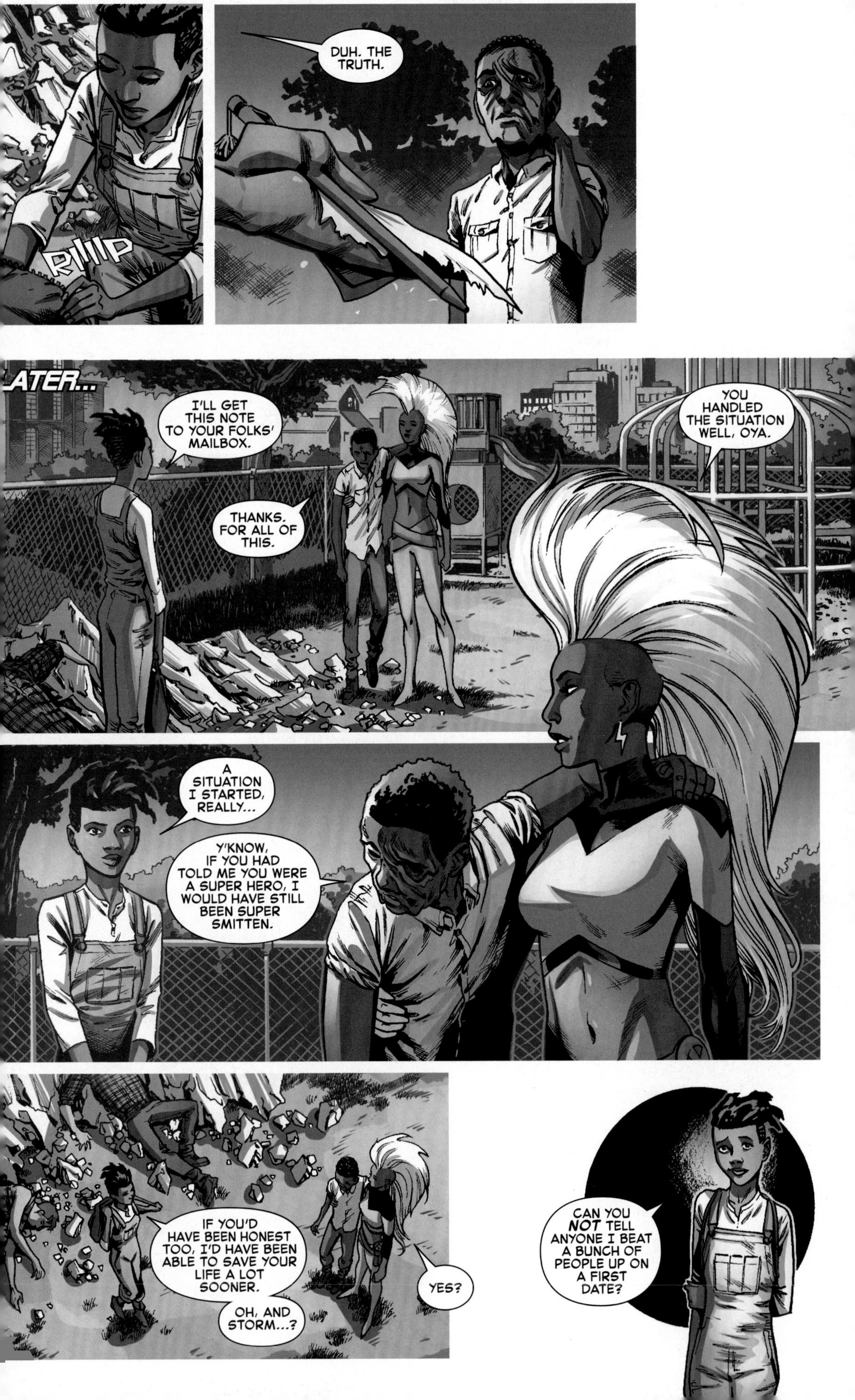
RIIIP
DUH. THE TRUTH.
LATER...
I'LL GET THIS NOTE TO YOUR FOLKS' MAILBOX.
THANKS. FOR ALL OF THIS.
YOU HANDLED THE SITUATION WELL, OYA.
A SITUATION I STARTED, REALLY...
Y'KNOW, IF YOU HAD TOLD ME YOU WERE A SUPER HERO, I WOULD HAVE STILL BEEN SUPER SMITTEN.
IF YOU'D HAVE BEEN HONEST TOO, I'D HAVE BEEN ABLE TO SAVE YOUR LIFE A LOT SOONER.
OH, AND STORM...?
YES?
CAN YOU NOT TELL ANYONE I BEAT A BUNCH OF PEOPLE UP ON A FIRST DATE?

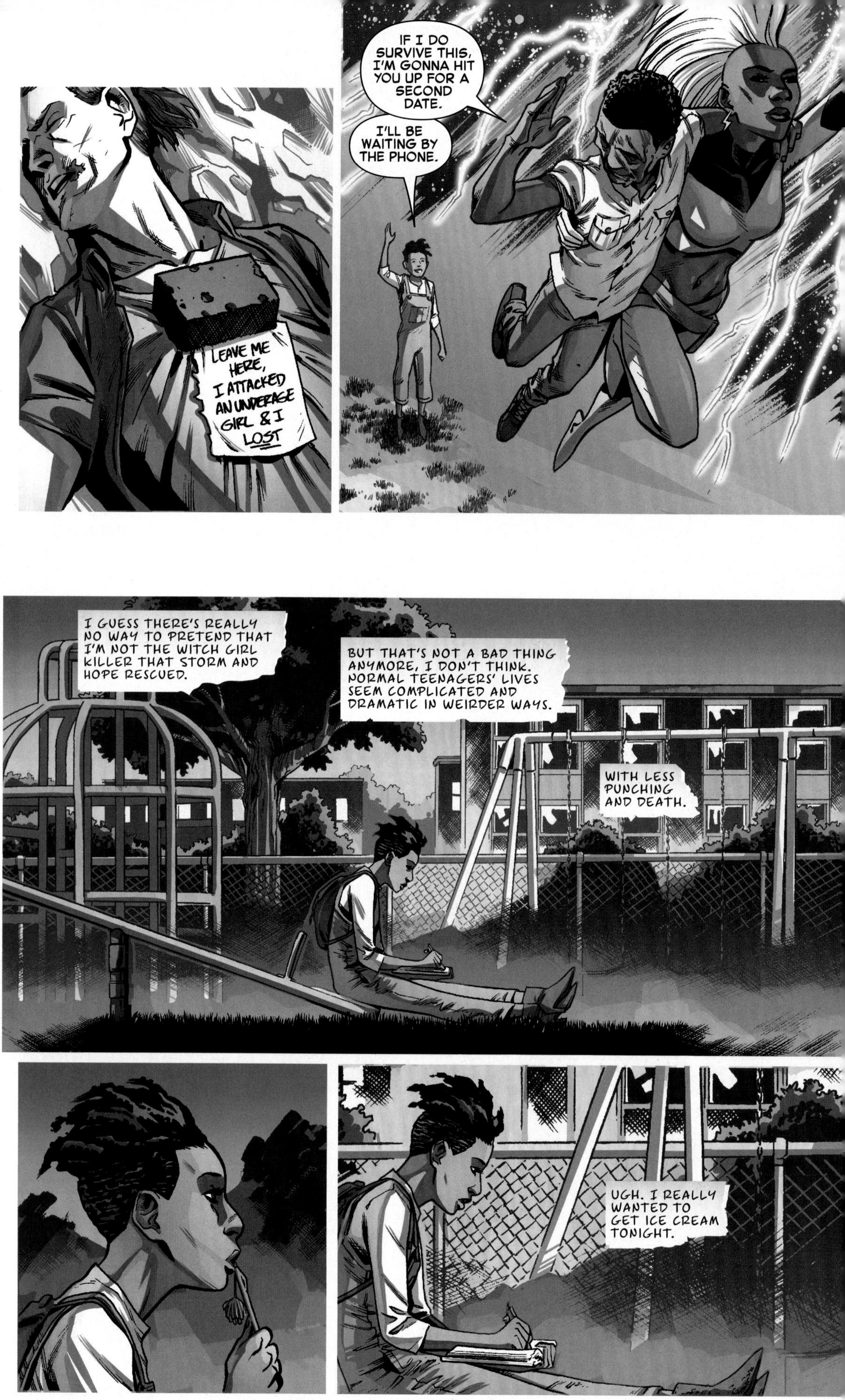
LEAVE ME HERE, I ATTACKED AN UNDERAGE GIRL & I LOST
IF I DO SURVIVE THIS, I'M GONNA HIT YOU UP FOR A SECOND DATE.
I'LL BE WAITING BY THE PHONE.
I GUESS THERE'S REALLY NO WAY TO PRETEND THAT I'M NOT THE WITCH GIRL KILLER THAT STORM AND HOPE RESCUED.
BUT THAT'S NOT A BAD THING ANYMORE, I DON'T THINK. NORMAL TEENAGERS' LIVES SEEM COMPLICATED AND DRAMATIC IN WEIRDER WAYS.
WITH LESS PUNCHING AND DEATH.
UGH. I REALLY WANTED TO GET ICE CREAM TONIGHT.

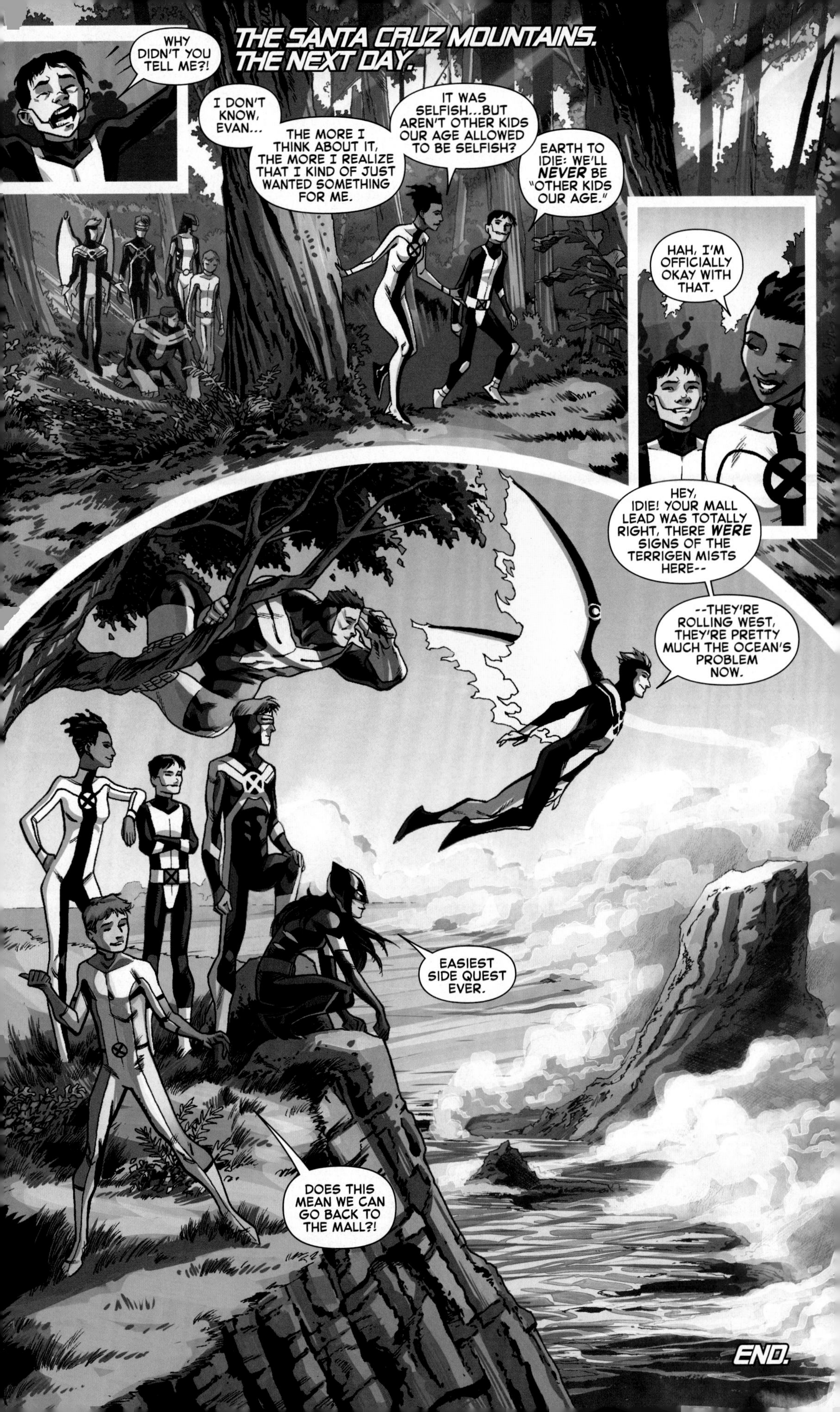

THE SANTA CRUZ MOUNTAINS. THE NEXT DAY.
WHY DIDN'T YOU TELL ME?!
I DON'T KNOW, EVAN...
THE MORE I THINK ABOUT IT, THE MORE I REALIZE THAT I KIND OF JUST WANTED SOMETHING FOR ME.
IT WAS SELFISH...BUT AREN'T OTHER KIDS OUR AGE ALLOWED TO BE SELFISH?
EARTH TO IDIE: WE'LL NEVER BE "OTHER KIDS OUR AGE."
HAH, I'M OFFICIALLY OKAY WITH THAT.
HEY, IDIE! YOUR MALL LEAD WAS TOTALLY RIGHT, THERE WERE SIGNS OF THE TERRIGEN MISTS HERE--
--THEY'RE ROLLING WEST, THEY'RE PRETTY MUCH THE OCEAN'S PROBLEM NOW.
EASIEST SIDE QUEST EVER.
DOES THIS MEAN WE CAN GO BACK TO THE MALL?!
END.

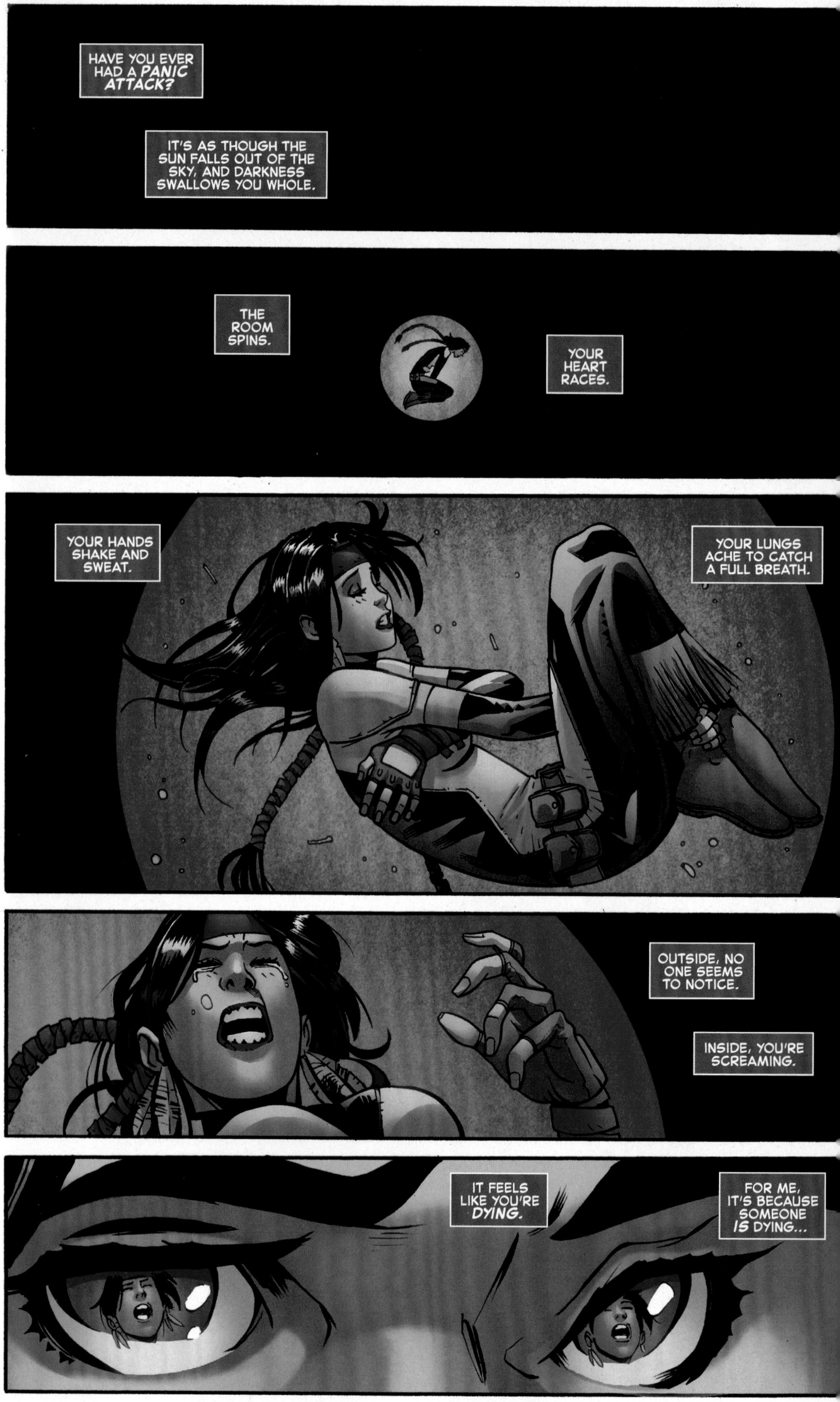
HAVE YOU EVER HAD A *PANIC ATTACK?*
IT'S AS THOUGH THE SUN FALLS OUT OF THE SKY, AND DARKNESS SWALLOWS YOU WHOLE.
THE ROOM SPINS.
YOUR HEART RACES.
YOUR HANDS SHAKE AND SWEAT.
YOUR LUNGS ACHE TO CATCH A FULL BREATH.
OUTSIDE, NO ONE SEEMS TO NOTICE.
INSIDE, YOU'RE SCREAMING.
IT FEELS LIKE YOU'RE *DYING.*
FOR ME, IT'S BECAUSE SOMEONE *IS* DYING...

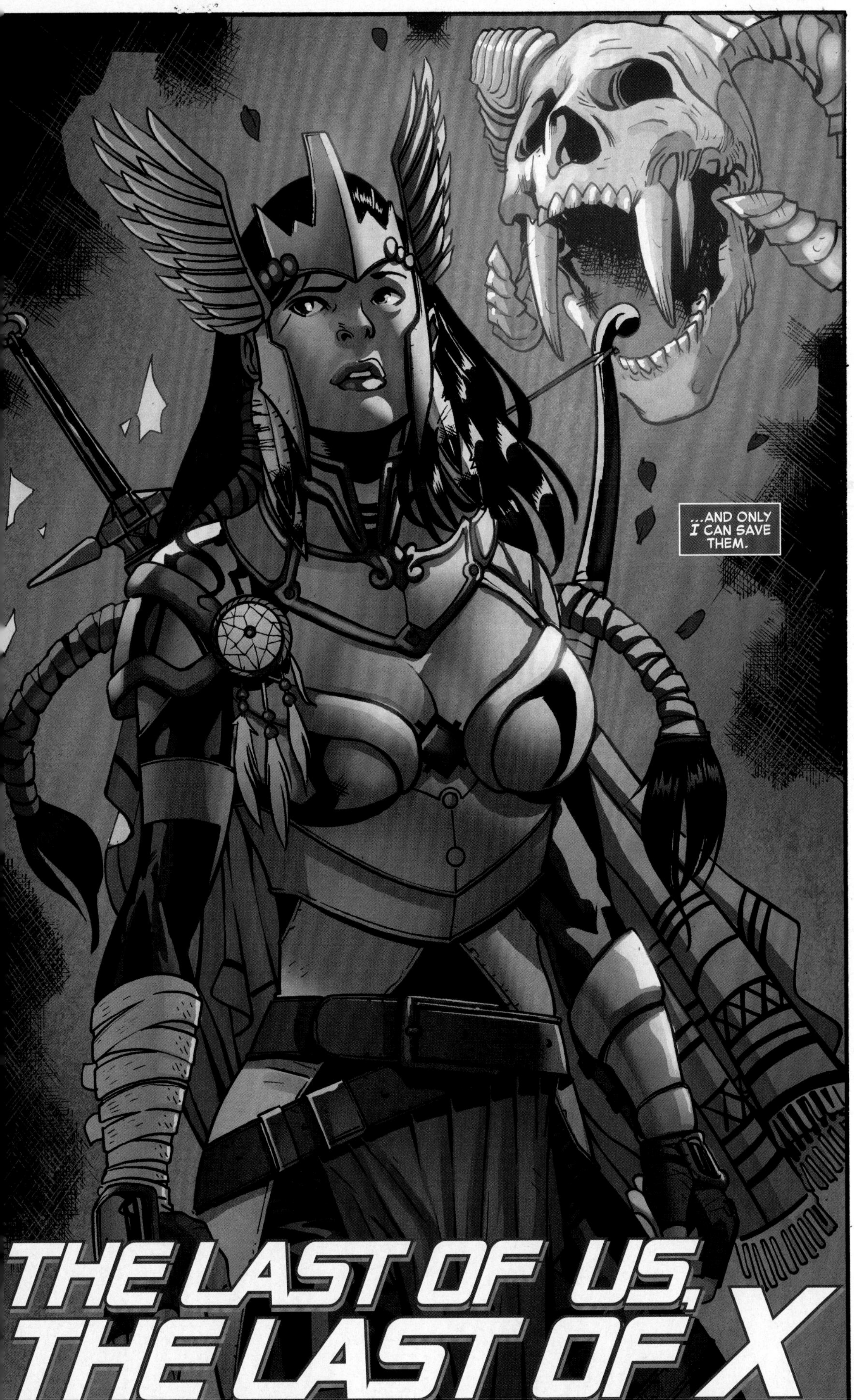
...AND ONLY I CAN SAVE THEM.
THE LAST OF US, THE LAST OF X

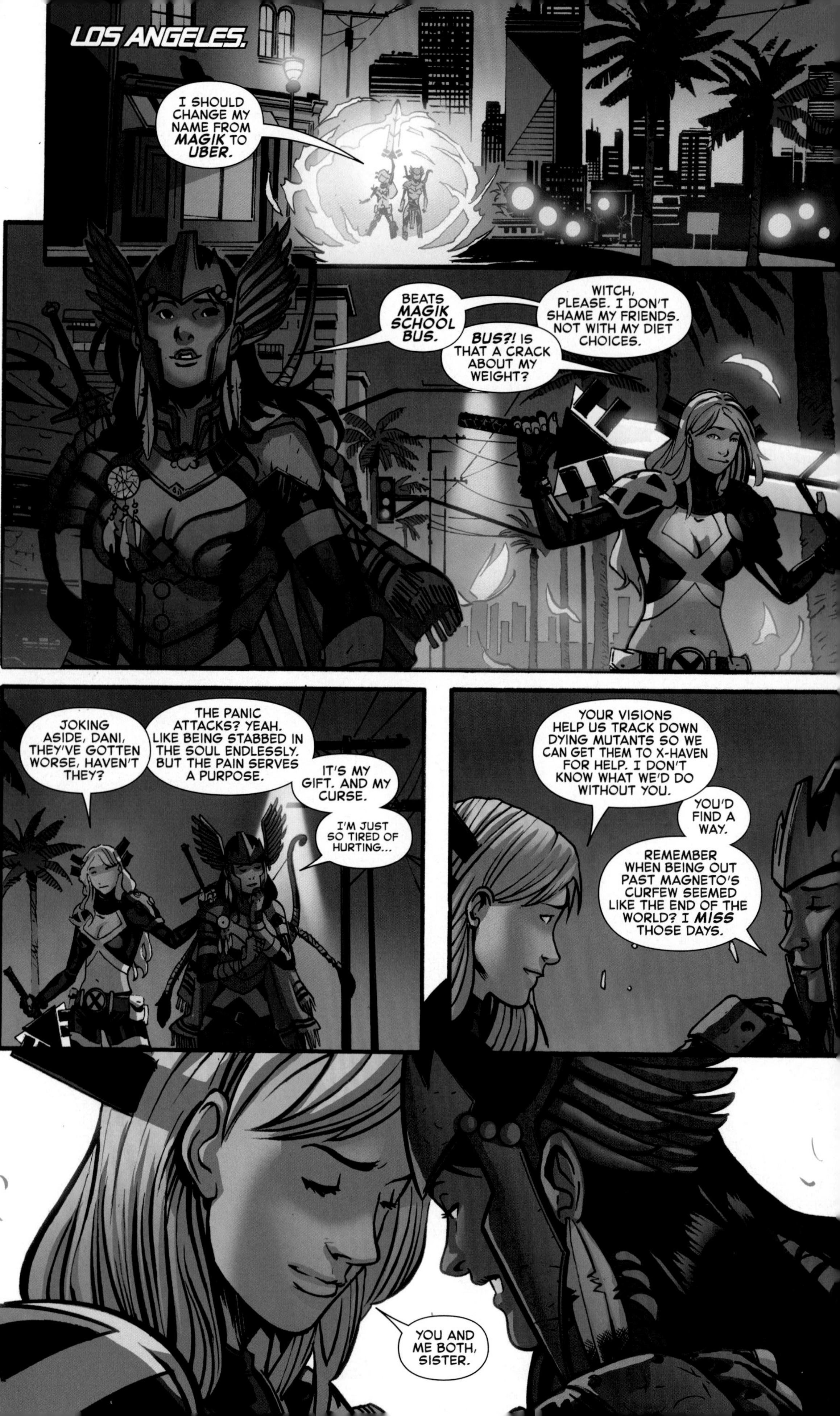

LOS ANGELES.
I SHOULD CHANGE MY NAME FROM MAGIK TO UBER.
BEATS MAGIK SCHOOL BUS.
BUS?! IS THAT A CRACK ABOUT MY WEIGHT?
WITCH, PLEASE. I DON'T SHAME MY FRIENDS. NOT WITH MY DIET CHOICES.
JOKING ASIDE, DANI, THEY'VE GOTTEN WORSE, HAVEN'T THEY?
THE PANIC ATTACKS? YEAH. LIKE BEING STABBED IN THE SOUL ENDLESSLY. BUT THE PAIN SERVES A PURPOSE.
IT'S MY GIFT. AND MY CURSE.
I'M JUST SO TIRED OF HURTING...
YOUR VISIONS HELP US TRACK DOWN DYING MUTANTS SO WE CAN GET THEM TO X-HAVEN FOR HELP. I DON'T KNOW WHAT WE'D DO WITHOUT YOU.
YOU'D FIND A WAY.
REMEMBER WHEN BEING OUT PAST MAGNETO'S CURFEW SEEMED LIKE THE END OF THE WORLD? I MISS THOSE DAYS.
YOU AND ME BOTH, SISTER.

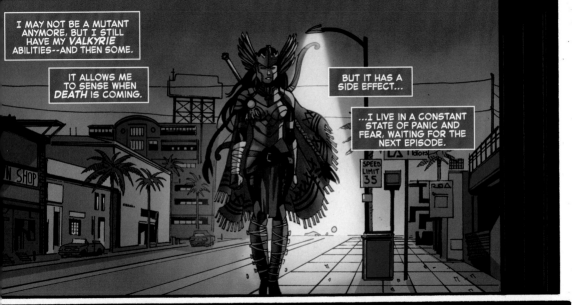

I MAY NOT BE A MUTANT ANYMORE, BUT I STILL HAVE MY VALKYRIE ABILITIES--AND THEN SOME.
IT ALLOWS ME TO SENSE WHEN DEATH IS COMING.
BUT IT HAS A SIDE EFFECT...
...I LIVE IN A CONSTANT STATE OF PANIC AND FEAR, WAITING FOR THE NEXT EPISODE.
SPEED LIMIT 35
SHOP
EVER SINCE M-POX GRIPPED THIS WORLD, I'M AFRAID ALL THE TIME.
I HATE BEING AFRAID.
I TELL MYSELF I AM NO STRANGER TO DEATH. I HAVE LOST FAMILY AND FRIENDS. IT IS INEVITABLE THAT I WILL LOSE MORE.
AND ONE DAY IT WILL BE MY TURN.
UNTIL THEN, I FIGHT. NOT JUST FOR MYSELF, BUT FOR ANYONE...
Medici's
OPEN
...NO MATTER HOW MUCH IT HURTS ME.
I CAME HERE BECAUSE ONE PERSON WAS DYING--NOW, EVERYONE IN THIS BUILDING HAS A DEATH SHROUD.
I HAVE TO HURRY...

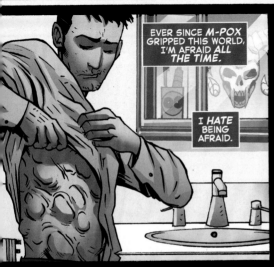

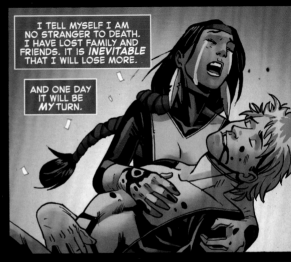

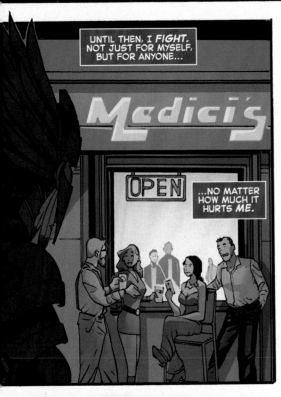

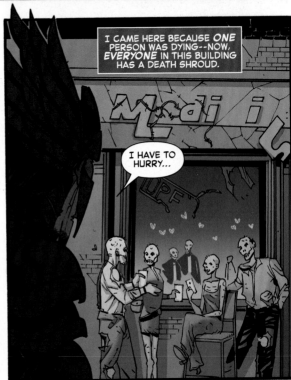

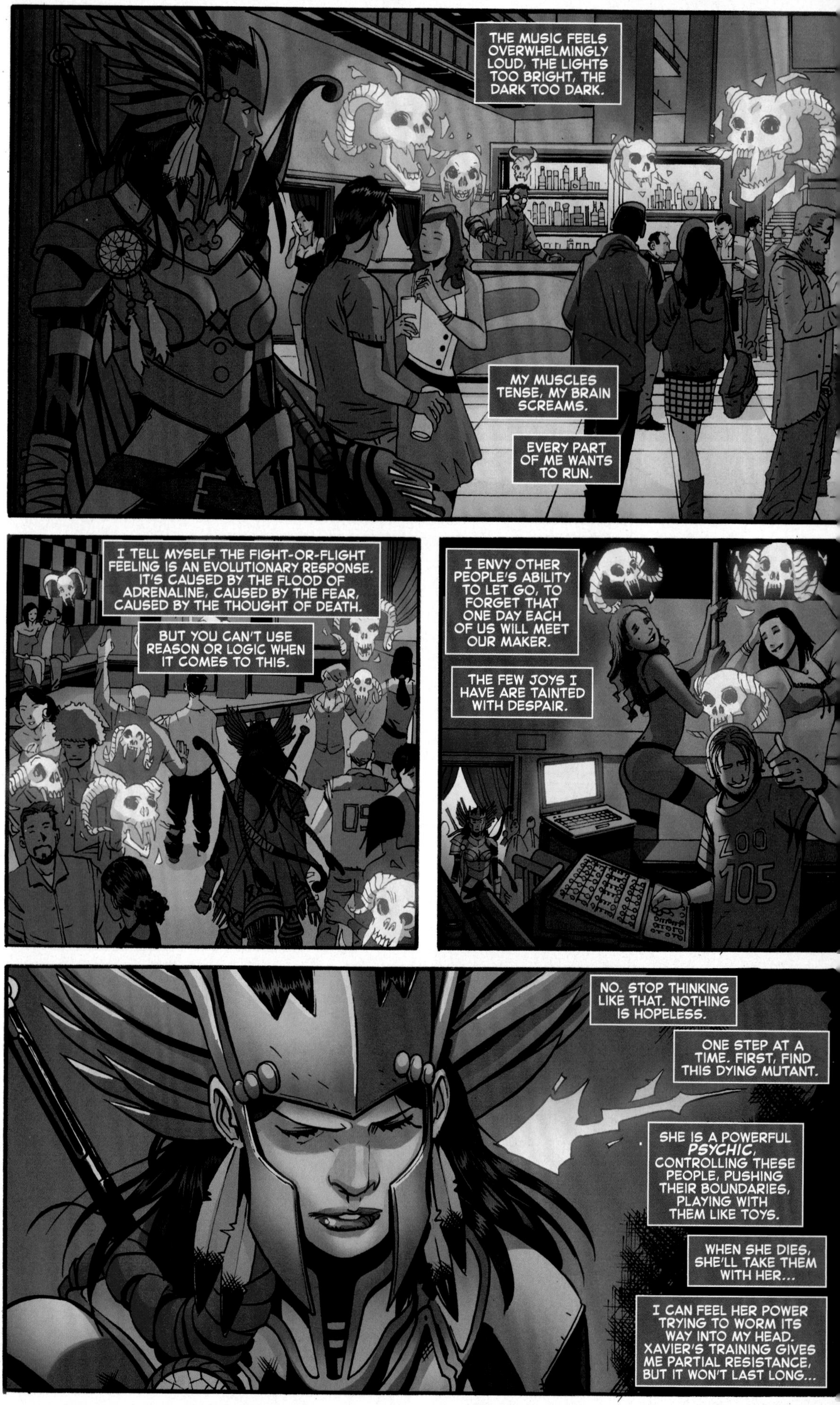
THE MUSIC FEELS OVERWHELMINGLY LOUD, THE LIGHTS TOO BRIGHT, THE DARK TOO DARK.
MY MUSCLES TENSE, MY BRAIN SCREAMS.
EVERY PART OF ME WANTS TO RUN.
I TELL MYSELF THE FIGHT-OR-FLIGHT FEELING IS AN EVOLUTIONARY RESPONSE. IT'S CAUSED BY THE FLOOD OF ADRENALINE, CAUSED BY THE FEAR, CAUSED BY THE THOUGHT OF DEATH.
BUT YOU CAN'T USE REASON OR LOGIC WHEN IT COMES TO THIS.
I ENVY OTHER PEOPLE'S ABILITY TO LET GO, TO FORGET THAT ONE DAY EACH OF US WILL MEET OUR MAKER.
THE FEW JOYS I HAVE ARE TAINTED WITH DESPAIR.
ZOO 105
NO. STOP THINKING LIKE THAT. NOTHING IS HOPELESS.
ONE STEP AT A TIME. FIRST, FIND THIS DYING MUTANT.
SHE IS A POWERFUL *PSYCHIC*, CONTROLLING THESE PEOPLE, PUSHING THEIR BOUNDARIES, PLAYING WITH THEM LIKE TOYS.
WHEN SHE DIES, SHE'LL TAKE THEM WITH HER...
I CAN FEEL HER POWER TRYING TO WORM ITS WAY INTO MY HEAD. XAVIER'S TRAINING GIVES ME PARTIAL RESISTANCE, BUT IT WON'T LAST LONG...

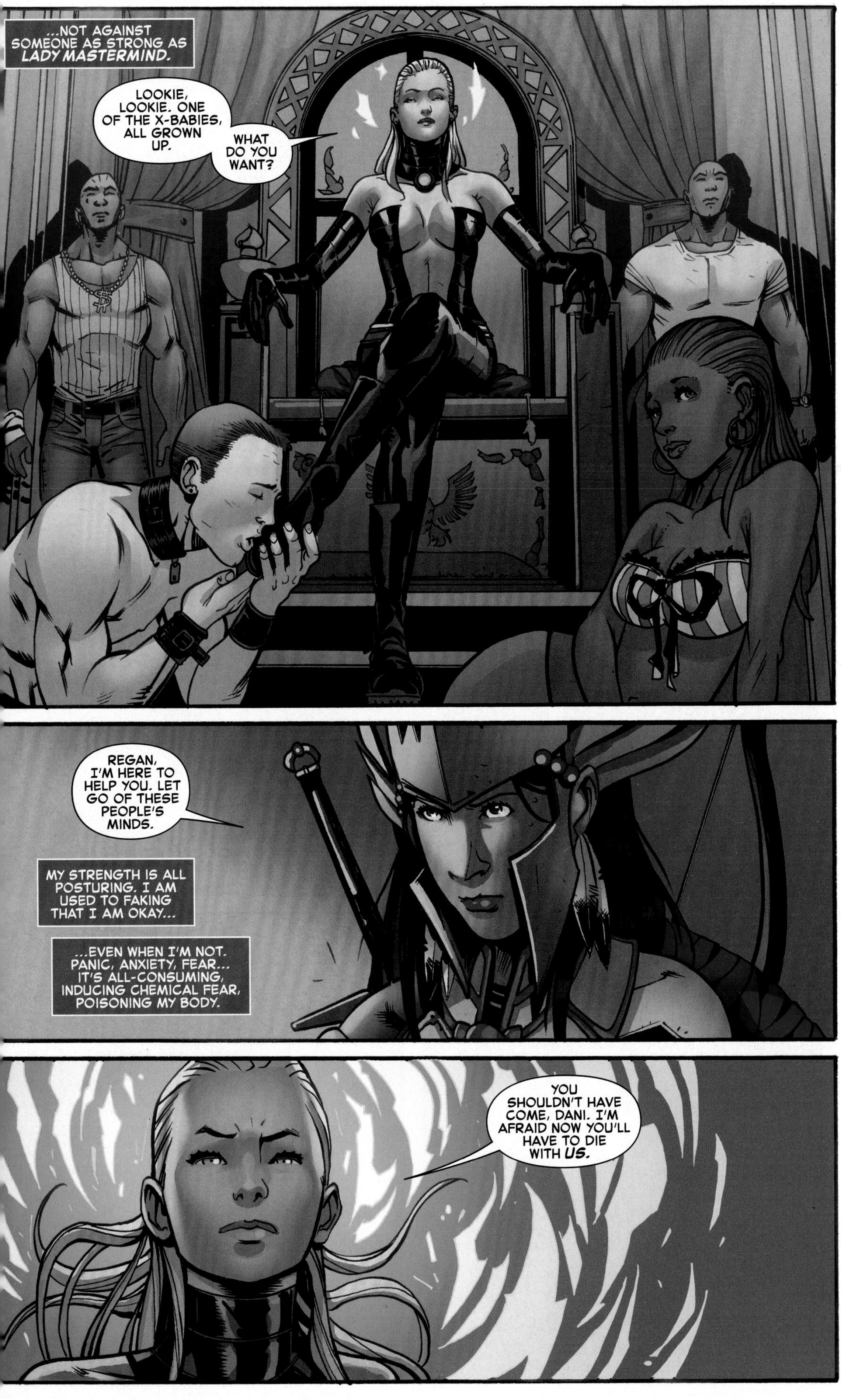

...NOT AGAINST SOMEONE AS STRONG AS LADY MASTERMIND.
LOOKIE, LOOKIE. ONE OF THE X-BABIES, ALL GROWN UP.
WHAT DO YOU WANT?
REGAN, I'M HERE TO HELP YOU. LET GO OF THESE PEOPLE'S MINDS.
MY STRENGTH IS ALL POSTURING. I AM USED TO FAKING THAT I AM OKAY...
...EVEN WHEN I'M NOT. PANIC, ANXIETY, FEAR... IT'S ALL-CONSUMING, INDUCING CHEMICAL FEAR, POISONING MY BODY.
YOU SHOULDN'T HAVE COME, DANI. I'M AFRAID NOW YOU'LL HAVE TO DIE WITH US.

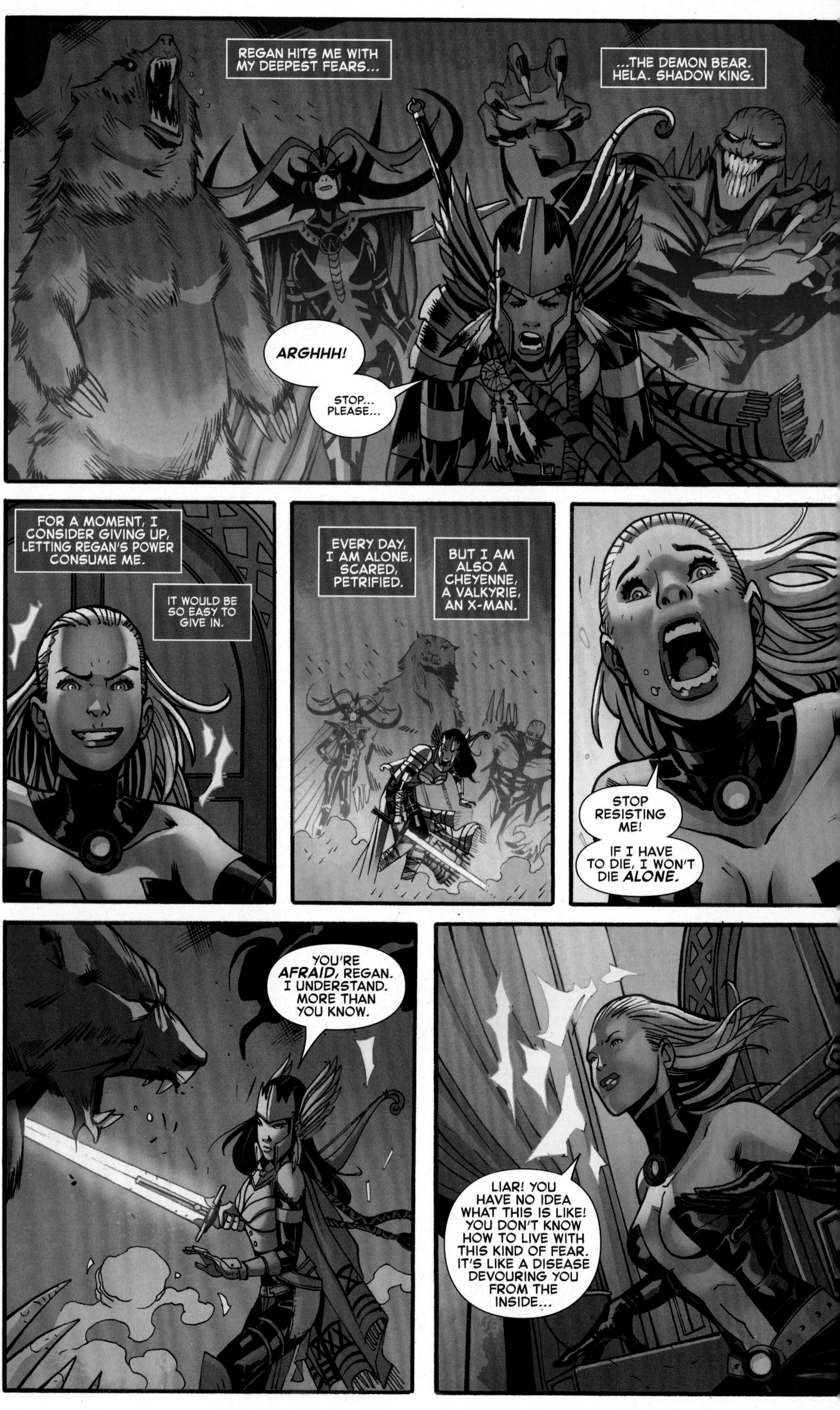
REGAN HITS ME WITH MY DEEPEST FEARS...
...THE DEMON BEAR. HELA. SHADOW KING.
ARGHHH!
STOP... PLEASE...
FOR A MOMENT, I CONSIDER GIVING UP, LETTING REGAN'S POWER CONSUME ME.
IT WOULD BE SO EASY TO GIVE IN.
EVERY DAY, I AM ALONE, SCARED, PETRIFIED.
BUT I AM ALSO A CHEYENNE, A VALKYRIE, AN X-MAN.
STOP RESISTING ME!
IF I HAVE TO DIE, I WON'T DIE ALONE.
YOU'RE AFRAID, REGAN. I UNDERSTAND. MORE THAN YOU KNOW.
LIAR! YOU HAVE NO IDEA WHAT THIS IS LIKE! YOU DON'T KNOW HOW TO LIVE WITH THIS KIND OF FEAR. IT'S LIKE A DISEASE DEVOURING YOU FROM THE INSIDE...

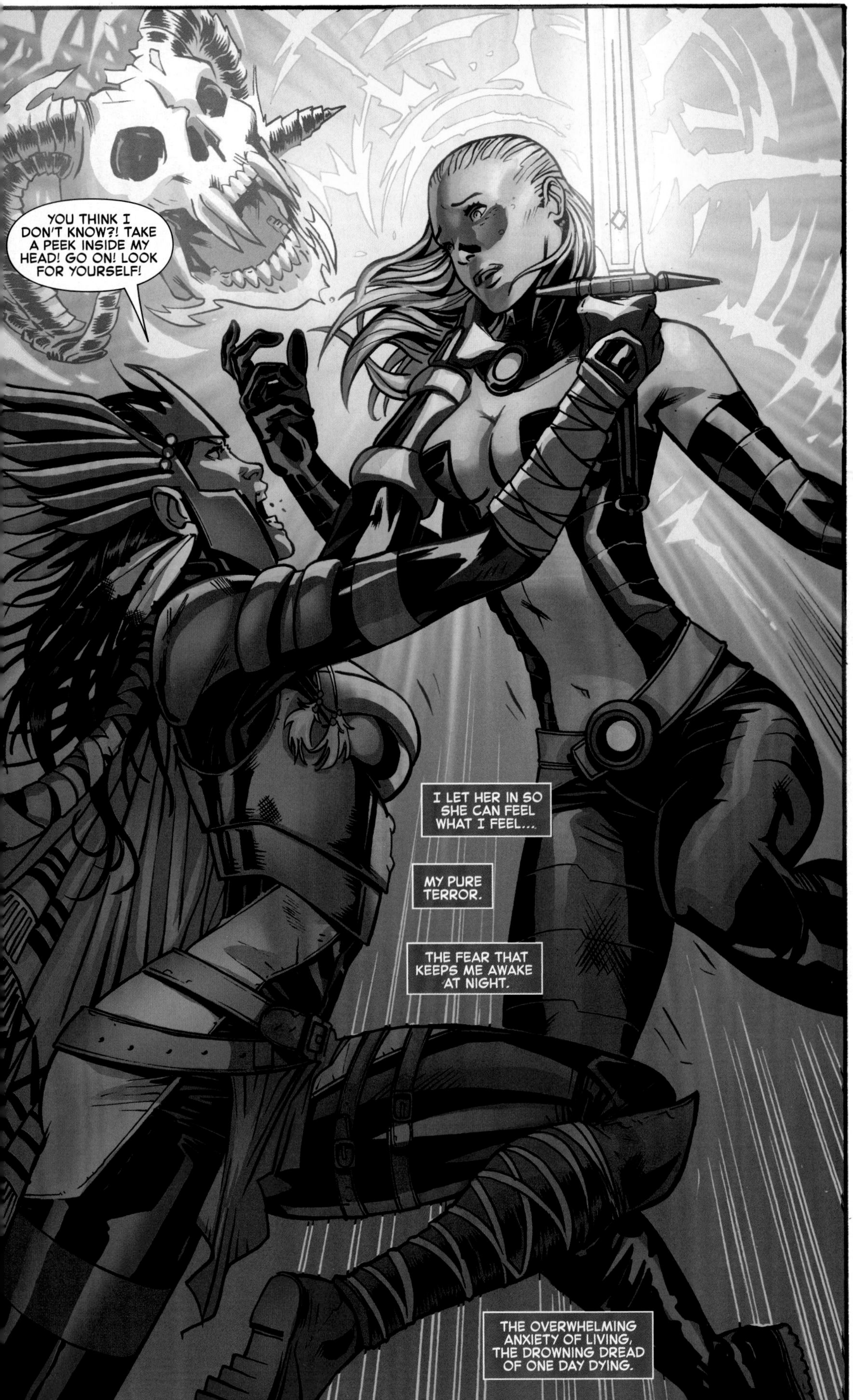
YOU THINK I DON'T KNOW?! TAKE A PEEK INSIDE MY HEAD! GO ON! LOOK FOR YOURSELF!
I LET HER IN SO SHE CAN FEEL WHAT I FEEL...
MY PURE TERROR.
THE FEAR THAT KEEPS ME AWAKE AT NIGHT.
THE OVERWHELMING ANXIETY OF LIVING, THE DROWNING DREAD OF ONE DAY DYING.

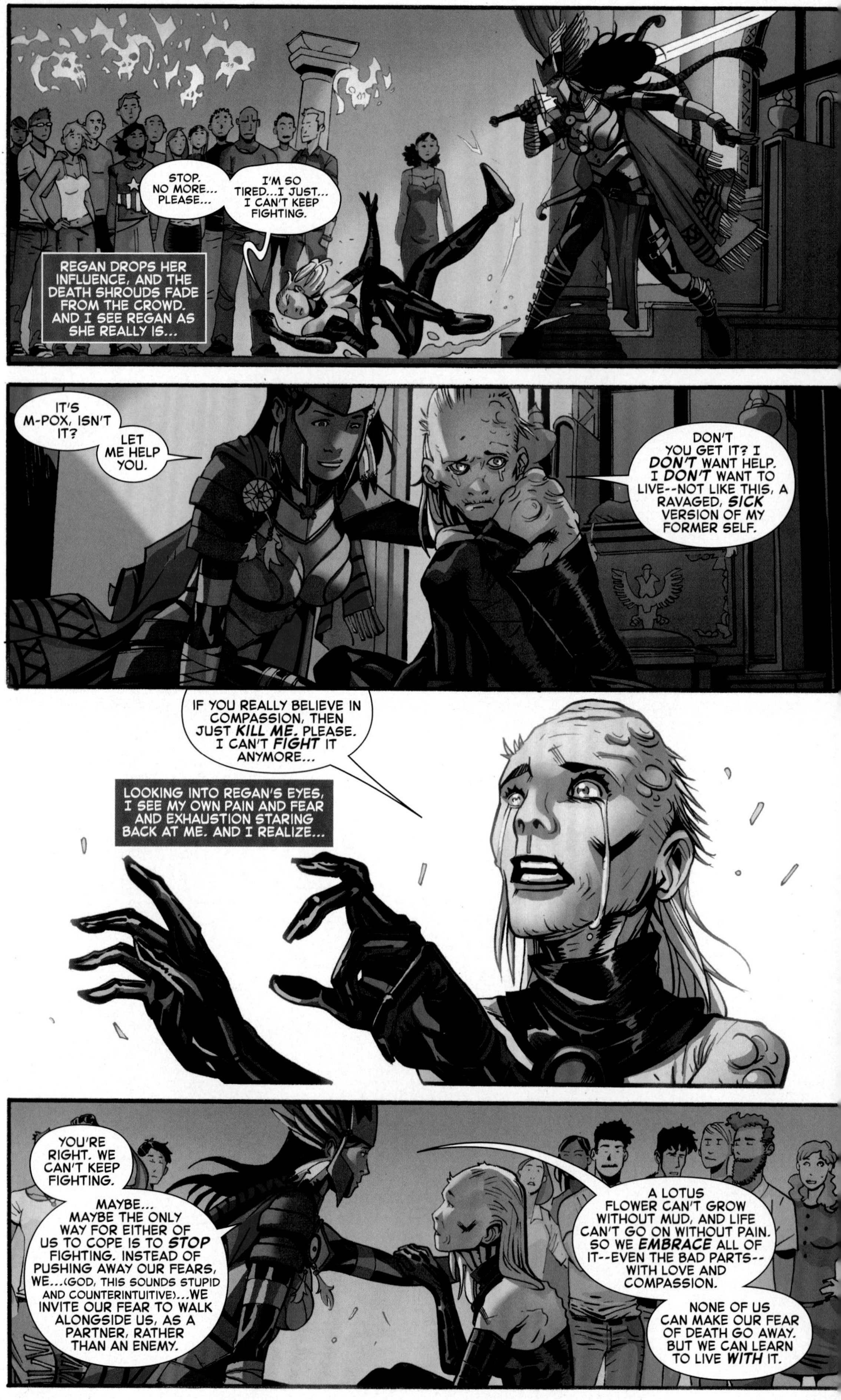

STOP. NO MORE... PLEASE...
I'M SO TIRED...I JUST... I CAN'T KEEP FIGHTING.
REGAN DROPS HER INFLUENCE, AND THE DEATH SHROUDS FADE FROM THE CROWD. AND I SEE REGAN AS SHE REALLY IS...
IT'S M-POX, ISN'T IT?
LET ME HELP YOU.
DON'T YOU GET IT? I DON'T WANT HELP. I DON'T WANT TO LIVE--NOT LIKE THIS, A RAVAGED, SICK VERSION OF MY FORMER SELF.
IF YOU REALLY BELIEVE IN COMPASSION, THEN JUST KILL ME. PLEASE. I CAN'T FIGHT IT ANYMORE...
LOOKING INTO REGAN'S EYES, I SEE MY OWN PAIN AND FEAR AND EXHAUSTION STARING BACK AT ME. AND I REALIZE...
YOU'RE RIGHT. WE CAN'T KEEP FIGHTING.
MAYBE... MAYBE THE ONLY WAY FOR EITHER OF US TO COPE IS TO STOP FIGHTING. INSTEAD OF PUSHING AWAY OUR FEARS, WE...(GOD, THIS SOUNDS STUPID AND COUNTERINTUITIVE)...WE INVITE OUR FEAR TO WALK ALONGSIDE US, AS A PARTNER, RATHER THAN AN ENEMY.
A LOTUS FLOWER CAN'T GROW WITHOUT MUD, AND LIFE CAN'T GO ON WITHOUT PAIN. SO WE EMBRACE ALL OF IT--EVEN THE BAD PARTS--WITH LOVE AND COMPASSION.
NONE OF US CAN MAKE OUR FEAR OF DEATH GO AWAY. BUT WE CAN LEARN TO LIVE WITH IT.

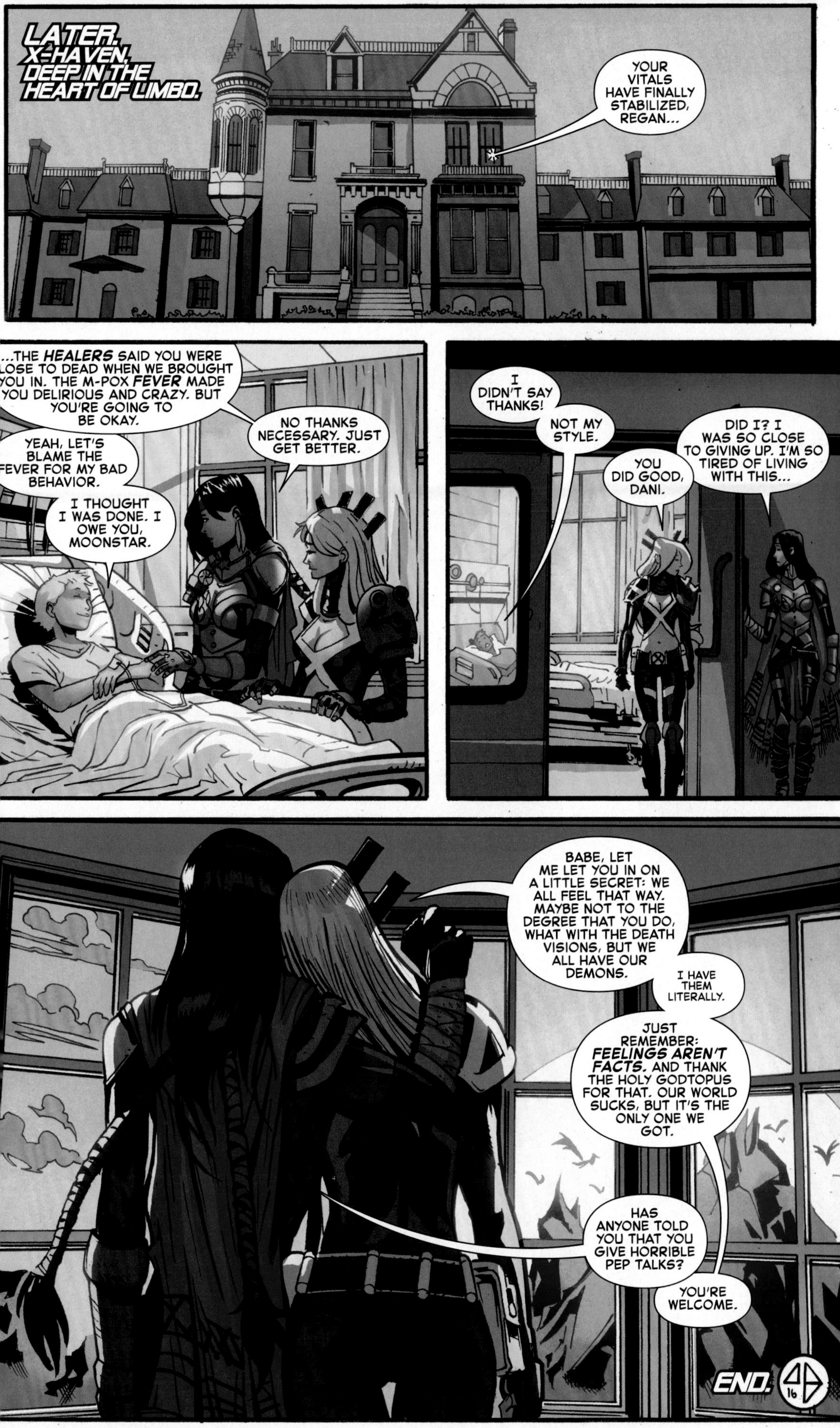
LATER. X-HAVEN, DEEP IN THE HEART OF LIMBO.
YOUR VITALS HAVE FINALLY STABILIZED, REGAN...
...THE HEALERS SAID YOU WERE CLOSE TO DEAD WHEN WE BROUGHT YOU IN. THE M-POX FEVER MADE YOU DELIRIOUS AND CRAZY. BUT YOU'RE GOING TO BE OKAY.
YEAH, LET'S BLAME THE FEVER FOR MY BAD BEHAVIOR.
I THOUGHT I WAS DONE. I OWE YOU, MOONSTAR.
NO THANKS NECESSARY. JUST GET BETTER.
I DIDN'T SAY THANKS!
NOT MY STYLE.
YOU DID GOOD, DANI.
DID I? I WAS SO CLOSE TO GIVING UP. I'M SO TIRED OF LIVING WITH THIS...
BABE, LET ME LET YOU IN ON A LITTLE SECRET: WE ALL FEEL THAT WAY. MAYBE NOT TO THE DEGREE THAT YOU DO, WHAT WITH THE DEATH VISIONS, BUT WE ALL HAVE OUR DEMONS.
I HAVE THEM LITERALLY.
JUST REMEMBER: FEELINGS AREN'T FACTS. AND THANK THE HOLY GODTOPUS FOR THAT. OUR WORLD SUCKS, BUT IT'S THE ONLY ONE WE GOT.
HAS ANYONE TOLD YOU THAT YOU GIVE HORRIBLE PEP TALKS?
YOU'RE WELCOME.
END.
16

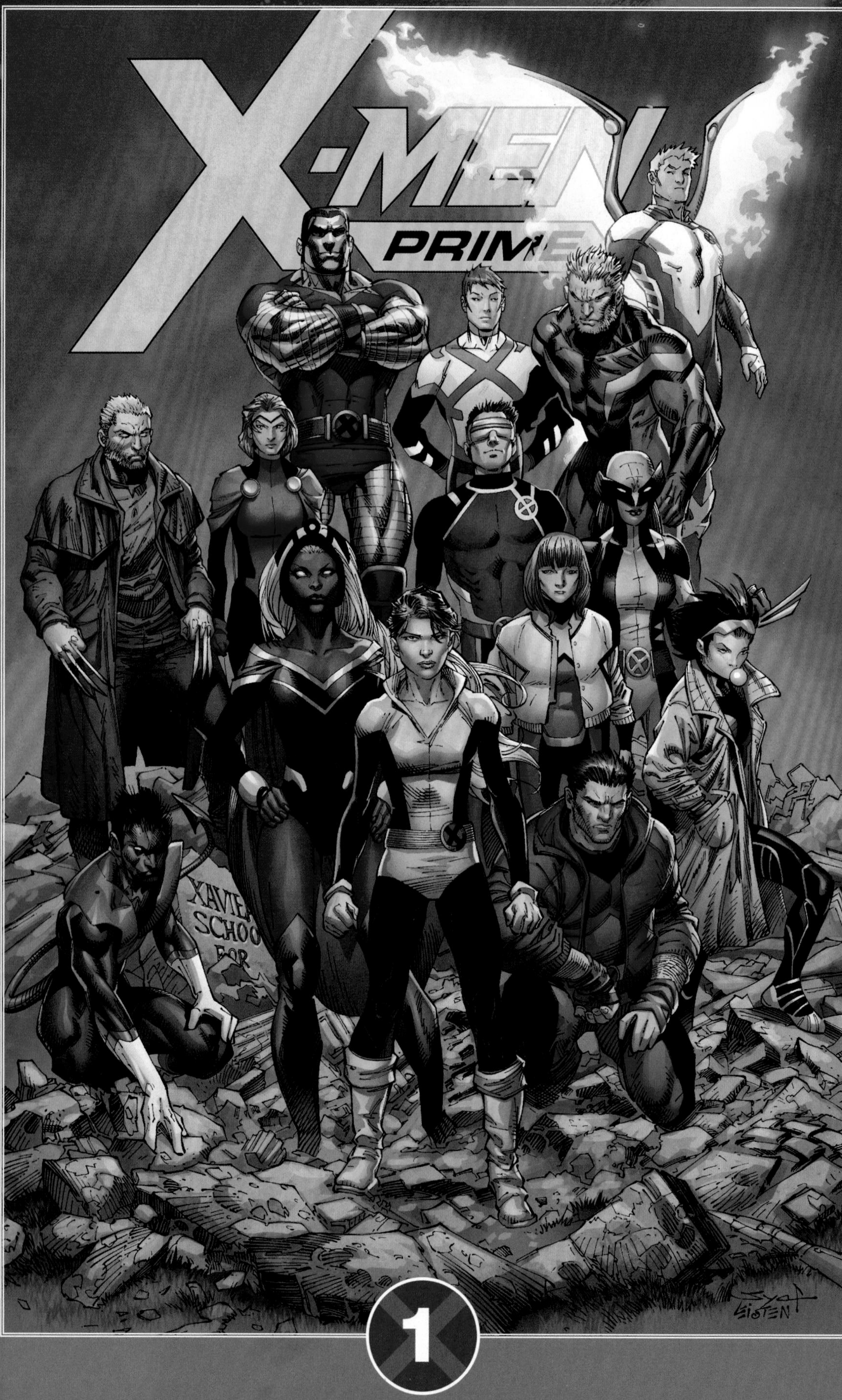
X-MEN
PRIME
XAVIER
SCHOO
FOR
1

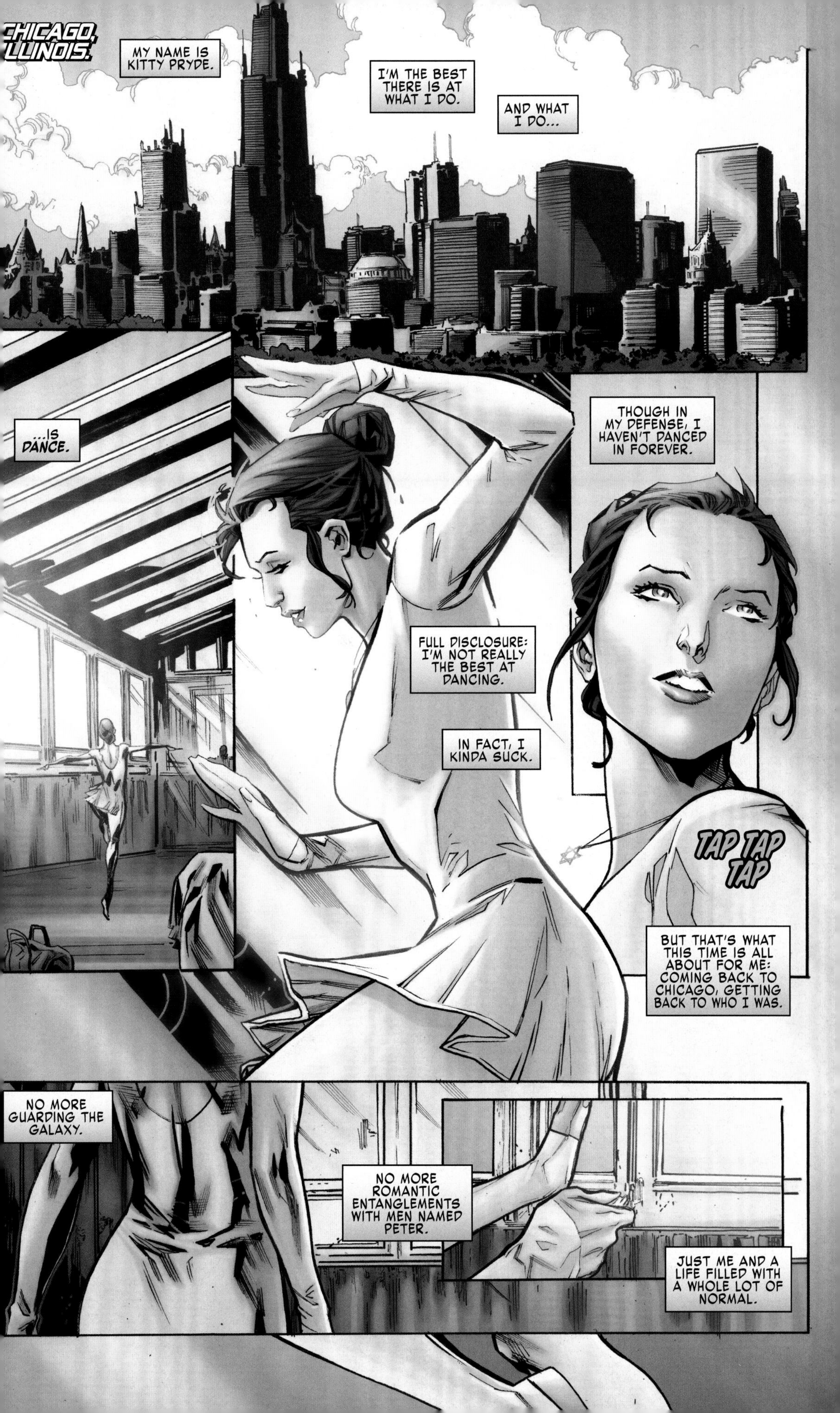
CHICAGO, ILLINOIS.
MY NAME IS KITTY PRYDE.
I'M THE BEST THERE IS AT WHAT I DO.
AND WHAT I DO...
...IS DANCE.
THOUGH IN MY DEFENSE, I HAVEN'T DANCED IN FOREVER.
FULL DISCLOSURE: I'M NOT REALLY THE BEST AT DANCING.
IN FACT, I KINDA SUCK.
TAP TAP TAP
BUT THAT'S WHAT THIS TIME IS ALL ABOUT FOR ME: COMING BACK TO CHICAGO, GETTING BACK TO WHO I WAS.
NO MORE GUARDING THE GALAXY.
NO MORE ROMANTIC ENTANGLEMENTS WITH MEN NAMED PETER.
JUST ME AND A LIFE FILLED WITH A WHOLE LOT OF NORMAL.

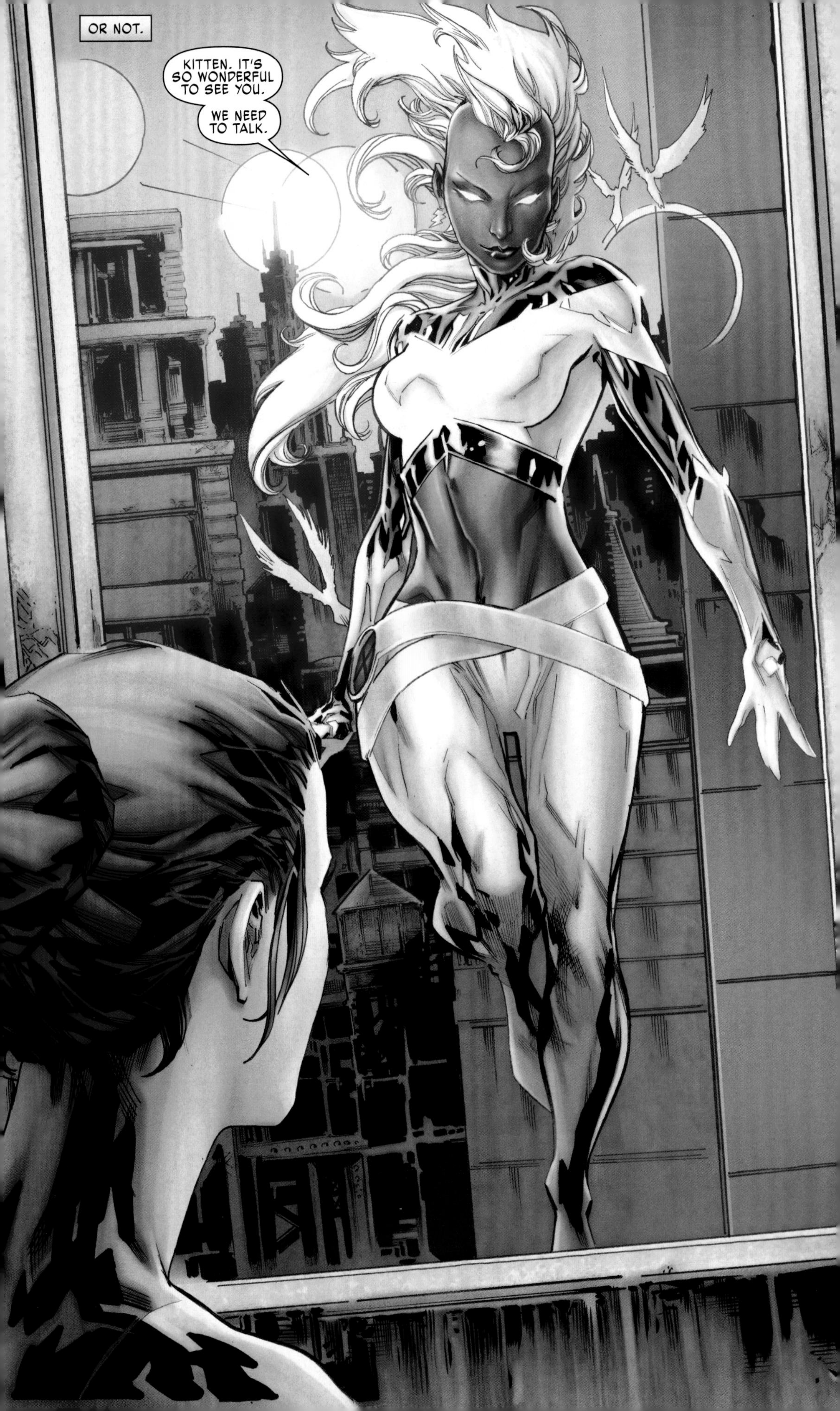
OR NOT.
KITTEN. IT'S SO WONDERFUL TO SEE YOU.
WE NEED TO TALK.

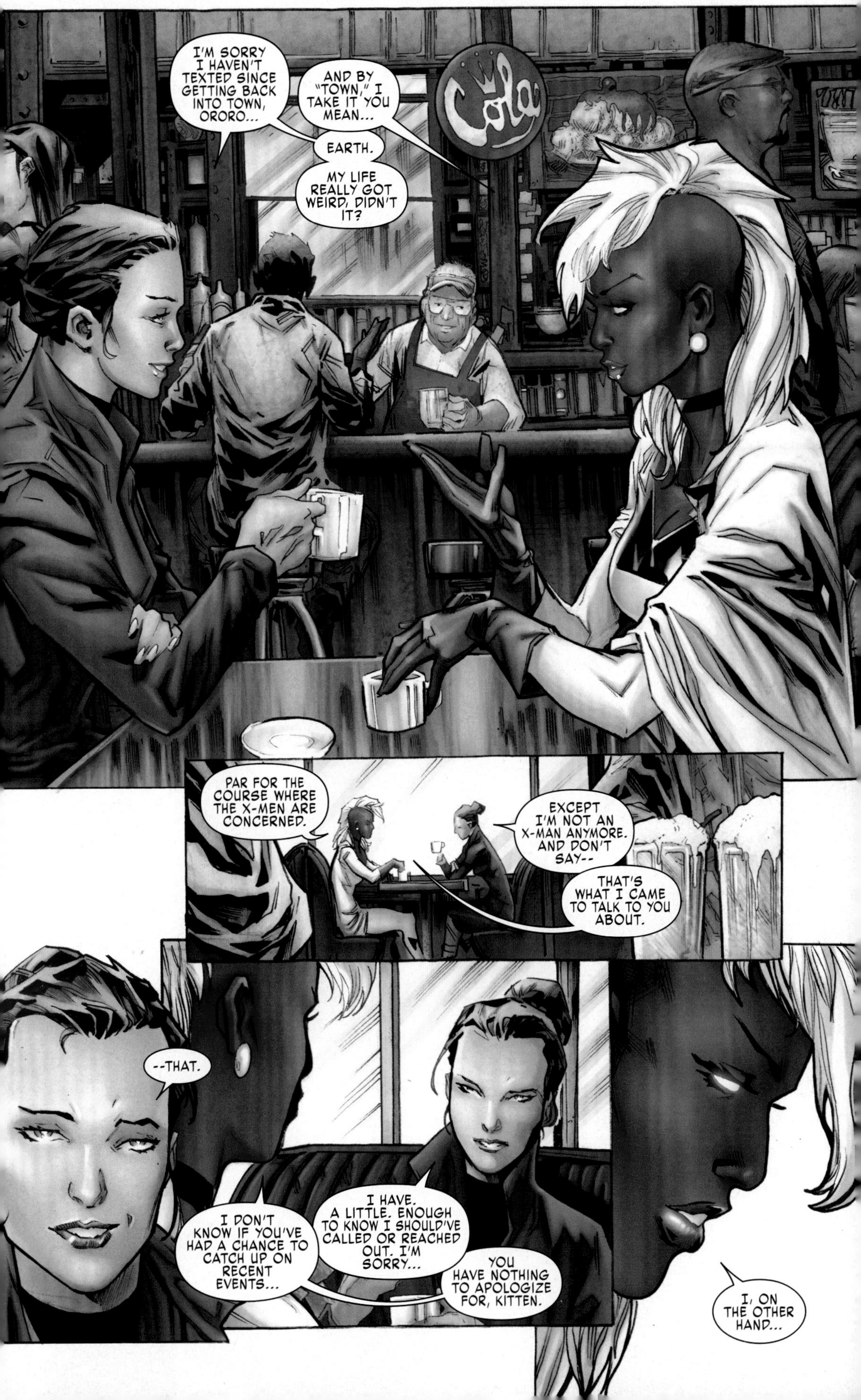
I'M SORRY I HAVEN'T TEXTED SINCE GETTING BACK INTO TOWN, ORORO...
AND BY "TOWN," I TAKE IT YOU MEAN...
EARTH.
MY LIFE REALLY GOT WEIRD, DIDN'T IT?
PAR FOR THE COURSE WHERE THE X-MEN ARE CONCERNED.
EXCEPT I'M NOT AN X-MAN ANYMORE. AND DON'T SAY--
THAT'S WHAT I CAME TO TALK TO YOU ABOUT.
--THAT.
I DON'T KNOW IF YOU'VE HAD A CHANCE TO CATCH UP ON RECENT EVENTS...
I HAVE. A LITTLE. ENOUGH TO KNOW I SHOULD'VE CALLED OR REACHED OUT. I'M SORRY...
YOU HAVE NOTHING TO APOLOGIZE FOR, KITTEN.
I, ON THE OTHER HAND...

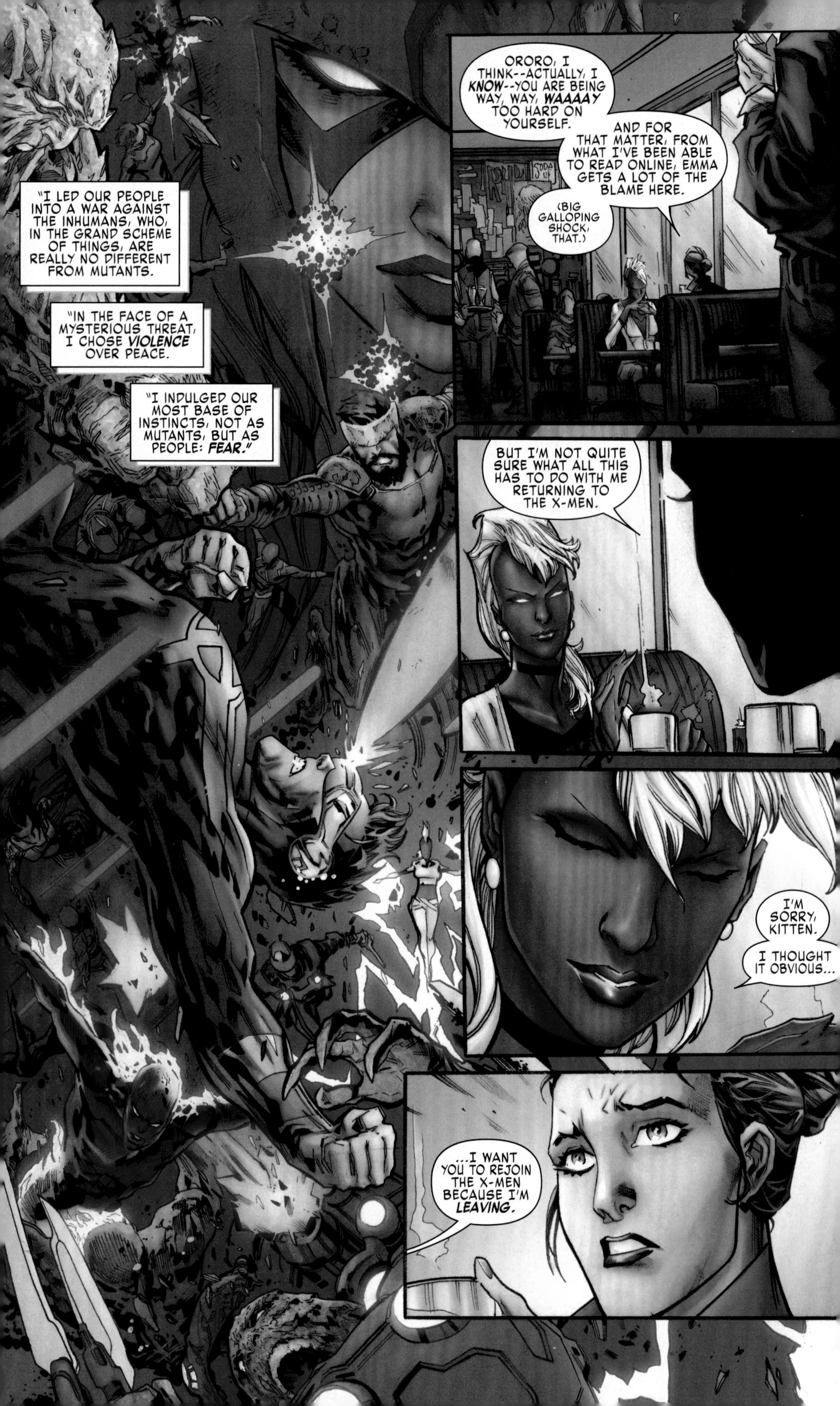

"I LED OUR PEOPLE INTO A WAR AGAINST THE INHUMANS, WHO, IN THE GRAND SCHEME OF THINGS, ARE REALLY NO DIFFERENT FROM MUTANTS.
"IN THE FACE OF A MYSTERIOUS THREAT, I CHOSE *VIOLENCE* OVER PEACE.
"I INDULGED OUR MOST BASE OF INSTINCTS, NOT AS MUTANTS, BUT AS PEOPLE: *FEAR.*"
ORORO, I THINK--ACTUALLY, I *KNOW*--YOU ARE BEING WAY, WAY, *WAAAAY* TOO HARD ON YOURSELF.
AND FOR THAT MATTER, FROM WHAT I'VE BEEN ABLE TO READ ONLINE, EMMA GETS A LOT OF THE BLAME HERE.
(BIG GALLOPING SHOCK, THAT.)
BUT I'M NOT QUITE SURE WHAT ALL THIS HAS TO DO WITH ME RETURNING TO THE X-MEN.
I'M SORRY, KITTEN.
I THOUGHT IT OBVIOUS...
...I WANT YOU TO REJOIN THE X-MEN BECAUSE I'M *LEAVING.*

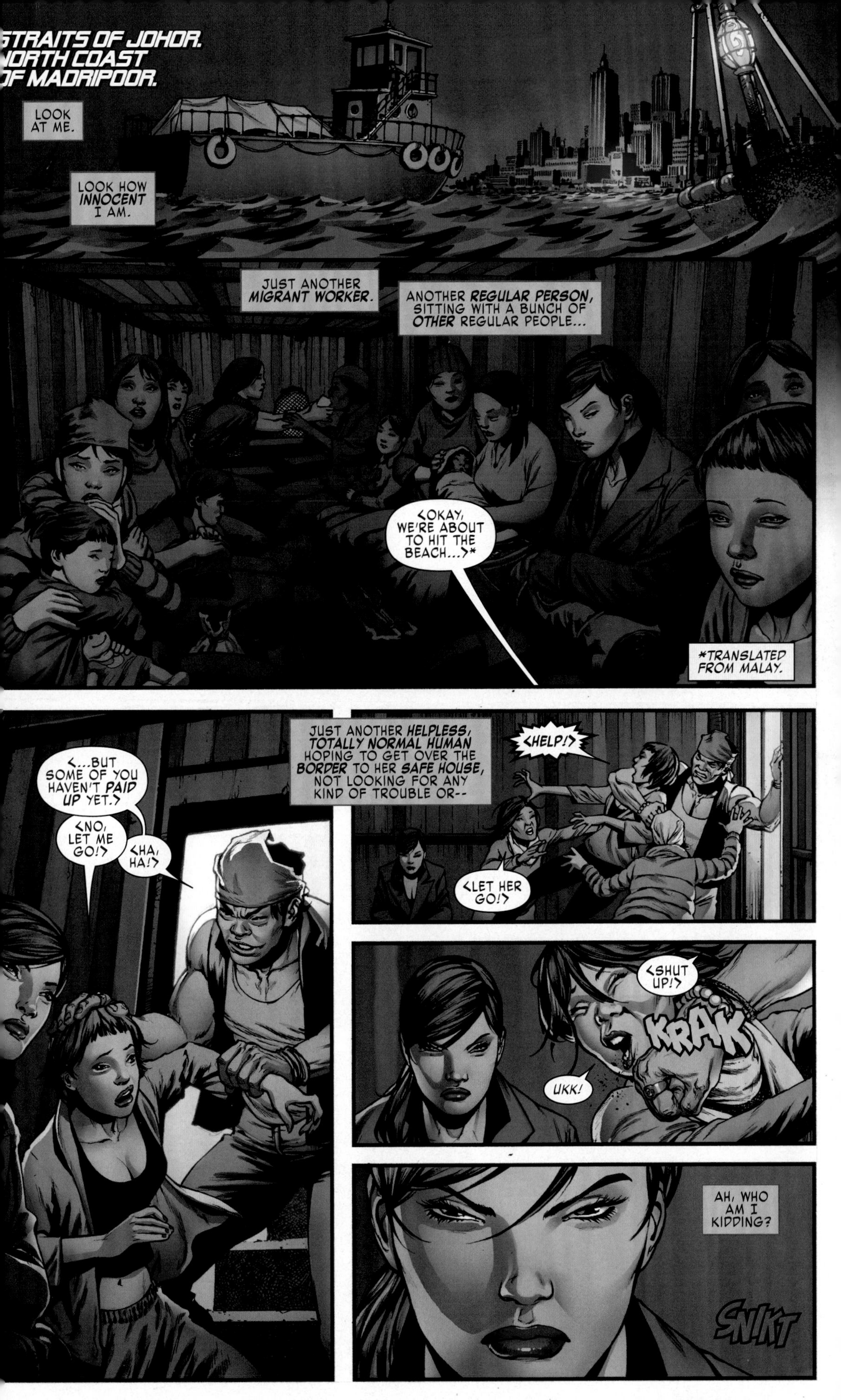
STRAITS OF JOHOR. NORTH COAST OF MADRIPOOR.
LOOK AT ME.
LOOK HOW INNOCENT I AM.
JUST ANOTHER MIGRANT WORKER.
ANOTHER REGULAR PERSON, SITTING WITH A BUNCH OF OTHER REGULAR PEOPLE...
<OKAY, WE'RE ABOUT TO HIT THE BEACH...>*
*TRANSLATED FROM MALAY.
<...BUT SOME OF YOU HAVEN'T PAID UP YET.>
<NO, LET ME GO!>
<HA, HA!>
JUST ANOTHER HELPLESS, TOTALLY NORMAL HUMAN HOPING TO GET OVER THE BORDER TO HER SAFE HOUSE, NOT LOOKING FOR ANY KIND OF TROUBLE OR--
<HELP!>
<LET HER GO!>
<SHUT UP!>
KRAK
UKK!
AH, WHO AM I KIDDING?
SNIKT

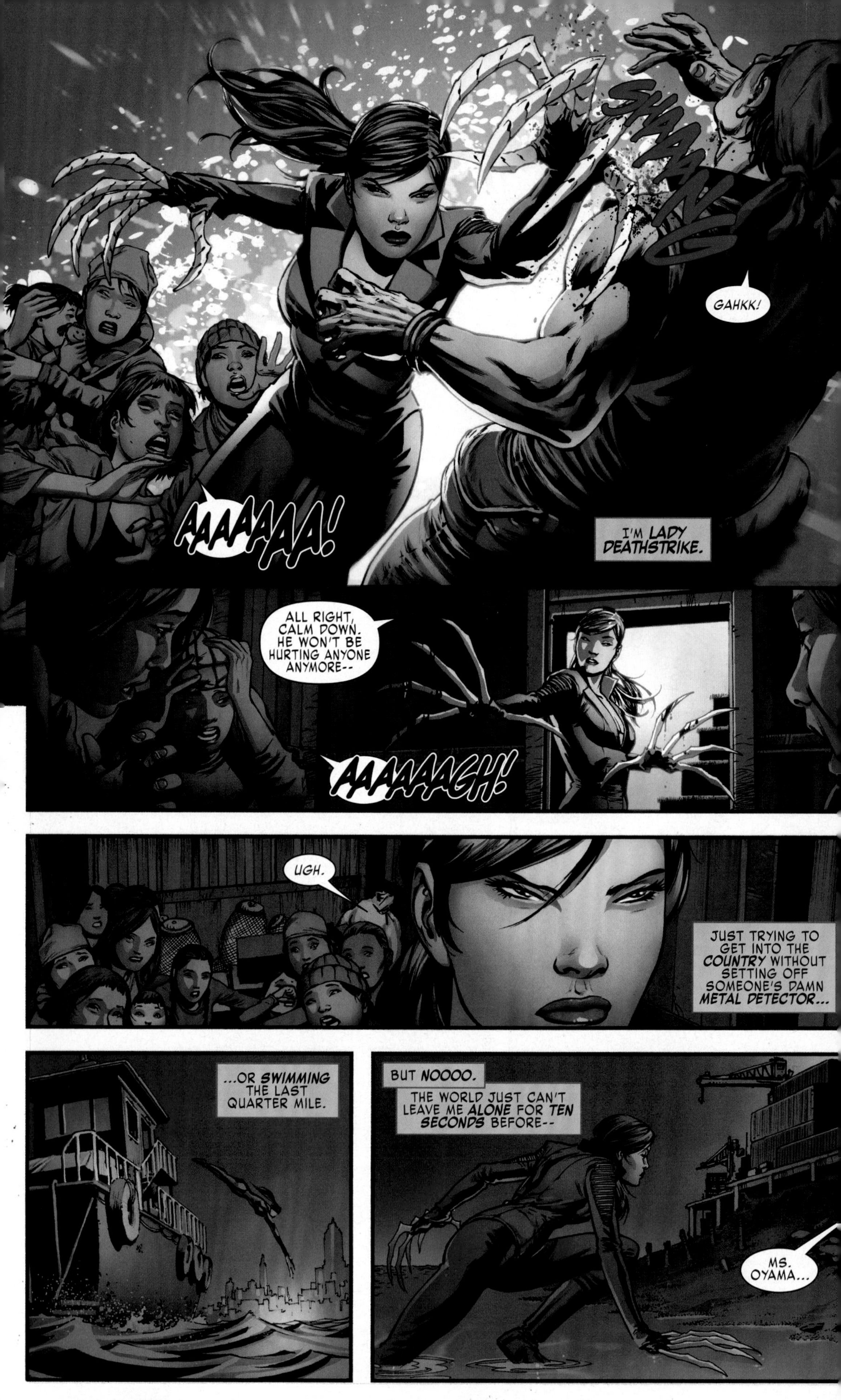
SHAAANG
GAHKK!
AAAAAAA!
I'M LADY DEATHSTRIKE.
ALL RIGHT, CALM DOWN. HE WON'T BE HURTING ANYONE ANYMORE--
AAAAAAGH!
UGH.
JUST TRYING TO GET INTO THE COUNTRY WITHOUT SETTING OFF SOMEONE'S DAMN METAL DETECTOR...
...OR SWIMMING THE LAST QUARTER MILE.
BUT NOOOO.
THE WORLD JUST CAN'T LEAVE ME ALONE FOR TEN SECONDS BEFORE--
MS. OYAMA...

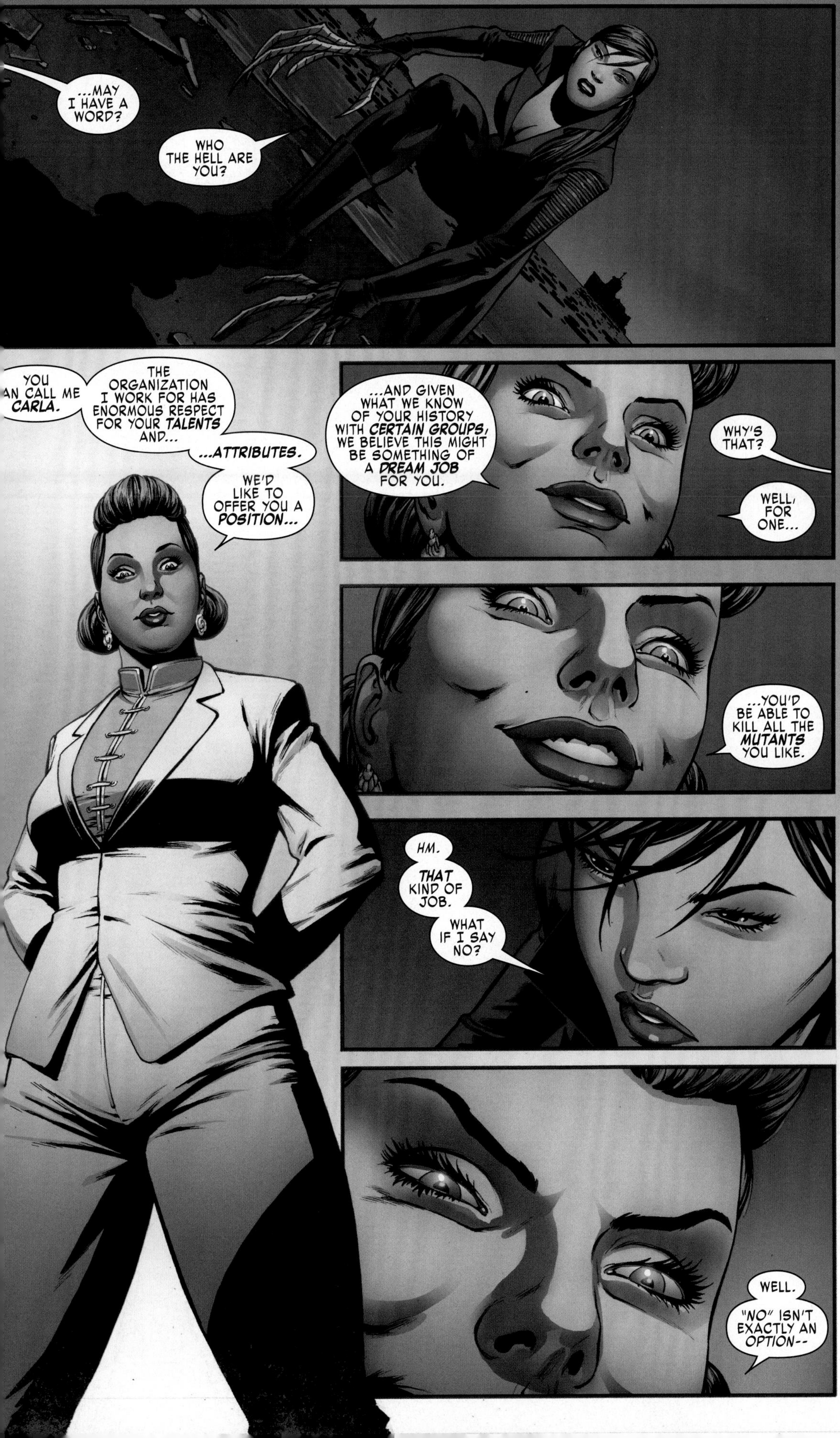
...MAY I HAVE A WORD?
WHO THE HELL ARE YOU?
YOU AN CALL ME CARLA.
THE ORGANIZATION I WORK FOR HAS ENORMOUS RESPECT FOR YOUR TALENTS AND...
...ATTRIBUTES.
WE'D LIKE TO OFFER YOU A POSITION...
...AND GIVEN WHAT WE KNOW OF YOUR HISTORY WITH CERTAIN GROUPS, WE BELIEVE THIS MIGHT BE SOMETHING OF A DREAM JOB FOR YOU.
WHY'S THAT?
WELL, FOR ONE...
...YOU'D BE ABLE TO KILL ALL THE MUTANTS YOU LIKE.
HM.
THAT KIND OF JOB.
WHAT IF I SAY NO?
WELL.
"NO" ISN'T EXACTLY AN OPTION--

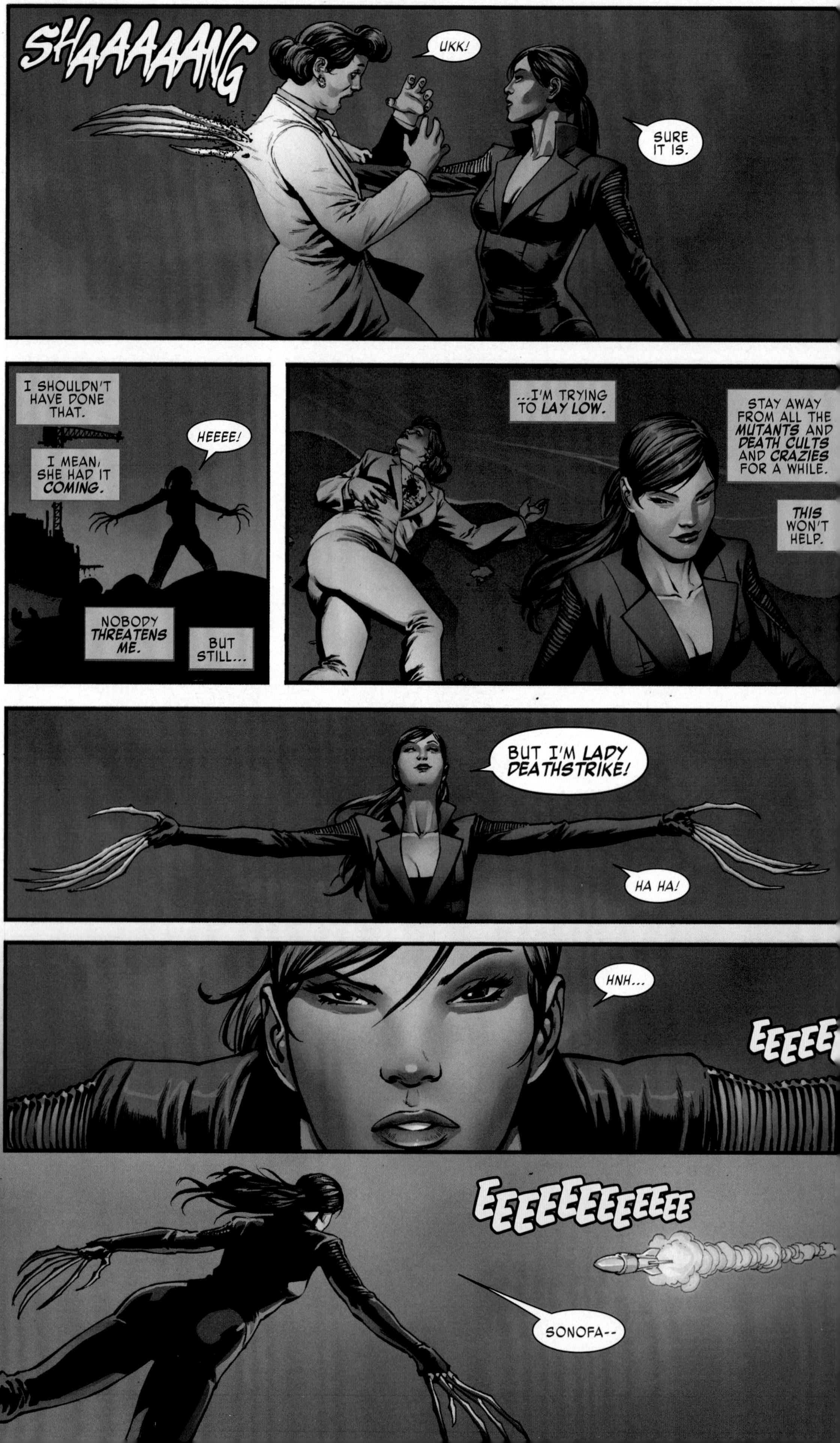
SHAAAAANG
UKK!
SURE IT IS.
I SHOULDN'T HAVE DONE THAT.
HEEEE!
I MEAN, SHE HAD IT COMING.
NOBODY THREATENS ME.
BUT STILL...
...I'M TRYING TO LAY LOW.
STAY AWAY FROM ALL THE MUTANTS AND DEATH CULTS AND CRAZIES FOR A WHILE.
THIS WON'T HELP.
BUT I'M LADY DEATHSTRIKE!
HA HA!
HNH...
EEEEE
EEEEEEEEEEEE
SONOFA--

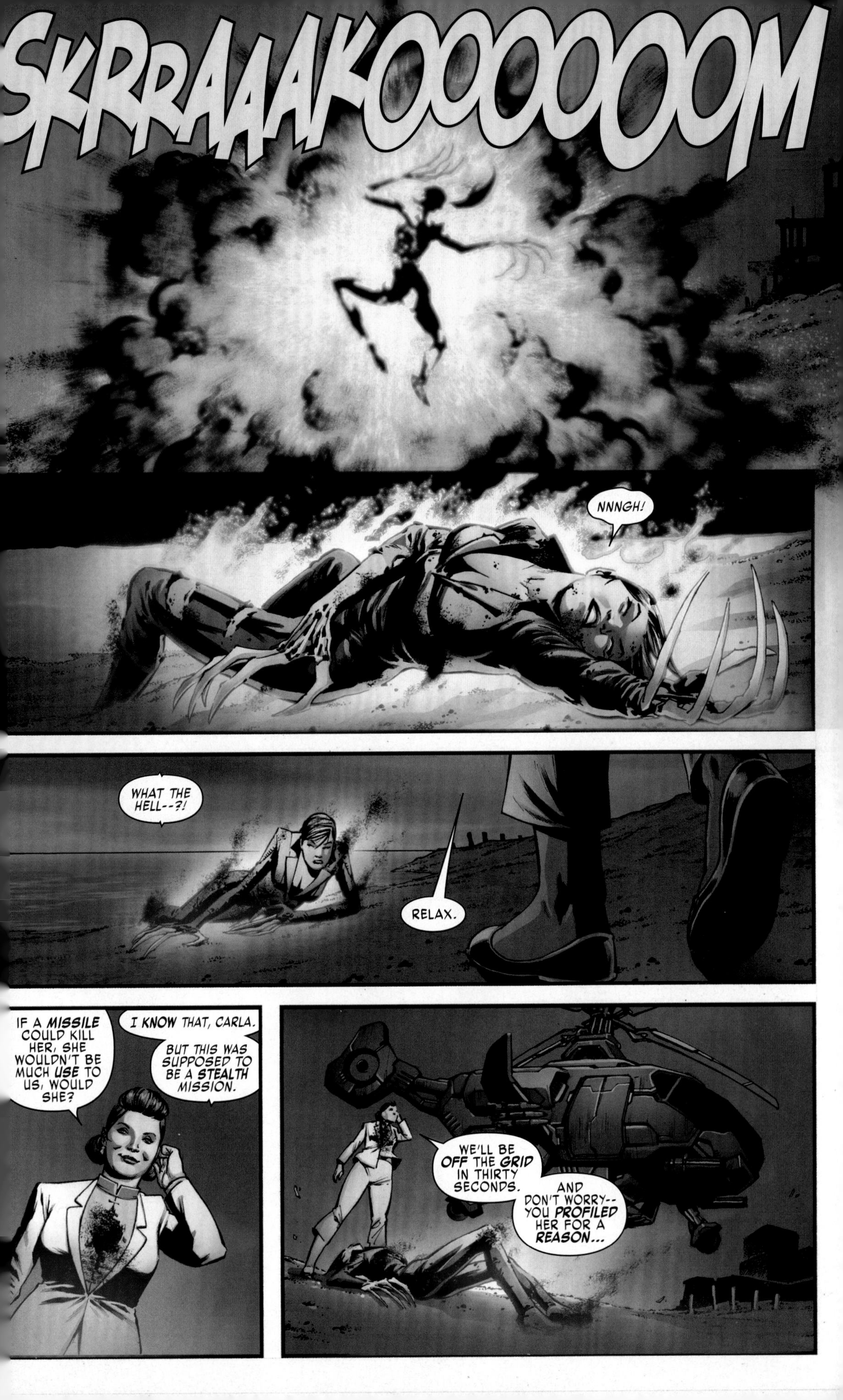
SKRRAAAKOOOOOOM
NNNGH!
WHAT THE HELL--?!
RELAX.
IF A MISSILE COULD KILL HER, SHE WOULDN'T BE MUCH USE TO US, WOULD SHE?
I KNOW THAT, CARLA.
BUT THIS WAS SUPPOSED TO BE A STEALTH MISSION.
WE'LL BE OFF THE GRID IN THIRTY SECONDS.
AND DON'T WORRY-- YOU PROFILED HER FOR A REASON...

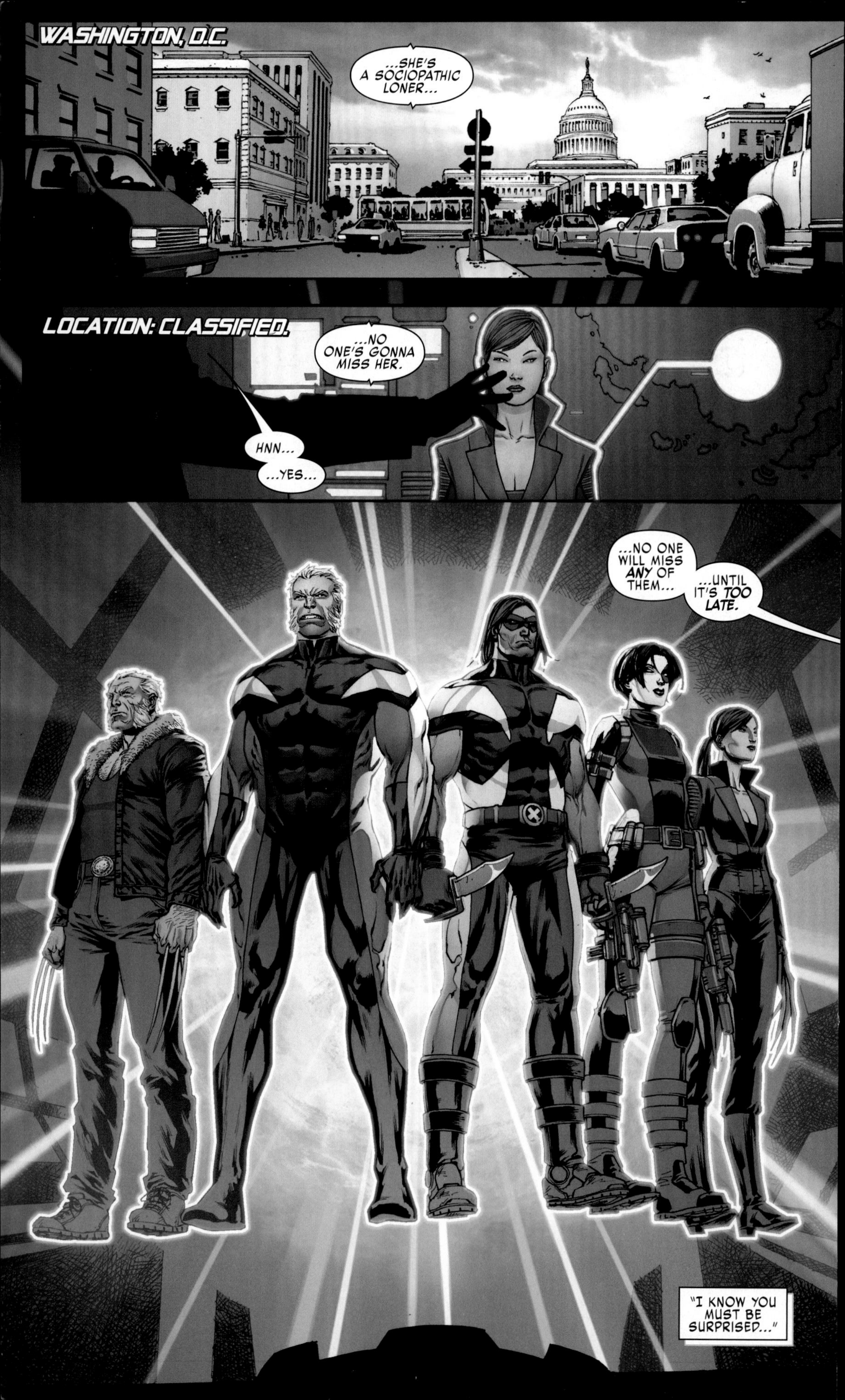
WASHINGTON, D.C.
...SHE'S A SOCIOPATHIC LONER...
LOCATION: CLASSIFIED.
...NO ONE'S GONNA MISS HER.
HNN...
...YES...
...NO ONE WILL MISS ANY OF THEM...
...UNTIL IT'S TOO LATE.
"I KNOW YOU MUST BE SURPRISED..."

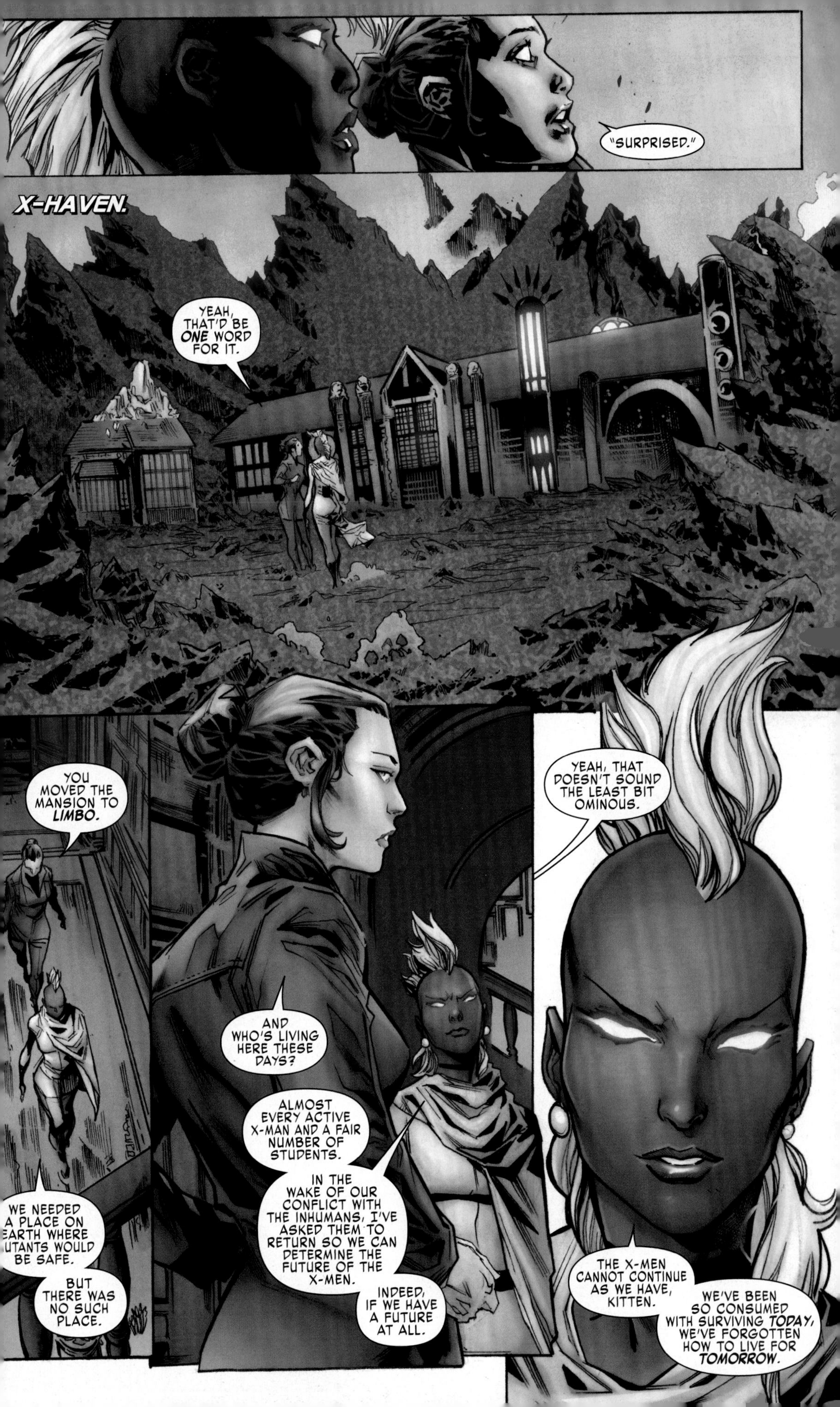
"SURPRISED."
X-HAVEN.
YEAH, THAT'D BE ONE WORD FOR IT.
YOU MOVED THE MANSION TO LIMBO.
WE NEEDED A PLACE ON EARTH WHERE UTANTS WOULD BE SAFE.
BUT THERE WAS NO SUCH PLACE.
AND WHO'S LIVING HERE THESE DAYS?
ALMOST EVERY ACTIVE X-MAN AND A FAIR NUMBER OF STUDENTS.
IN THE WAKE OF OUR CONFLICT WITH THE INHUMANS, I'VE ASKED THEM TO RETURN SO WE CAN DETERMINE THE FUTURE OF THE X-MEN.
INDEED, IF WE HAVE A FUTURE AT ALL.
YEAH, THAT DOESN'T SOUND THE LEAST BIT OMINOUS.
THE X-MEN CANNOT CONTINUE AS WE HAVE, KITTEN.
WE'VE BEEN SO CONSUMED WITH SURVIVING TODAY, WE'VE FORGOTTEN HOW TO LIVE FOR TOMORROW.

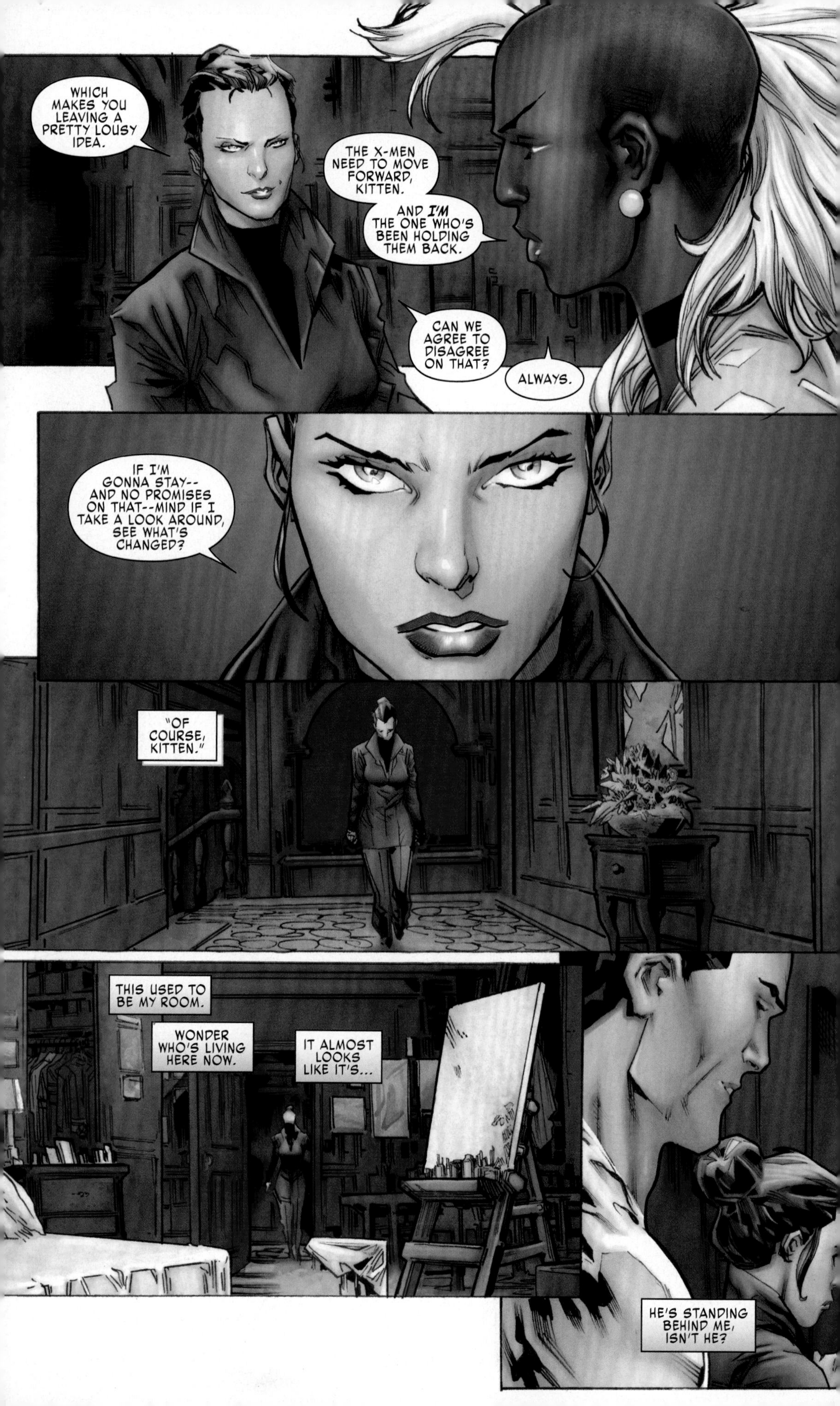
WHICH MAKES YOU LEAVING A PRETTY LOUSY IDEA.
THE X-MEN NEED TO MOVE FORWARD, KITTEN.
AND I'M THE ONE WHO'S BEEN HOLDING THEM BACK.
CAN WE AGREE TO DISAGREE ON THAT?
ALWAYS.
IF I'M GONNA STAY-- AND NO PROMISES ON THAT--MIND IF I TAKE A LOOK AROUND, SEE WHAT'S CHANGED?
"OF COURSE, KITTEN."
THIS USED TO BE MY ROOM.
WONDER WHO'S LIVING HERE NOW.
IT ALMOST LOOKS LIKE IT'S...
HE'S STANDING BEHIND ME, ISN'T HE?

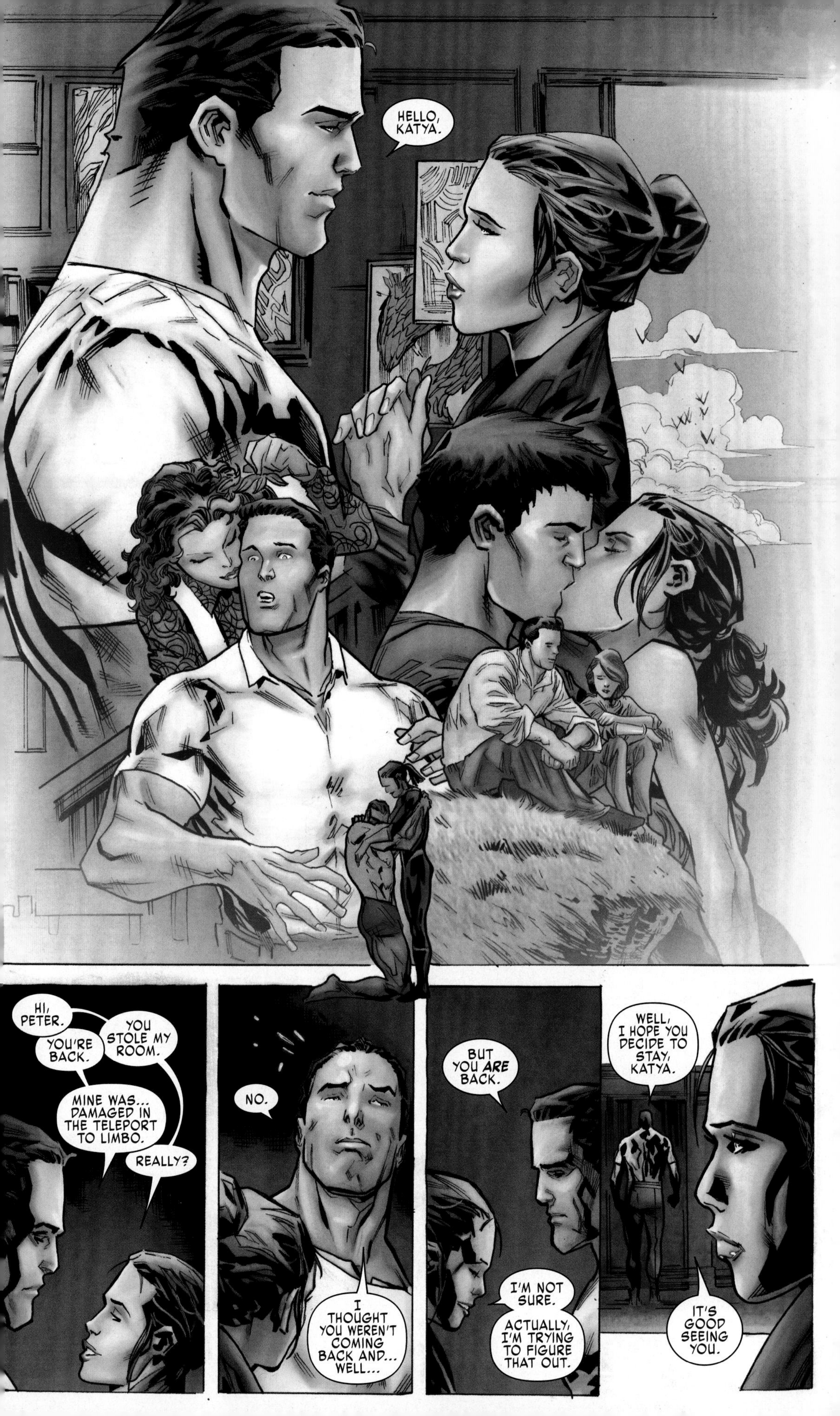
HELLO, KATYA.
HI, PETER.
YOU STOLE MY ROOM.
YOU'RE BACK.
MINE WAS... DAMAGED IN THE TELEPORT TO LIMBO.
REALLY?
NO.
I THOUGHT YOU WEREN'T COMING BACK AND... WELL...
BUT YOU ARE BACK.
I'M NOT SURE.
ACTUALLY, I'M TRYING TO FIGURE THAT OUT.
WELL, I HOPE YOU DECIDE TO STAY, KATYA.
IT'S GOOD SEEING YOU.

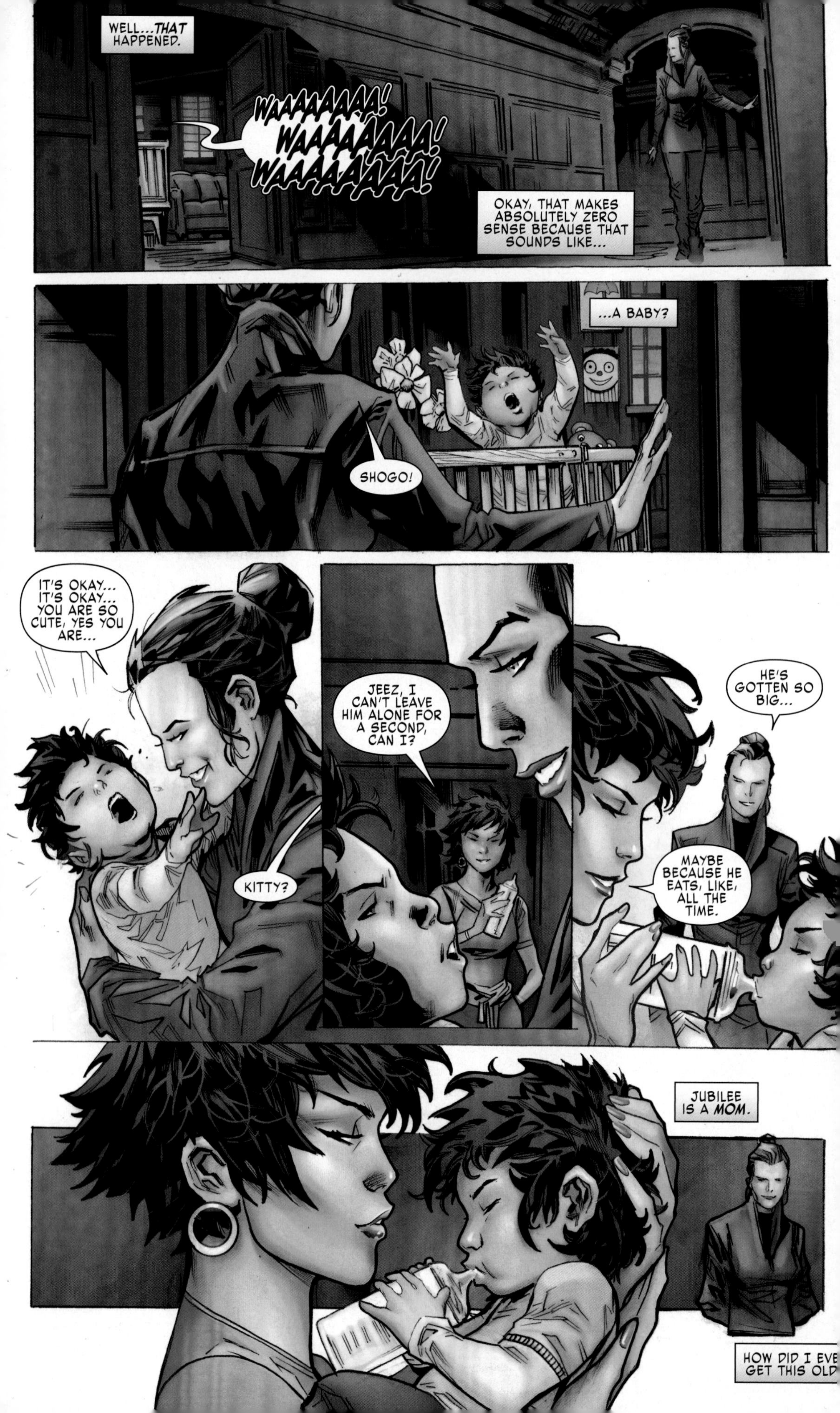
WELL...THAT HAPPENED.
WAAAAAAAA! WAAAAAAAA! WAAAAAAAA!
OKAY, THAT MAKES ABSOLUTELY ZERO SENSE BECAUSE THAT SOUNDS LIKE...
...A BABY?
SHOGO!
IT'S OKAY... IT'S OKAY... YOU ARE SO CUTE, YES YOU ARE...
KITTY?
JEEZ, I CAN'T LEAVE HIM ALONE FOR A SECOND, CAN I?
HE'S GOTTEN SO BIG...
MAYBE BECAUSE HE EATS, LIKE, ALL THE TIME.
JUBILEE IS A MOM.
HOW DID I EVE
GET THIS OLD

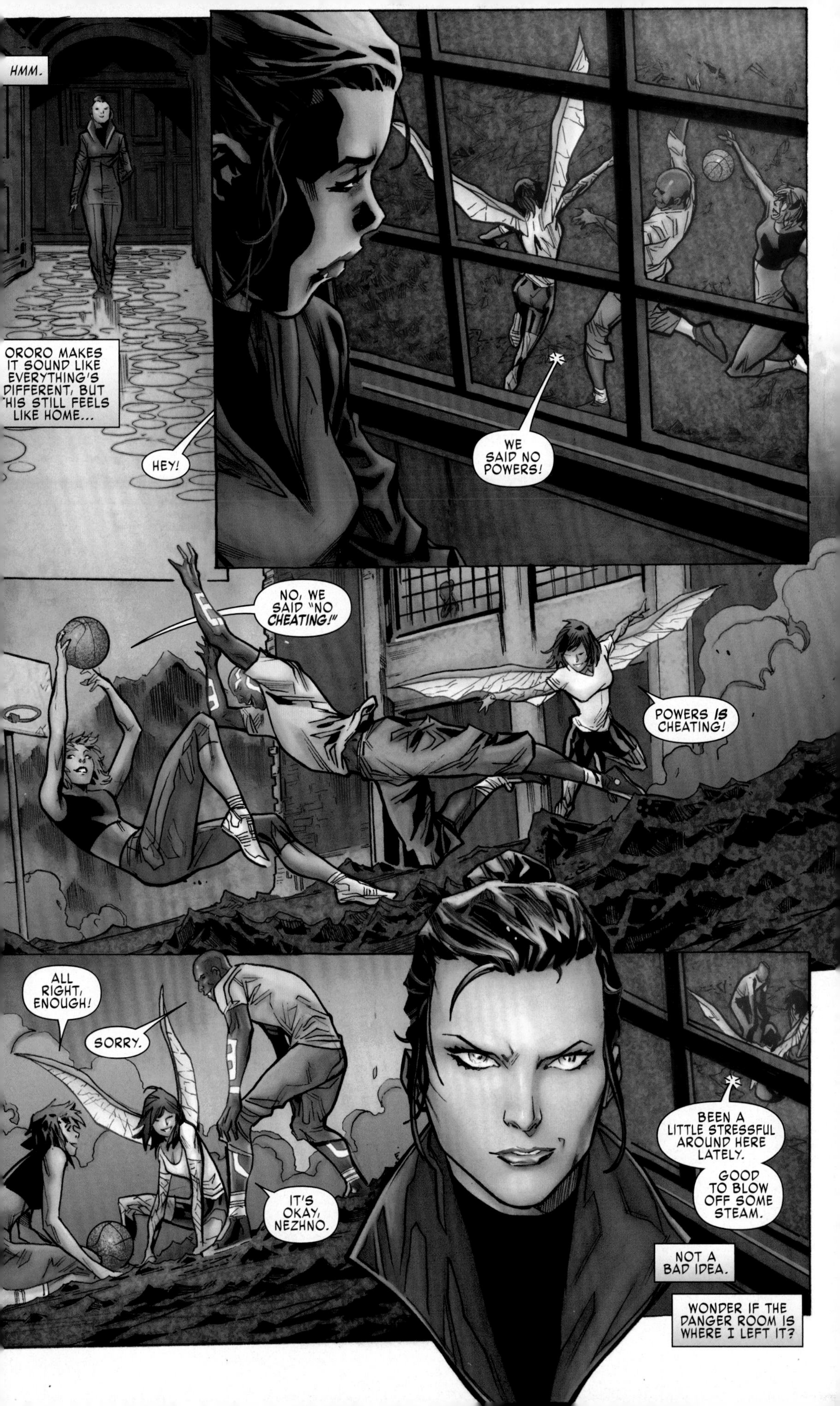
HMM.
ORORO MAKES IT SOUND LIKE EVERYTHING'S DIFFERENT, BUT THIS STILL FEELS LIKE HOME...
HEY!
WE SAID NO POWERS!
NO, WE SAID "NO CHEATING!"
POWERS IS CHEATING!
ALL RIGHT, ENOUGH!
SORRY.
IT'S OKAY, NEZHNO.
BEEN A LITTLE STRESSFUL AROUND HERE LATELY.
GOOD TO BLOW OFF SOME STEAM.
NOT A BAD IDEA.
WONDER IF THE DANGER ROOM IS WHERE I LEFT IT?

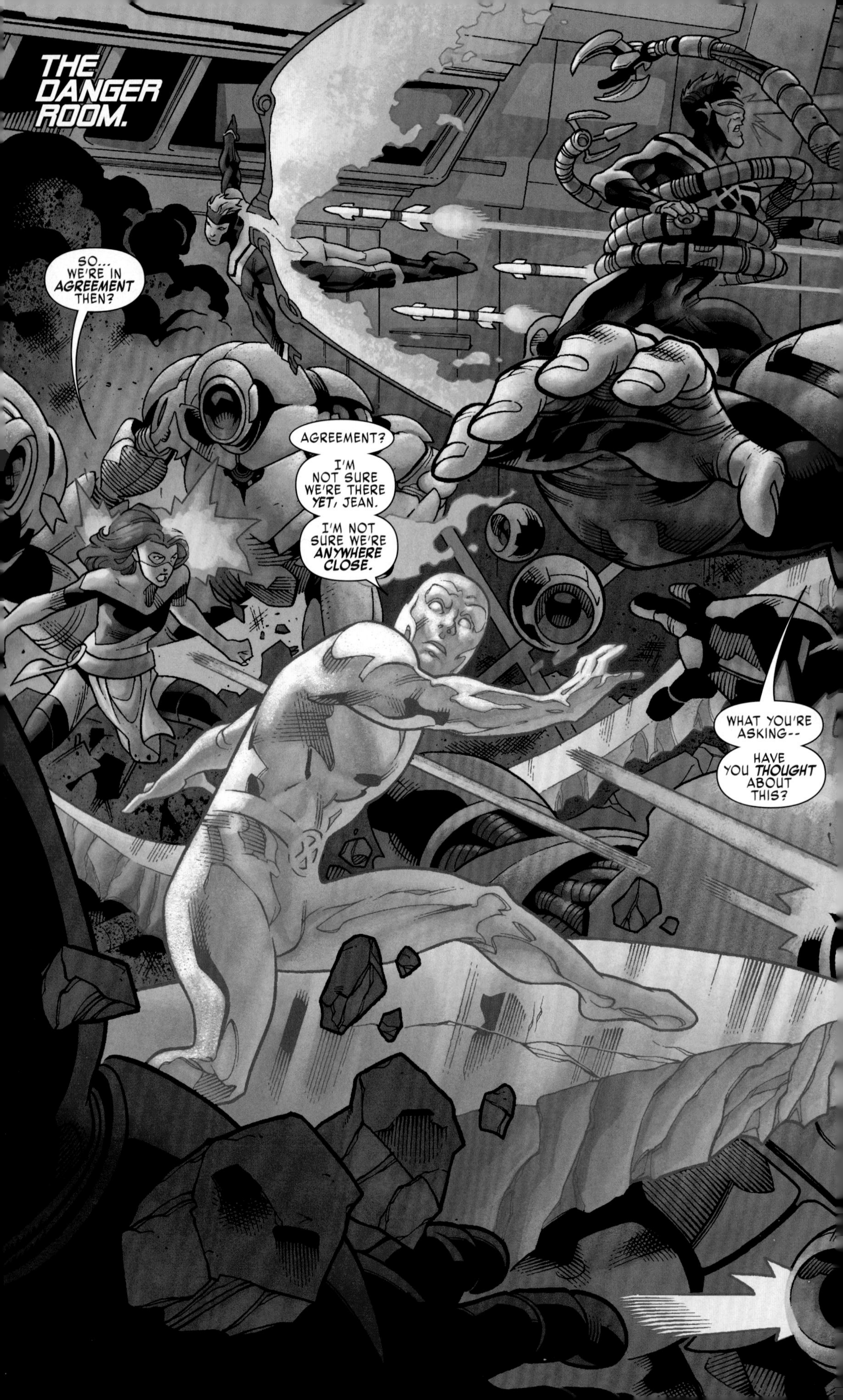
THE DANGER ROOM.
SO... WE'RE IN AGREEMENT THEN?
AGREEMENT?
I'M NOT SURE WE'RE THERE YET, JEAN.
I'M NOT SURE WE'RE ANYWHERE CLOSE.
WHAT YOU'RE ASKING--
HAVE YOU THOUGHT ABOUT THIS?

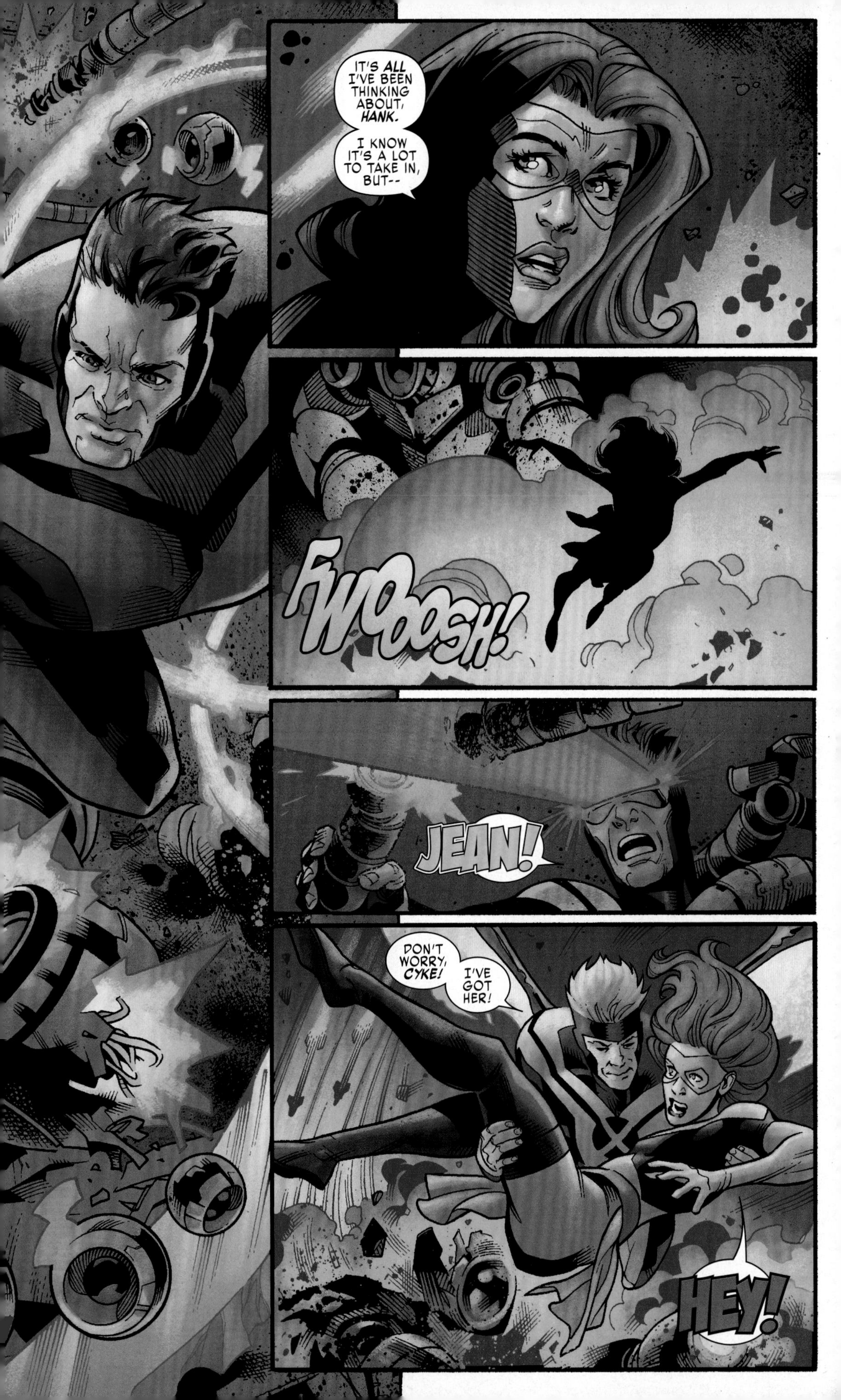
IT'S ALL I'VE BEEN THINKING ABOUT, HANK.
I KNOW IT'S A LOT TO TAKE IN, BUT--
FWOOOSH!
JEAN!
DON'T WORRY, CYKE!
I'VE GOT HER!
HEY!

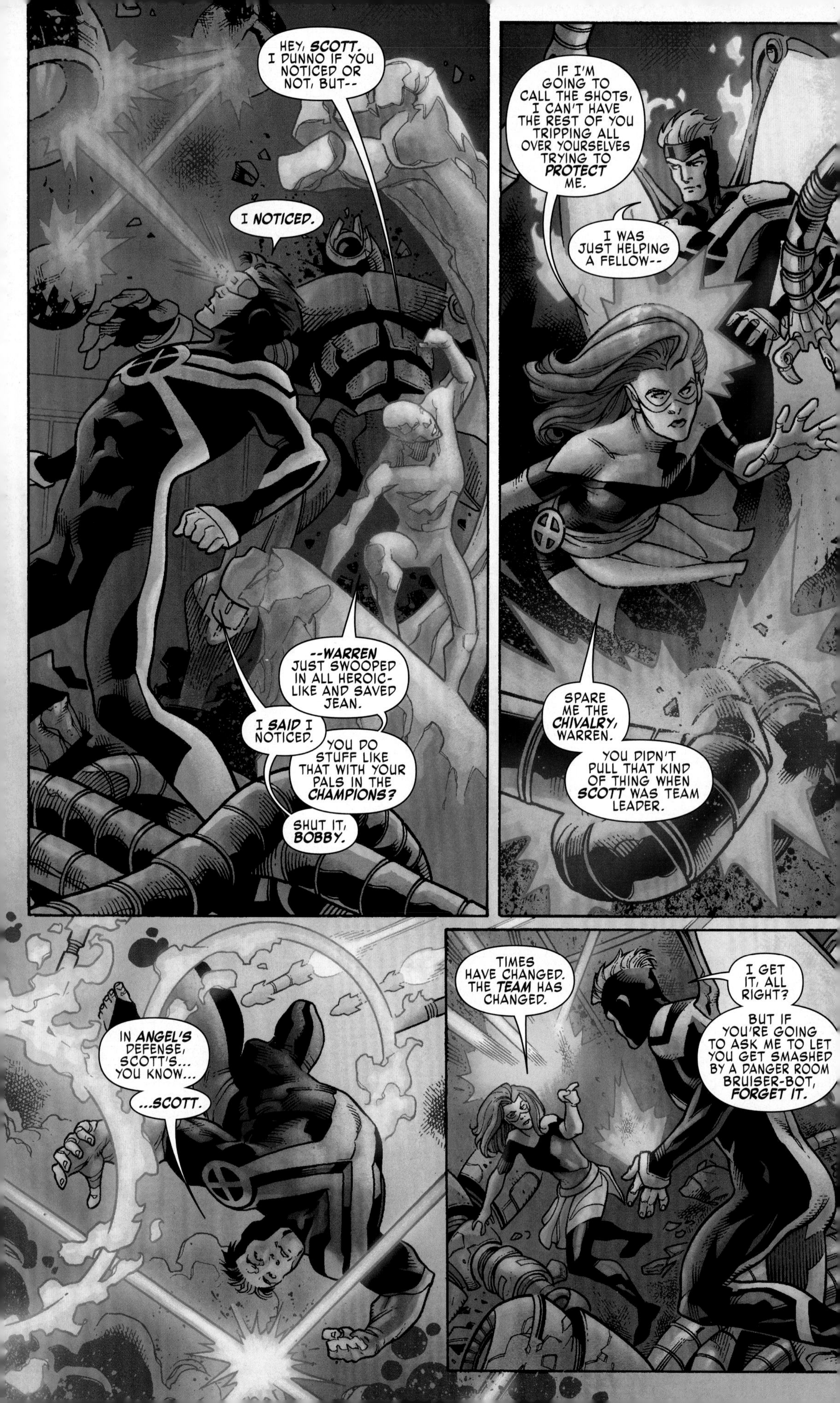
HEY, SCOTT. I DUNNO IF YOU NOTICED OR NOT, BUT--
I NOTICED.
--WARREN JUST SWOOPED IN ALL HEROIC-LIKE AND SAVED JEAN.
I SAID I NOTICED.
YOU DO STUFF LIKE THAT WITH YOUR PALS IN THE CHAMPIONS?
SHUT IT, BOBBY.
IF I'M GOING TO CALL THE SHOTS, I CAN'T HAVE THE REST OF YOU TRIPPING ALL OVER YOURSELVES TRYING TO PROTECT ME.
I WAS JUST HELPING A FELLOW--
SPARE ME THE CHIVALRY, WARREN.
YOU DIDN'T PULL THAT KIND OF THING WHEN SCOTT WAS TEAM LEADER.
IN ANGEL'S DEFENSE, SCOTT'S... YOU KNOW...
...SCOTT.
TIMES HAVE CHANGED. THE TEAM HAS CHANGED.
I GET IT, ALL RIGHT?
BUT IF YOU'RE GOING TO ASK ME TO LET YOU GET SMASHED BY A DANGER ROOM BRUISER-BOT, FORGET IT.

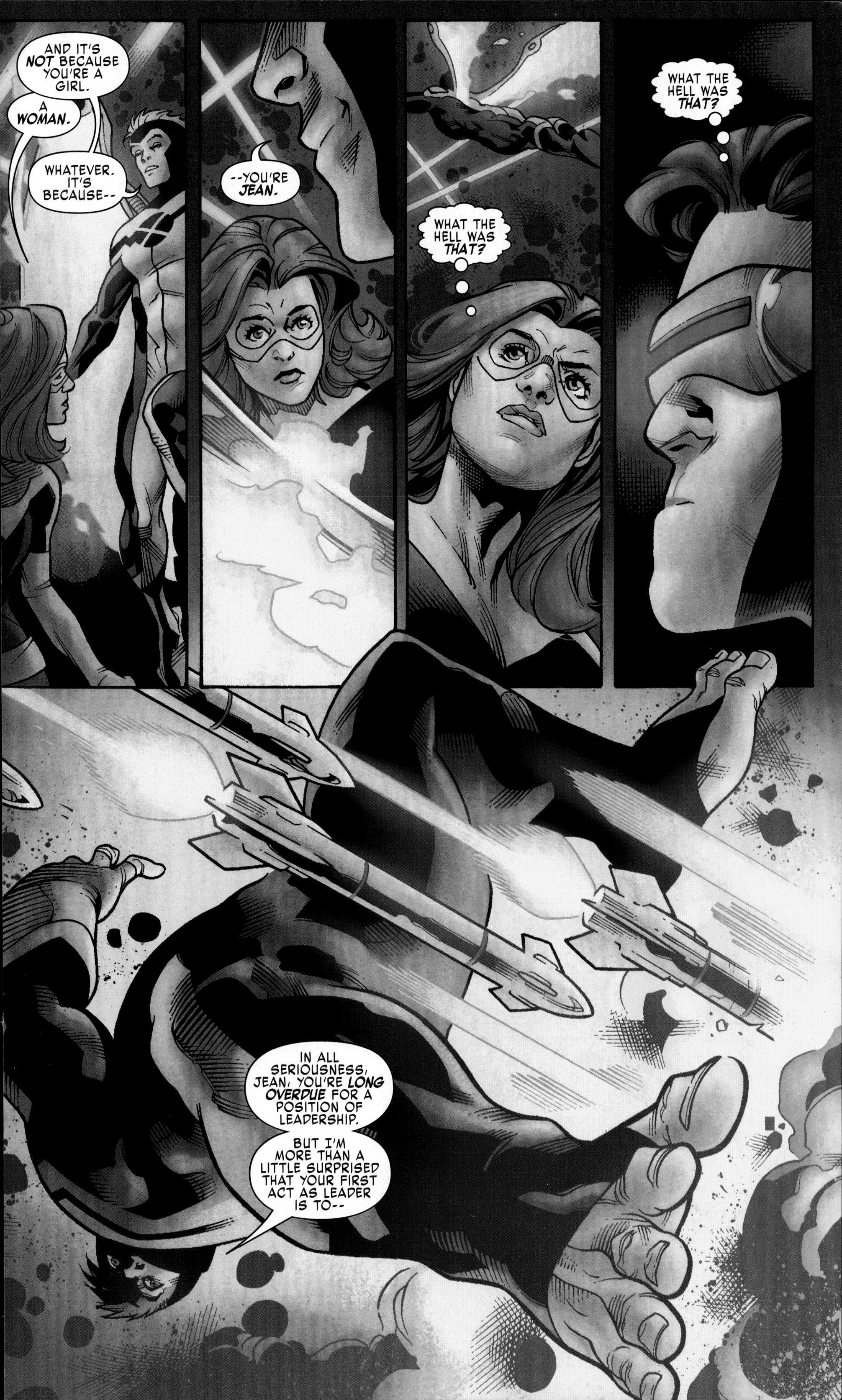

AND IT'S NOT BECAUSE YOU'RE A GIRL.
A WOMAN.
WHATEVER. IT'S BECAUSE--
--YOU'RE JEAN.
WHAT THE HELL WAS THAT?
WHAT THE HELL WAS THAT?
IN ALL SERIOUSNESS, JEAN, YOU'RE LONG OVERDUE FOR A POSITION OF LEADERSHIP.
BUT I'M MORE THAN A LITTLE SURPRISED THAT YOUR FIRST ACT AS LEADER IS TO--

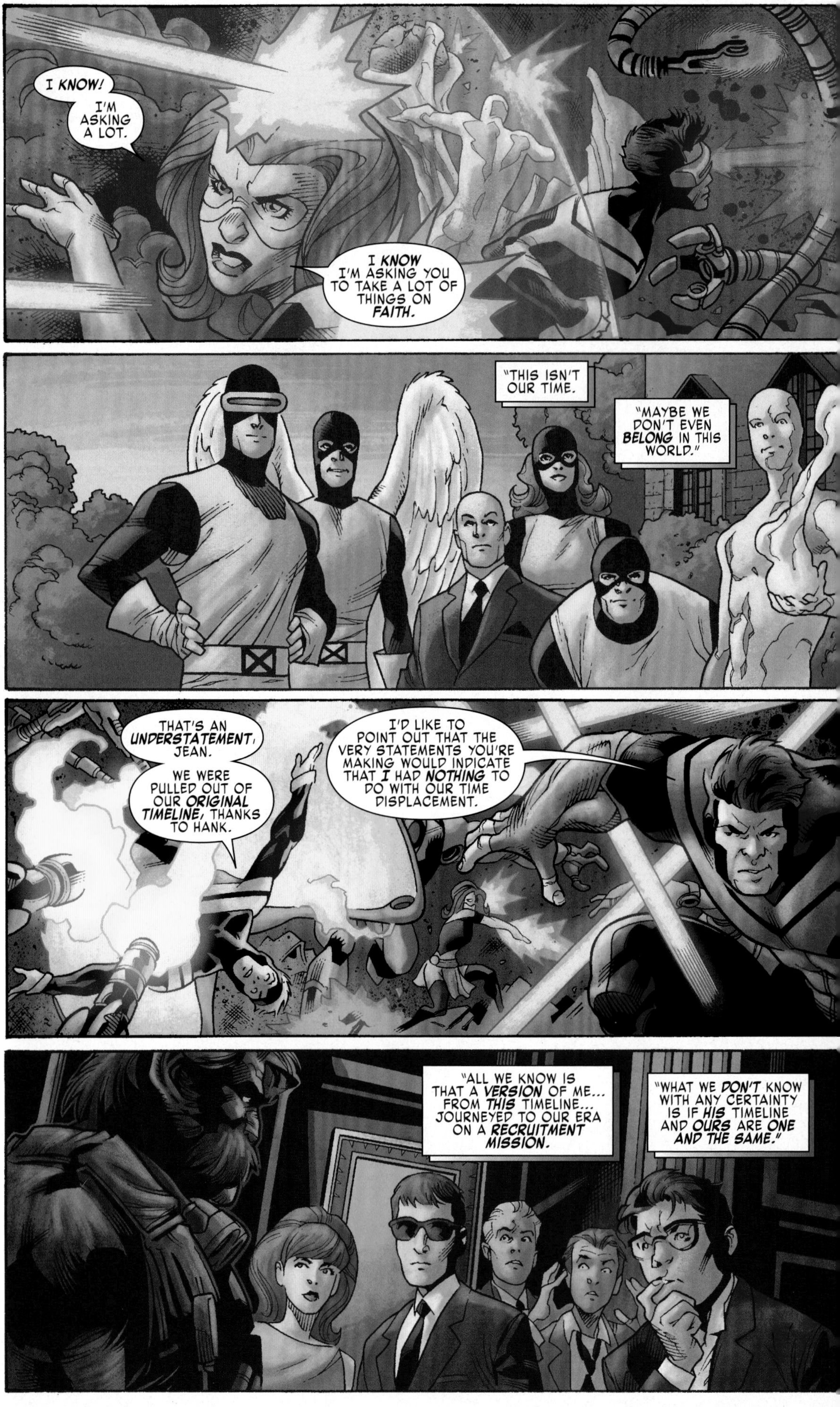
I KNOW!
I'M ASKING A LOT.
I KNOW I'M ASKING YOU TO TAKE A LOT OF THINGS ON FAITH.
"THIS ISN'T OUR TIME.
"MAYBE WE DON'T EVEN BELONG IN THIS WORLD."
THAT'S AN UNDERSTATEMENT, JEAN.
WE WERE PULLED OUT OF OUR ORIGINAL TIMELINE, THANKS TO HANK.
I'D LIKE TO POINT OUT THAT THE VERY STATEMENTS YOU'RE MAKING WOULD INDICATE THAT I HAD NOTHING TO DO WITH OUR TIME DISPLACEMENT.
"ALL WE KNOW IS THAT A VERSION OF ME... FROM THIS TIMELINE... JOURNEYED TO OUR ERA ON A RECRUITMENT MISSION.
"WHAT WE DON'T KNOW WITH ANY CERTAINTY IS IF HIS TIMELINE AND OURS ARE ONE AND THE SAME."

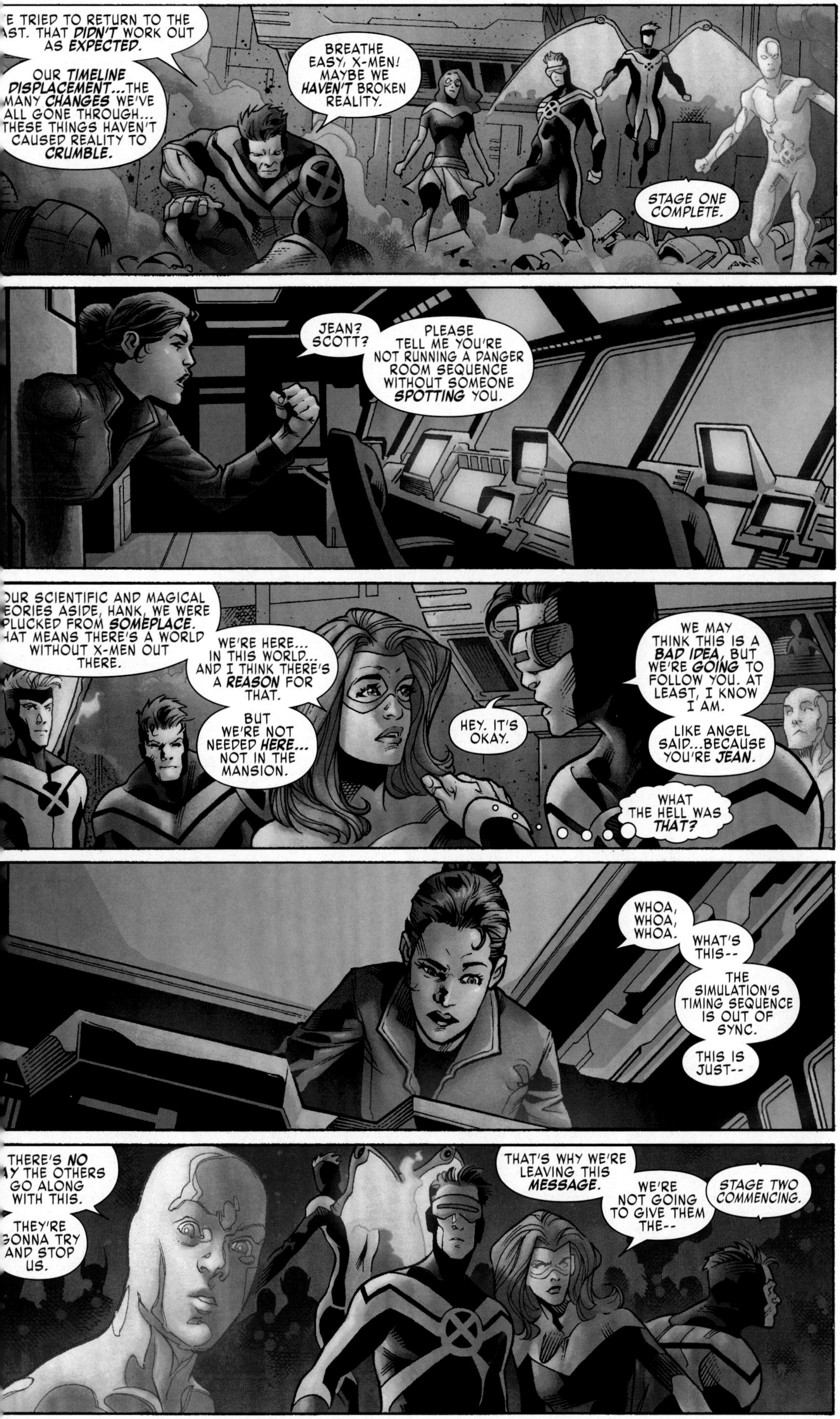
E TRIED TO RETURN TO THE
AST. THAT DIDN'T WORK OUT AS EXPECTED.
OUR TIMELINE DISPLACEMENT...THE MANY CHANGES WE'VE ALL GONE THROUGH... THESE THINGS HAVEN'T CAUSED REALITY TO CRUMBLE.
BREATHE EASY, X-MEN! MAYBE WE HAVEN'T BROKEN REALITY.
STAGE ONE COMPLETE.
JEAN? SCOTT?
PLEASE TELL ME YOU'RE NOT RUNNING A DANGER ROOM SEQUENCE WITHOUT SOMEONE SPOTTING YOU.
OUR SCIENTIFIC AND MAGICAL
EORIES ASIDE, HANK, WE WERE PLUCKED FROM SOMEPLACE.
HAT MEANS THERE'S A WORLD WITHOUT X-MEN OUT THERE.
WE'RE HERE... IN THIS WORLD... AND I THINK THERE'S A REASON FOR THAT.
BUT WE'RE NOT NEEDED HERE... NOT IN THE MANSION.
HEY. IT'S OKAY.
WE MAY THINK THIS IS A BAD IDEA, BUT WE'RE GOING TO FOLLOW YOU. AT LEAST, I KNOW I AM.
LIKE ANGEL SAID...BECAUSE YOU'RE JEAN.
WHAT THE HELL WAS THAT?
WHOA, WHOA, WHOA.
WHAT'S THIS--
THE SIMULATION'S TIMING SEQUENCE IS OUT OF SYNC.
THIS IS JUST--
THERE'S NO
Y THE OTHERS GO ALONG WITH THIS.
THEY'RE
GONNA TRY AND STOP US.
THAT'S WHY WE'RE LEAVING THIS MESSAGE.
WE'RE NOT GOING TO GIVE THEM THE--
STAGE TWO COMMENCING.

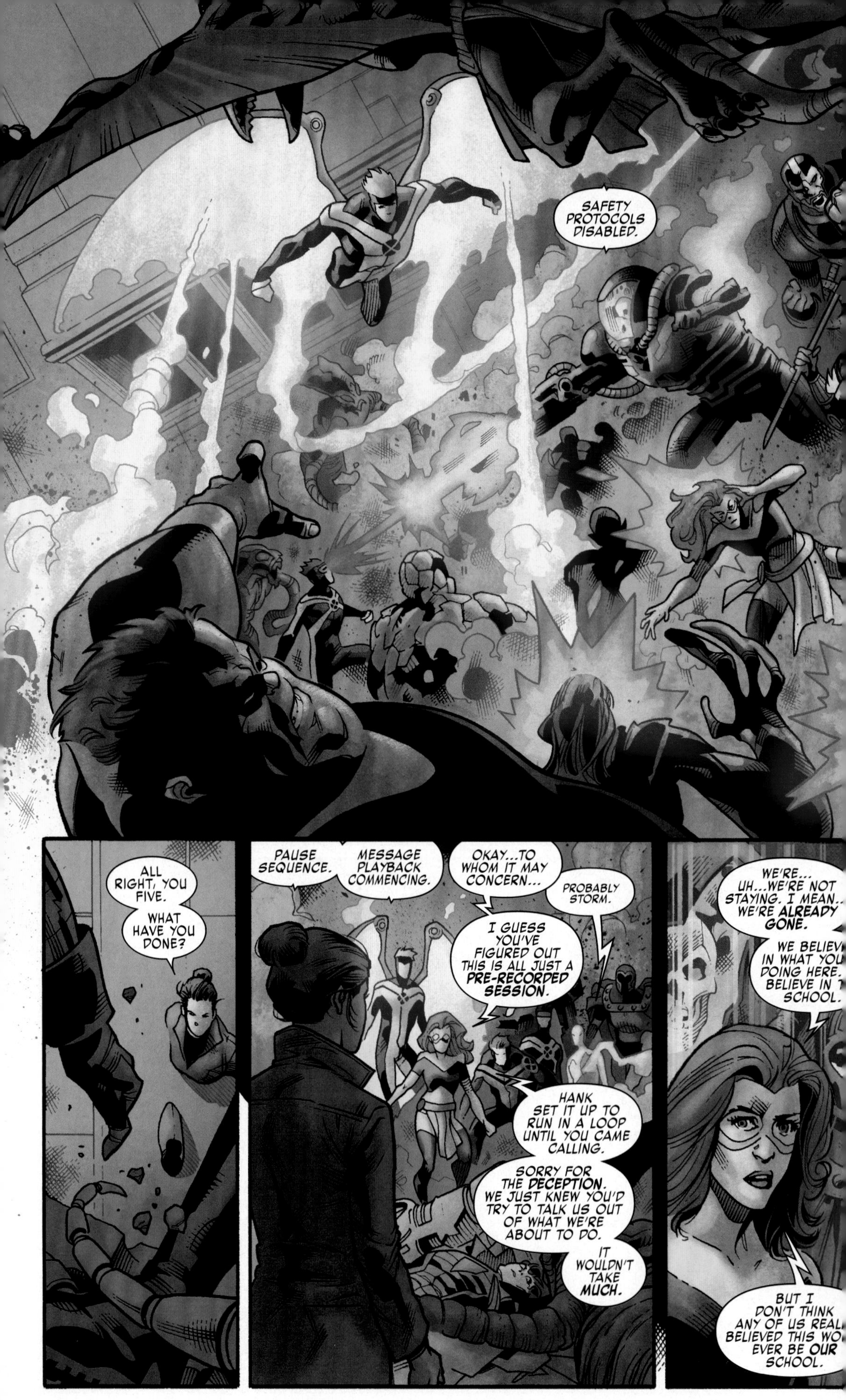
SAFETY PROTOCOLS DISABLED.
ALL RIGHT, YOU FIVE.
WHAT HAVE YOU DONE?
PAUSE SEQUENCE.
MESSAGE PLAYBACK COMMENCING.
OKAY...TO WHOM IT MAY CONCERN...
PROBABLY STORM.
I GUESS YOU'VE FIGURED OUT THIS IS ALL JUST A **PRE-RECORDED SESSION**.
HANK SET IT UP TO RUN IN A LOOP UNTIL YOU CAME CALLING.
SORRY FOR THE **DECEPTION**. WE JUST KNEW YOU'D TRY TO TALK US OUT OF WHAT WE'RE ABOUT TO DO.
IT WOULDN'T TAKE **MUCH**.
WE'RE... UH...WE'RE NOT STAYING. I MEAN... WE'RE **ALREADY GONE**.
WE BELIEV IN WHAT YOU DOING HERE. BELIEVE IN SCHOOL.
BUT I DON'T THINK ANY OF US REAL BELIEVED THIS WO EVER BE **OUR** SCHOOL.

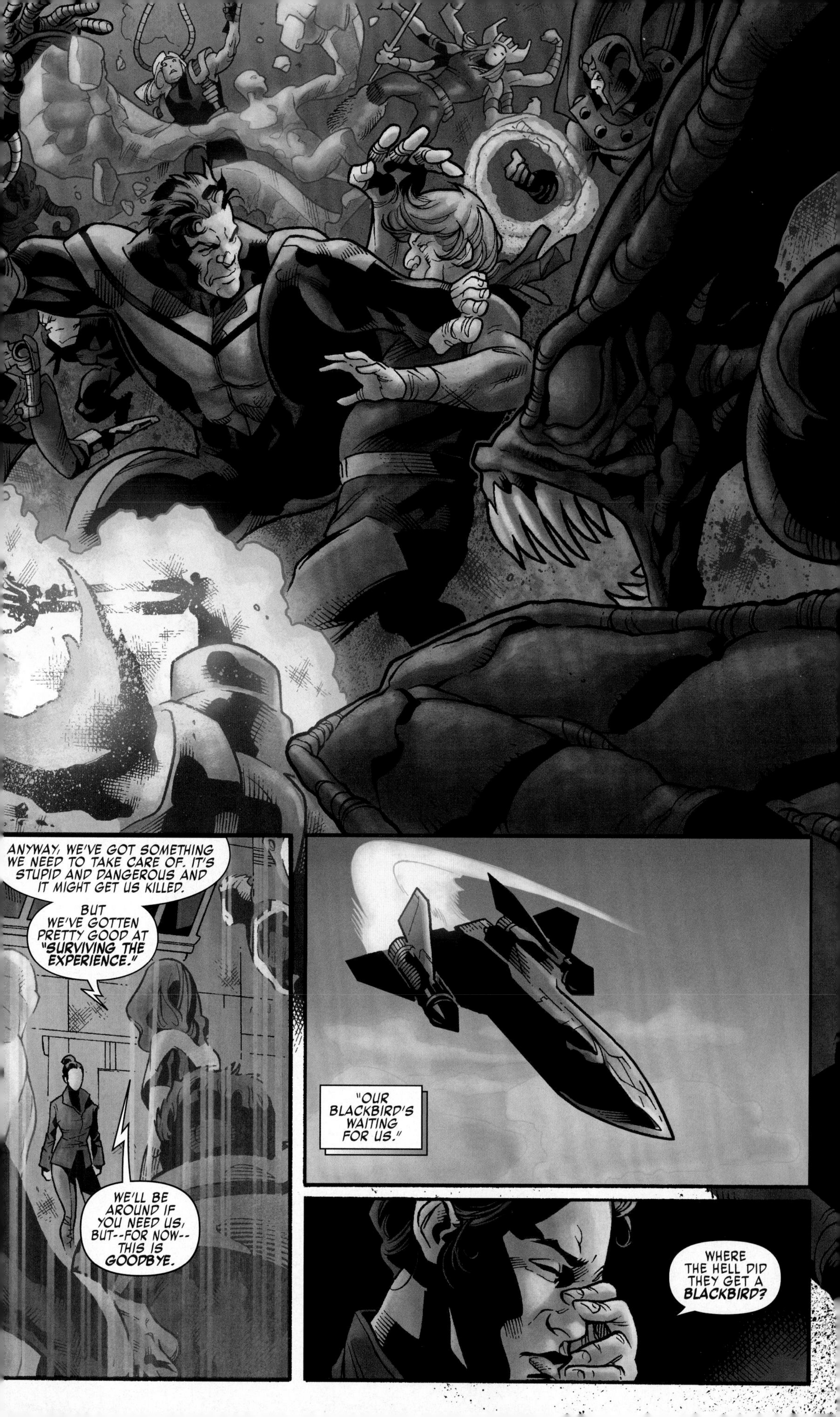
ANYWAY, WE'VE GOT SOMETHING WE NEED TO TAKE CARE OF. IT'S STUPID AND DANGEROUS AND IT MIGHT GET US KILLED.
BUT WE'VE GOTTEN PRETTY GOOD AT "SURVIVING THE EXPERIENCE."
WE'LL BE AROUND IF YOU NEED US, BUT--FOR NOW--THIS IS GOODBYE.
"OUR BLACKBIRD'S WAITING FOR US."
WHERE THE HELL DID THEY GET A BLACKBIRD?

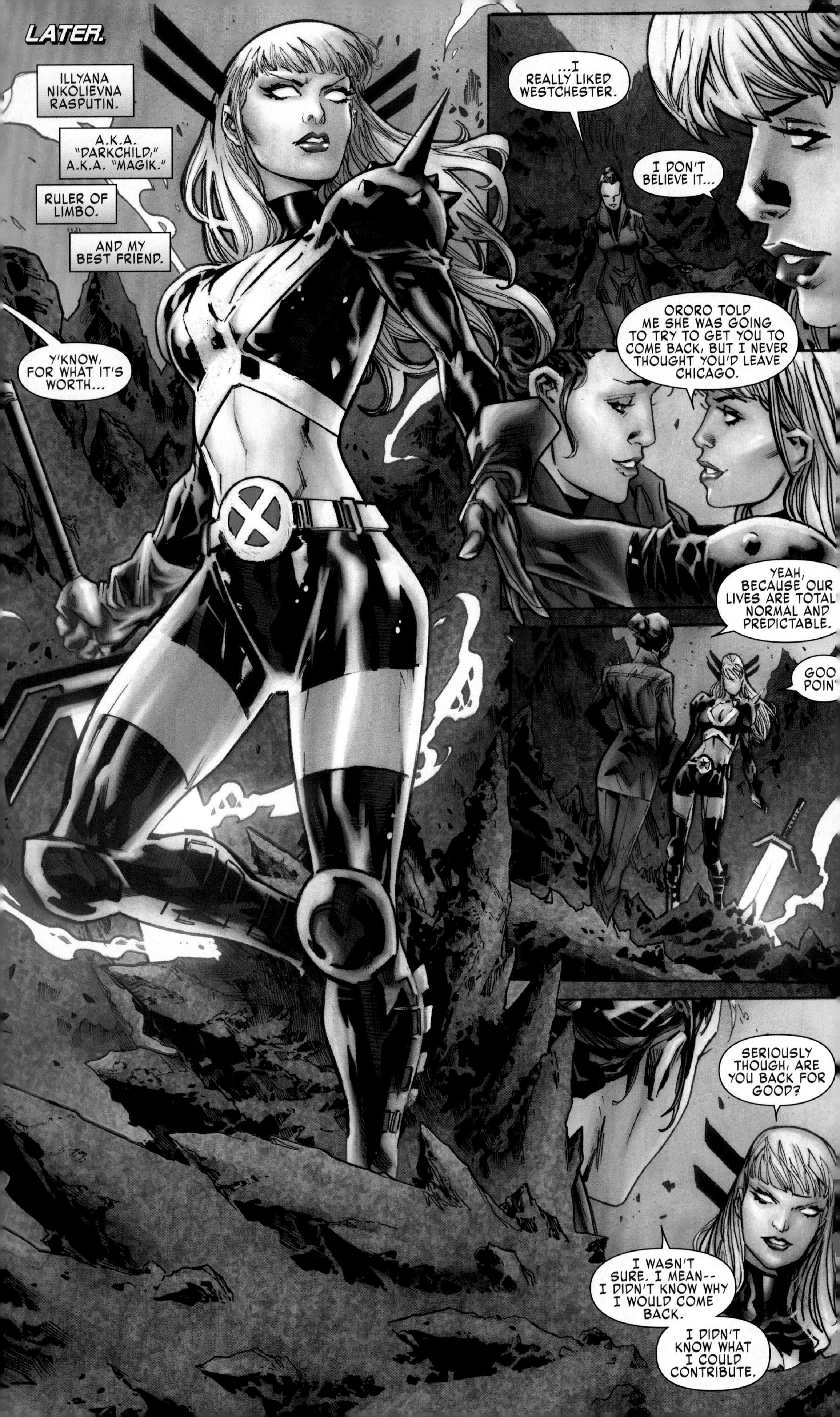
LATER.
ILLYANA NIKOLIEVNA RASPUTIN.
A.K.A. "DARKCHILD," A.K.A. "MAGIK."
RULER OF LIMBO.
AND MY BEST FRIEND.
Y'KNOW, FOR WHAT IT'S WORTH...
...I REALLY LIKED WESTCHESTER.
I DON'T BELIEVE IT...
ORORO TOLD ME SHE WAS GOING TO TRY TO GET YOU TO COME BACK, BUT I NEVER THOUGHT YOU'D LEAVE CHICAGO.
YEAH, BECAUSE OUR LIVES ARE TOTAL NORMAL AND PREDICTABLE.
GOO POIN
SERIOUSLY THOUGH, ARE YOU BACK FOR GOOD?
I WASN'T SURE. I MEAN-- I DIDN'T KNOW WHY I WOULD COME BACK.
I DIDN'T KNOW WHAT I COULD CONTRIBUTE.

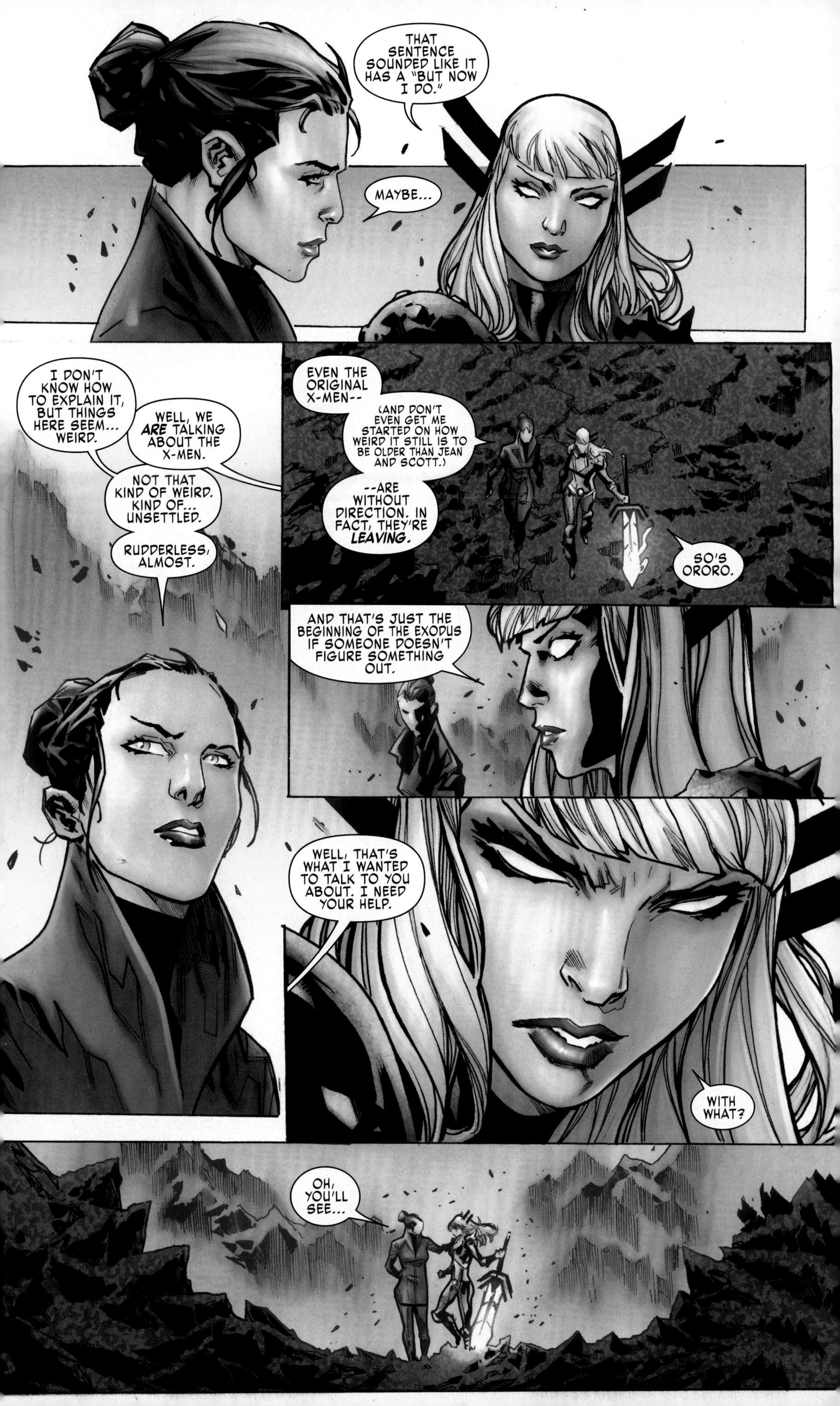

THAT SENTENCE SOUNDED LIKE IT HAS A "BUT NOW I DO."
MAYBE...
I DON'T KNOW HOW TO EXPLAIN IT, BUT THINGS HERE SEEM... WEIRD.
WELL, WE ARE TALKING ABOUT THE X-MEN.
NOT THAT KIND OF WEIRD. KIND OF... UNSETTLED.
RUDDERLESS, ALMOST.
EVEN THE ORIGINAL X-MEN--
(AND DON'T EVEN GET ME STARTED ON HOW WEIRD IT STILL IS TO BE OLDER THAN JEAN AND SCOTT.)
--ARE WITHOUT DIRECTION. IN FACT, THEY'RE LEAVING.
SO'S ORORO.
AND THAT'S JUST THE BEGINNING OF THE EXODUS IF SOMEONE DOESN'T FIGURE SOMETHING OUT.
WELL, THAT'S WHAT I WANTED TO TALK TO YOU ABOUT. I NEED YOUR HELP.
WITH WHAT?
OH, YOU'LL SEE...

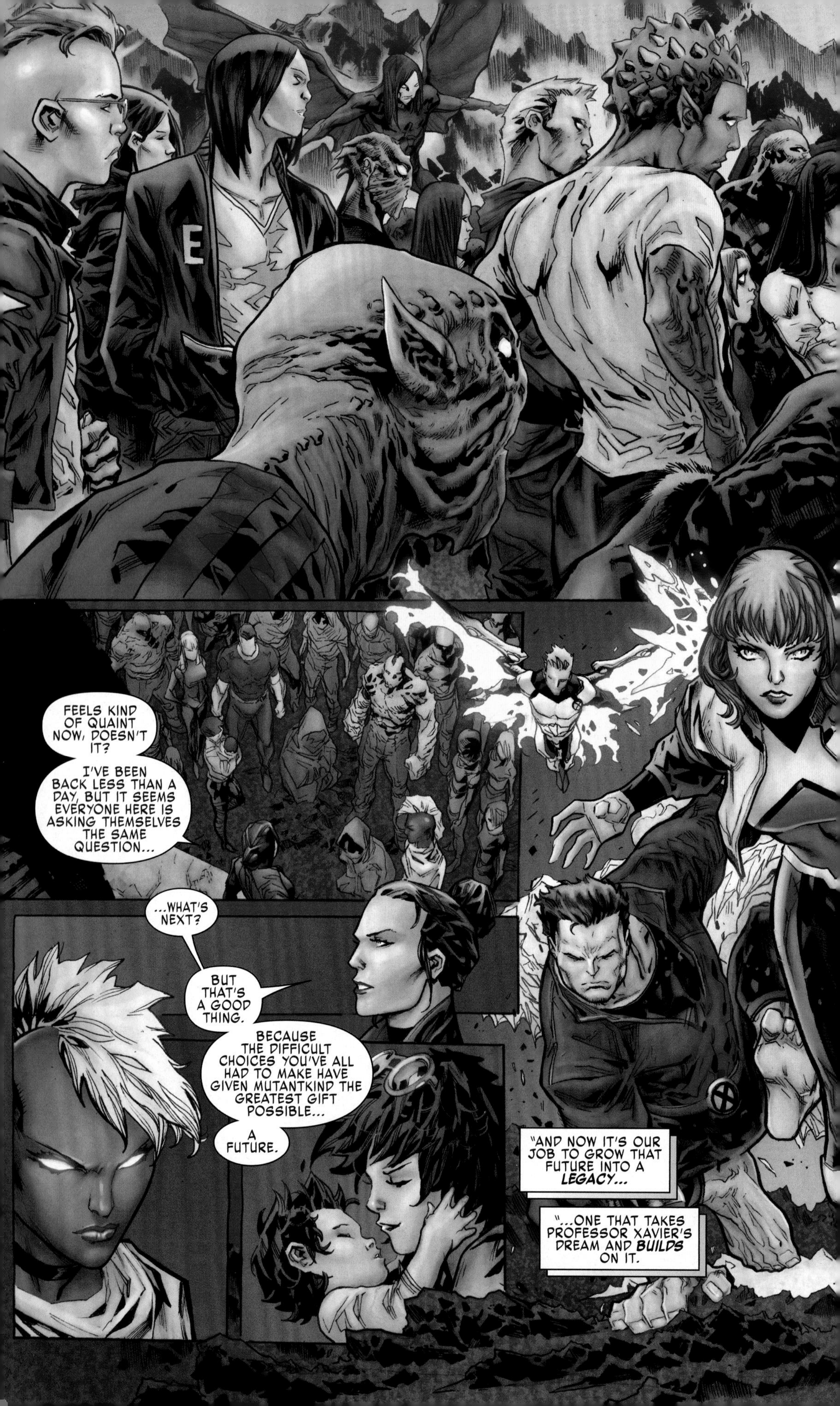

FEELS KIND OF QUAINT NOW, DOESN'T IT?
I'VE BEEN BACK LESS THAN A DAY, BUT IT SEEMS EVERYONE HERE IS ASKING THEMSELVES THE SAME QUESTION...
...WHAT'S NEXT?
BUT THAT'S A GOOD THING.
BECAUSE THE DIFFICULT CHOICES YOU'VE ALL HAD TO MAKE HAVE GIVEN MUTANTKIND THE GREATEST GIFT POSSIBLE...
A FUTURE.
"AND NOW IT'S OUR JOB TO GROW THAT FUTURE INTO A LEGACY...
"...ONE THAT TAKES PROFESSOR XAVIER'S DREAM AND BUILDS ON IT.

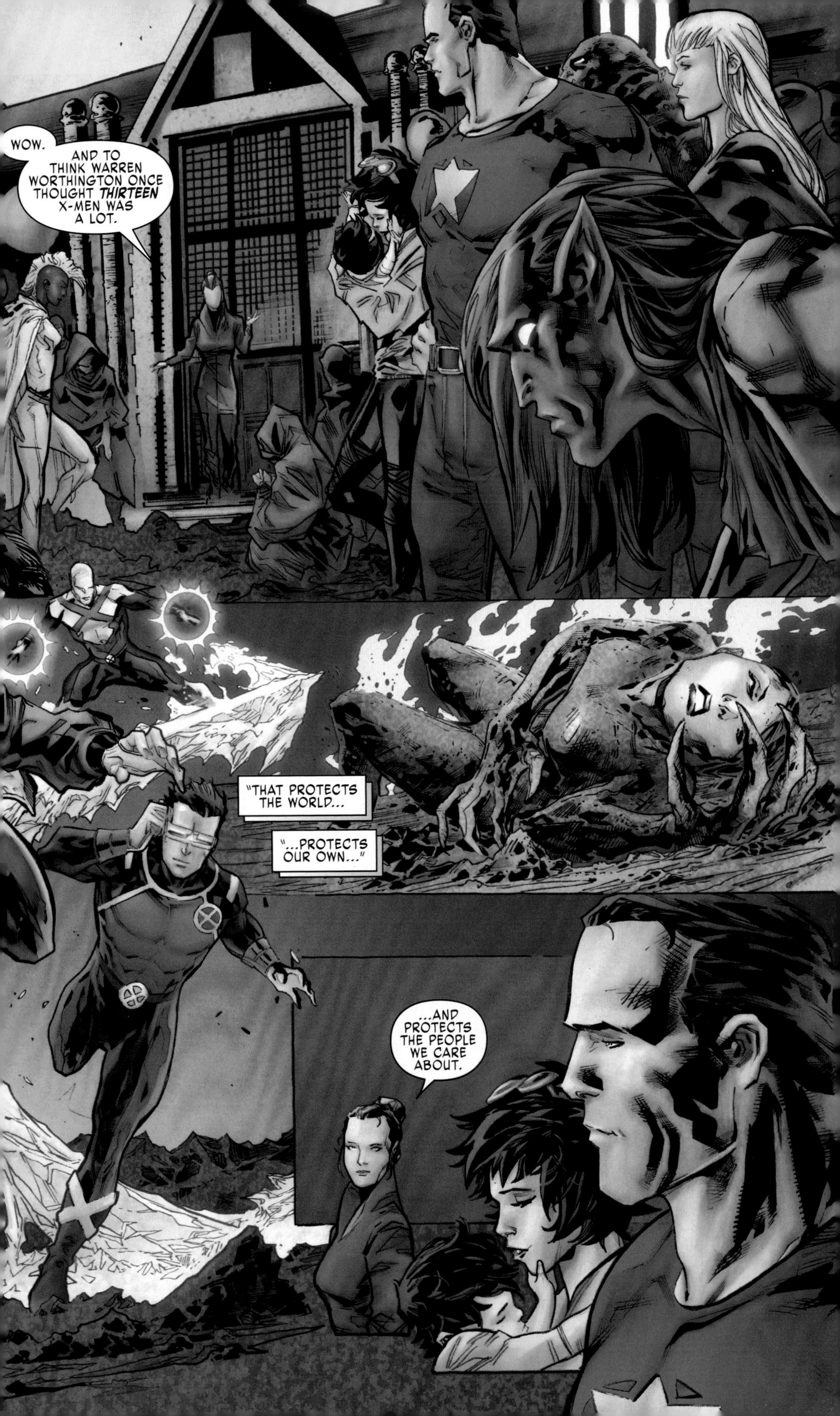
WOW.
AND TO THINK WARREN WORTHINGTON ONCE THOUGHT THIRTEEN X-MEN WAS A LOT.
"THAT PROTECTS THE WORLD...
"...PROTECTS OUR OWN..."
...AND PROTECTS THE PEOPLE WE CARE ABOUT.

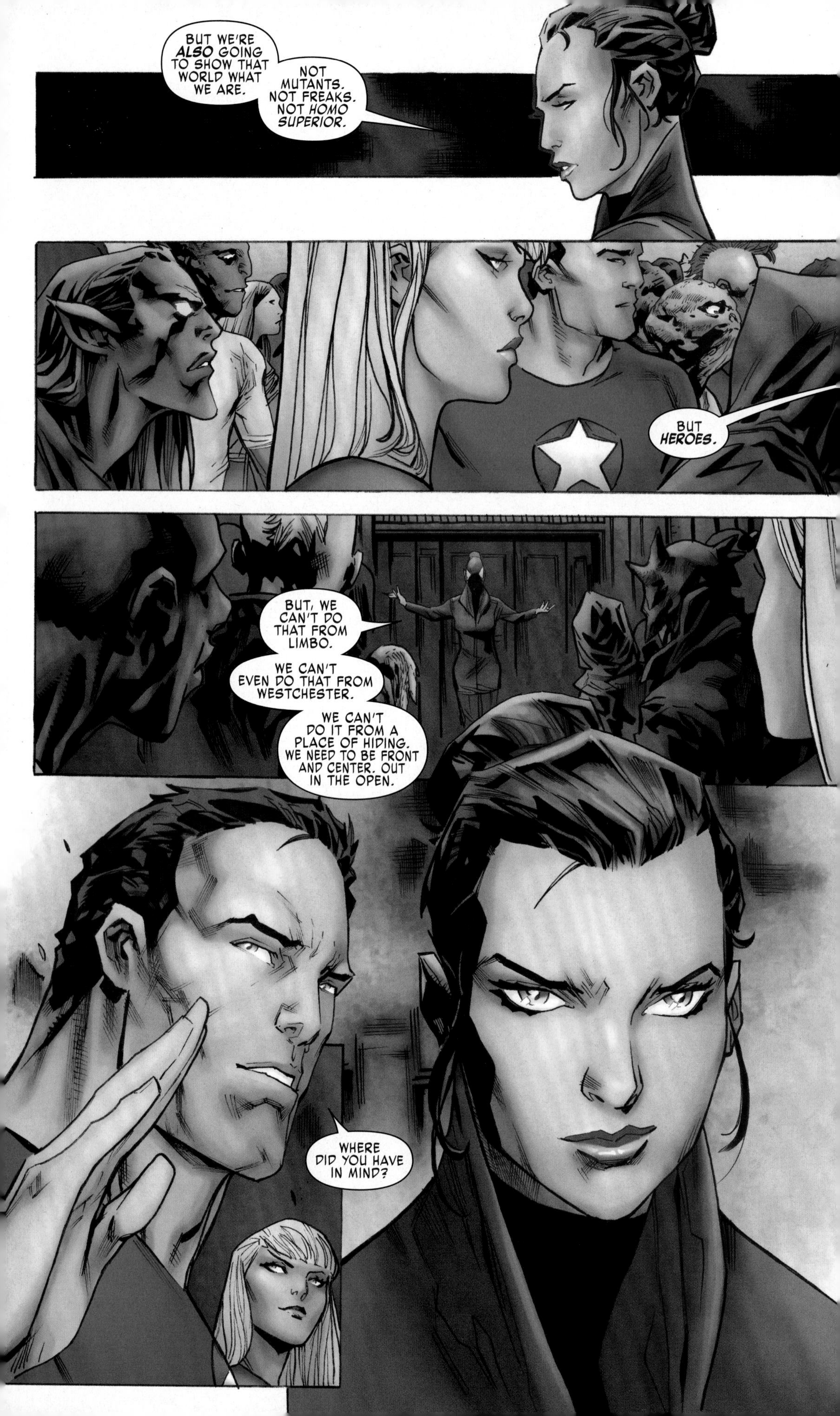
BUT WE'RE ALSO GOING TO SHOW THAT WORLD WHAT WE ARE.
NOT MUTANTS. NOT FREAKS. NOT HOMO SUPERIOR.
BUT HEROES.
BUT, WE CAN'T DO THAT FROM LIMBO.
WE CAN'T EVEN DO THAT FROM WESTCHESTER.
WE CAN'T DO IT FROM A PLACE OF HIDING. WE NEED TO BE FRONT AND CENTER. OUT IN THE OPEN.
WHERE DID YOU HAVE IN MIND?

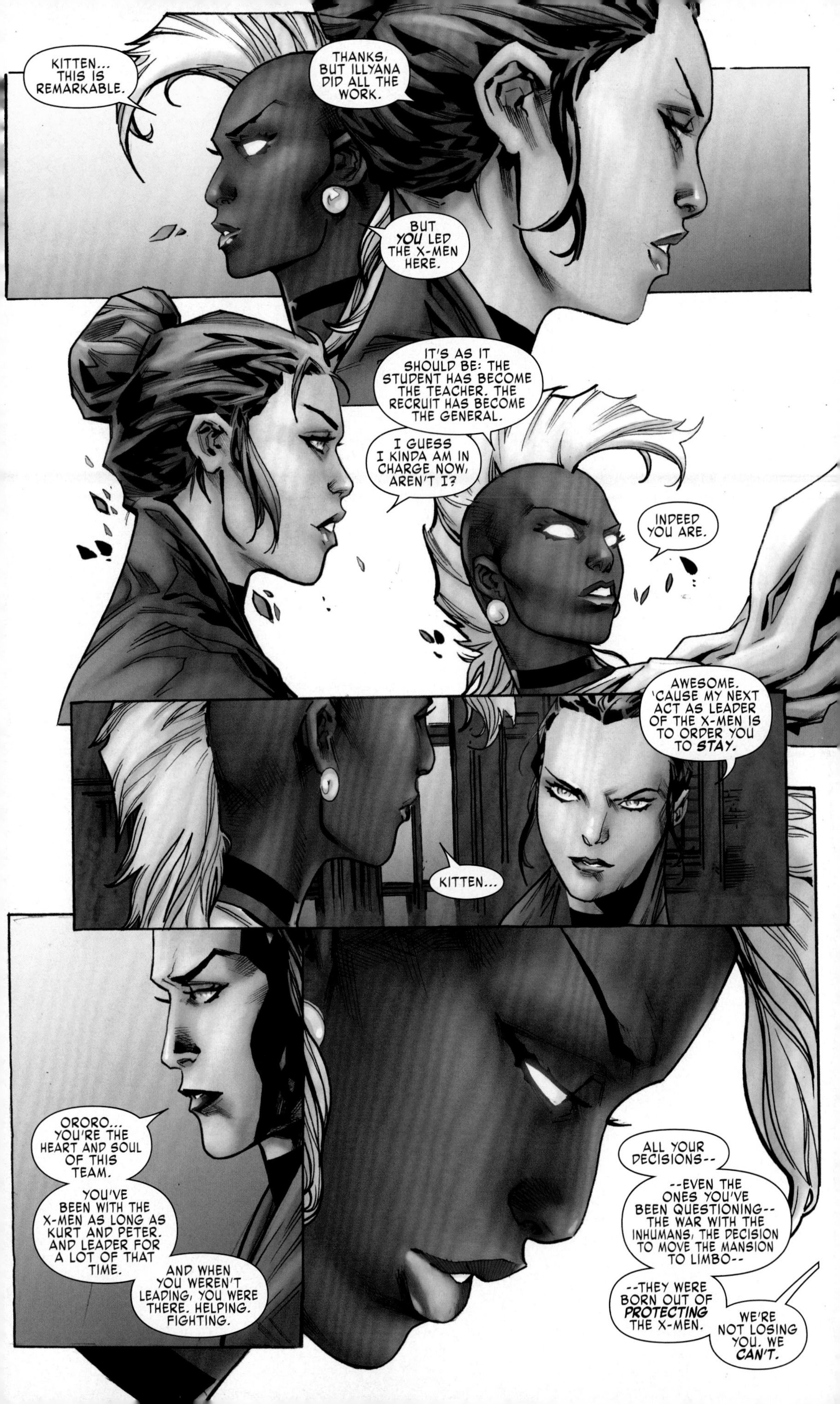
KITTEN... THIS IS REMARKABLE.
THANKS, BUT ILLYANA DID ALL THE WORK.
BUT YOU LED THE X-MEN HERE.
IT'S AS IT SHOULD BE: THE STUDENT HAS BECOME THE TEACHER. THE RECRUIT HAS BECOME THE GENERAL.
I GUESS I KINDA AM IN CHARGE NOW, AREN'T I?
INDEED YOU ARE.
AWESOME. 'CAUSE MY NEXT ACT AS LEADER OF THE X-MEN IS TO ORDER YOU TO STAY.
KITTEN...
ORORO... YOU'RE THE HEART AND SOUL OF THIS TEAM.
YOU'VE BEEN WITH THE X-MEN AS LONG AS KURT AND PETER. AND LEADER FOR A LOT OF THAT TIME.
AND WHEN YOU WEREN'T LEADING, YOU WERE THERE. HELPING. FIGHTING.
ALL YOUR DECISIONS--
--EVEN THE ONES YOU'VE BEEN QUESTIONING-- THE WAR WITH THE INHUMANS, THE DECISION TO MOVE THE MANSION TO LIMBO--
--THEY WERE BORN OUT OF PROTECTING THE X-MEN.
WE'RE NOT LOSING YOU. WE CAN'T.

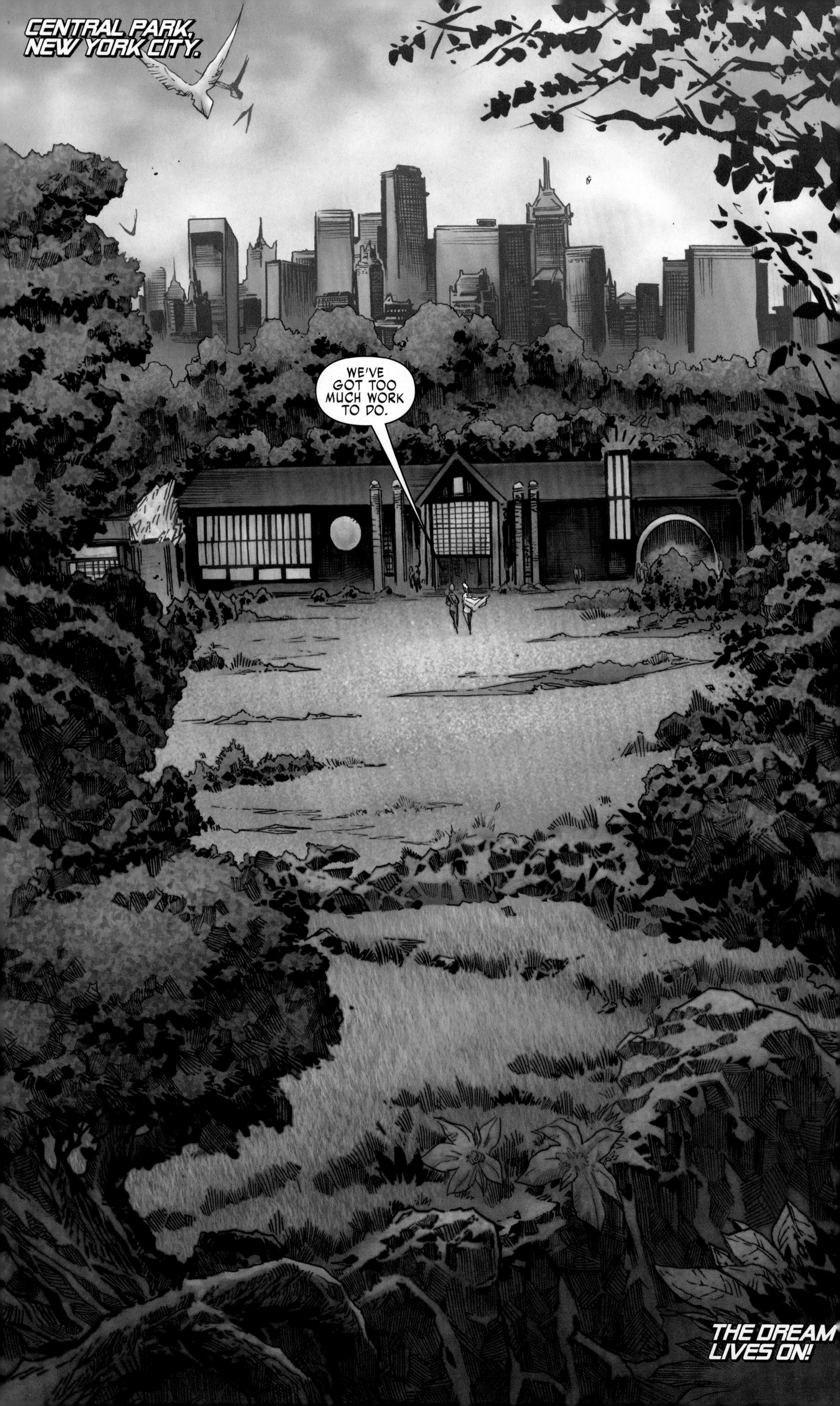
CENTRAL PARK, NEW YORK CITY.
WE'VE GOT TOO MUCH WORK TO DO.
THE DREAM LIVES ON!

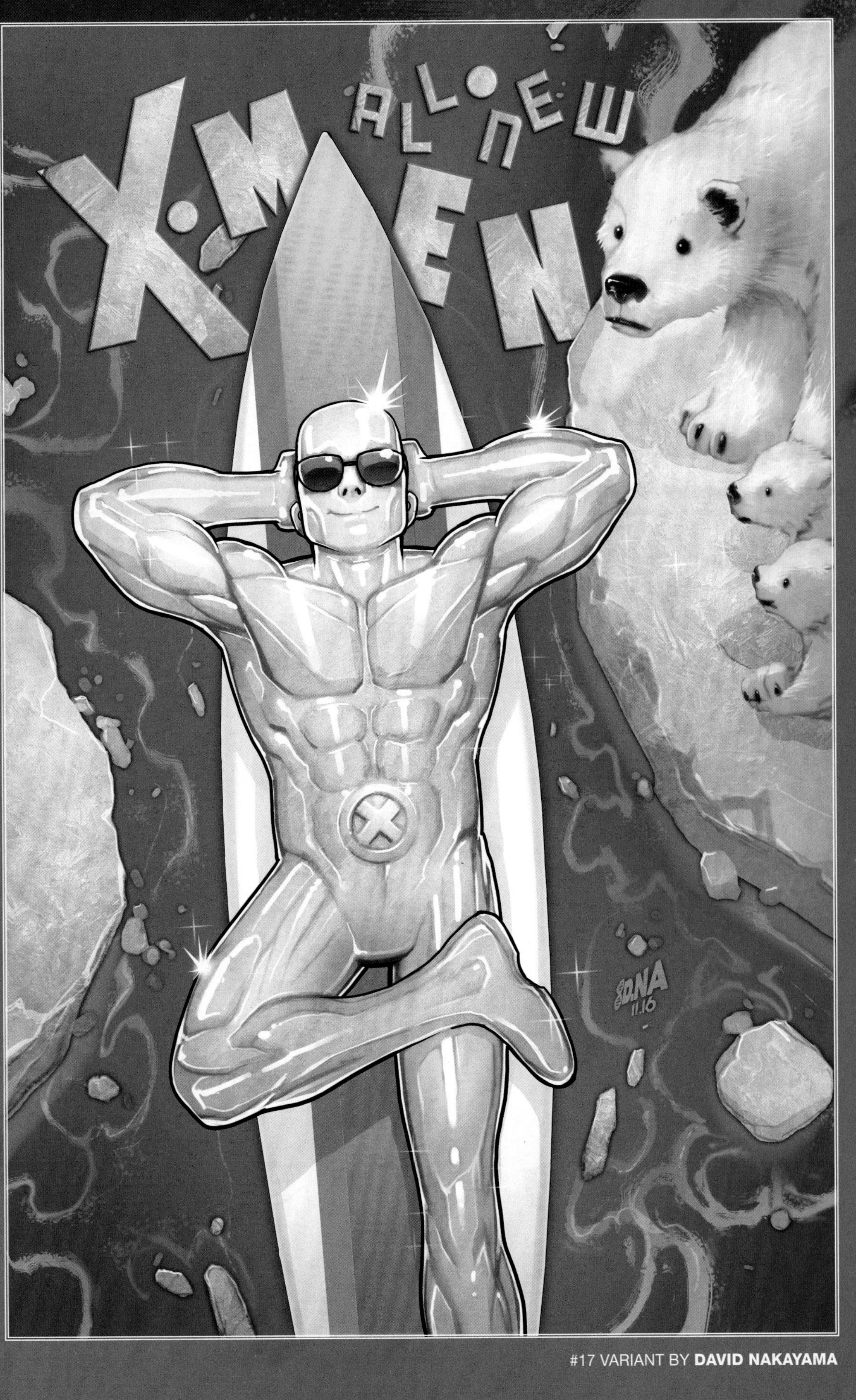
ALL NEW
X-MEN
D.NA
11.16

#17 VARIANT BY **DAVID NAKAYAMA**

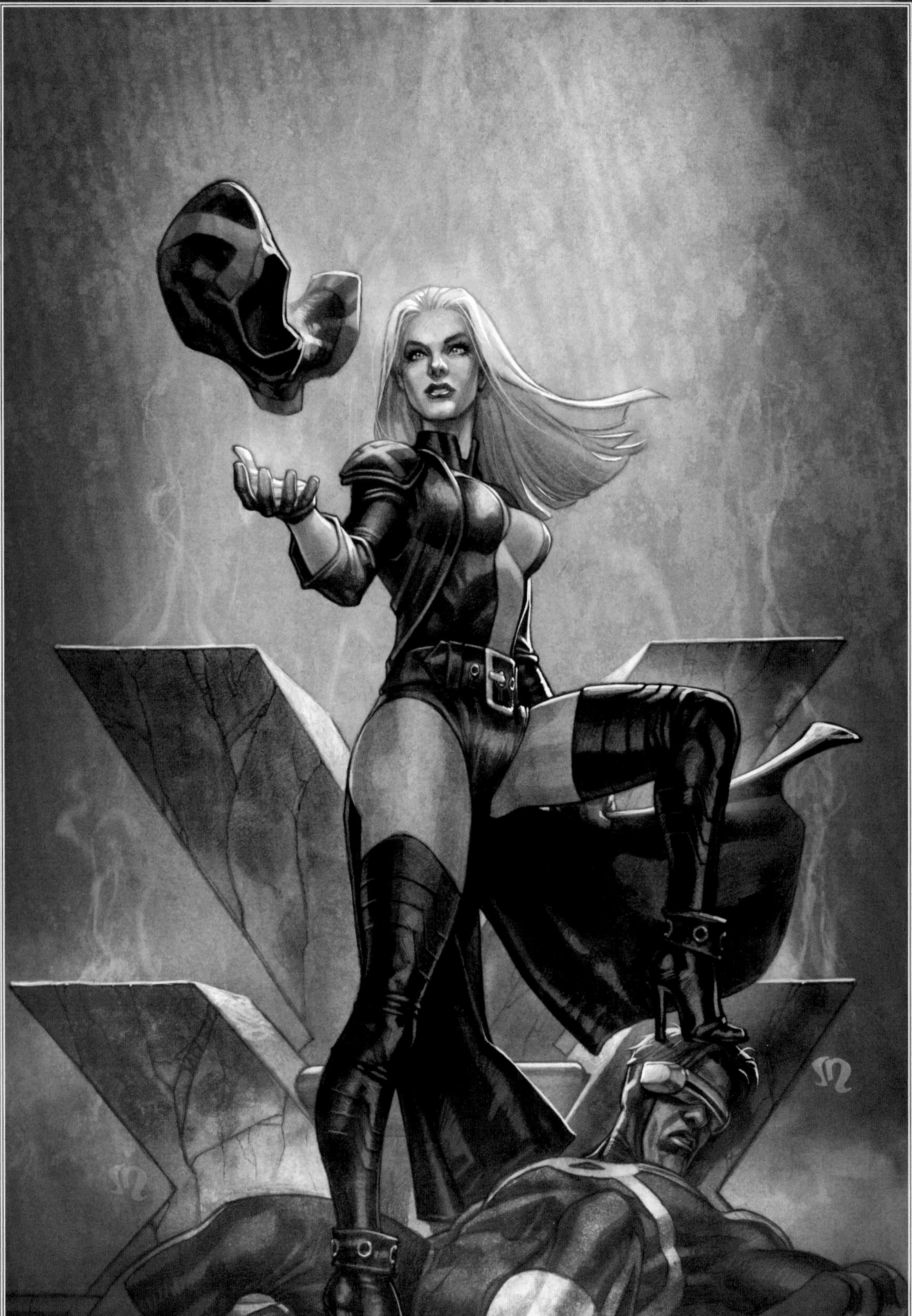

#18 VARIANT BY **STEPHANE ROUX**

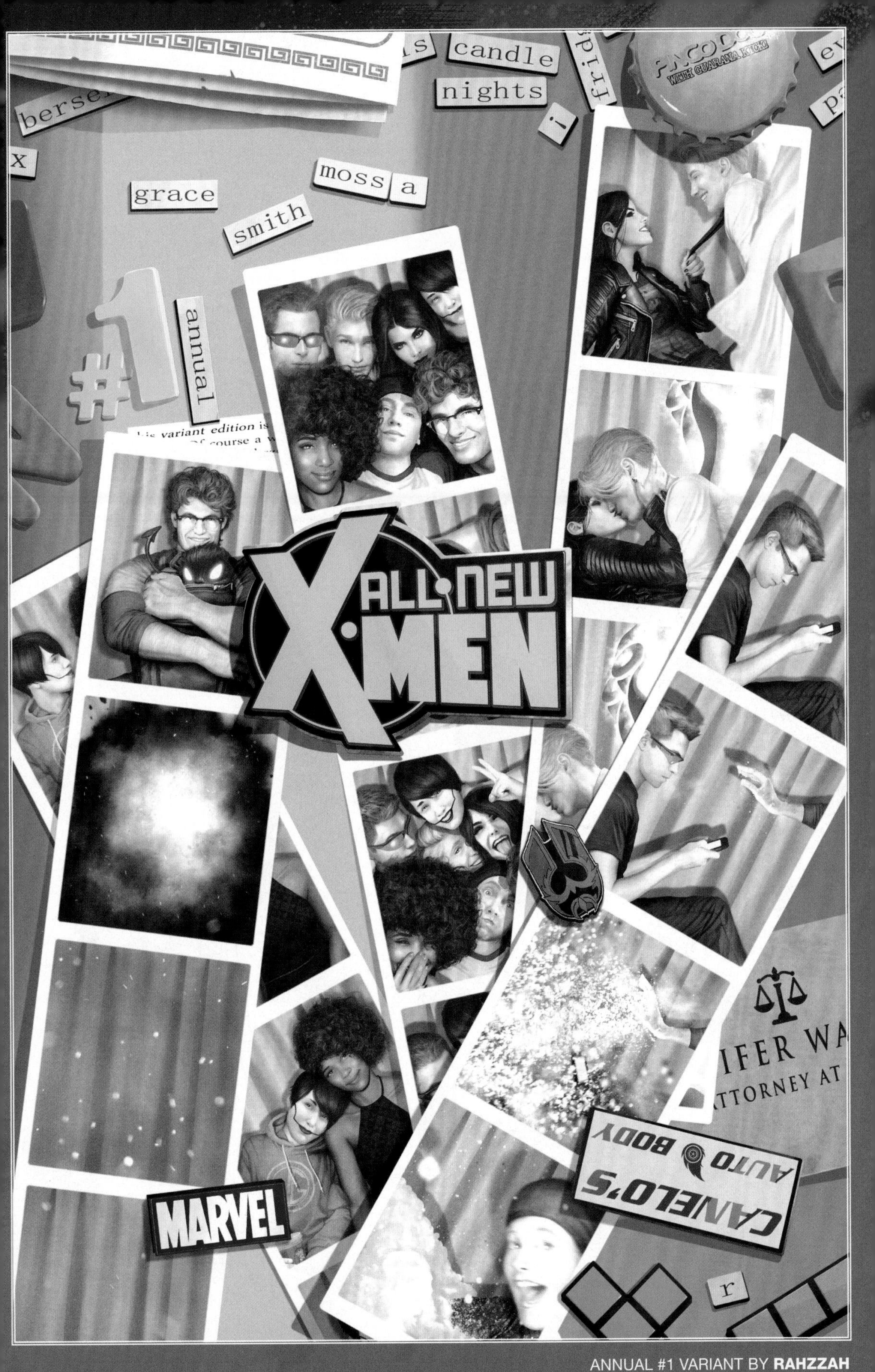
candle
nights
grace
moss
a
smith
annual
#1
ALL-NEW X-MEN
MARVEL
CANELO'S AUTO BODY
ATTORNEY AT

ANNUAL #1 VARIANT BY **RAHZZAH**

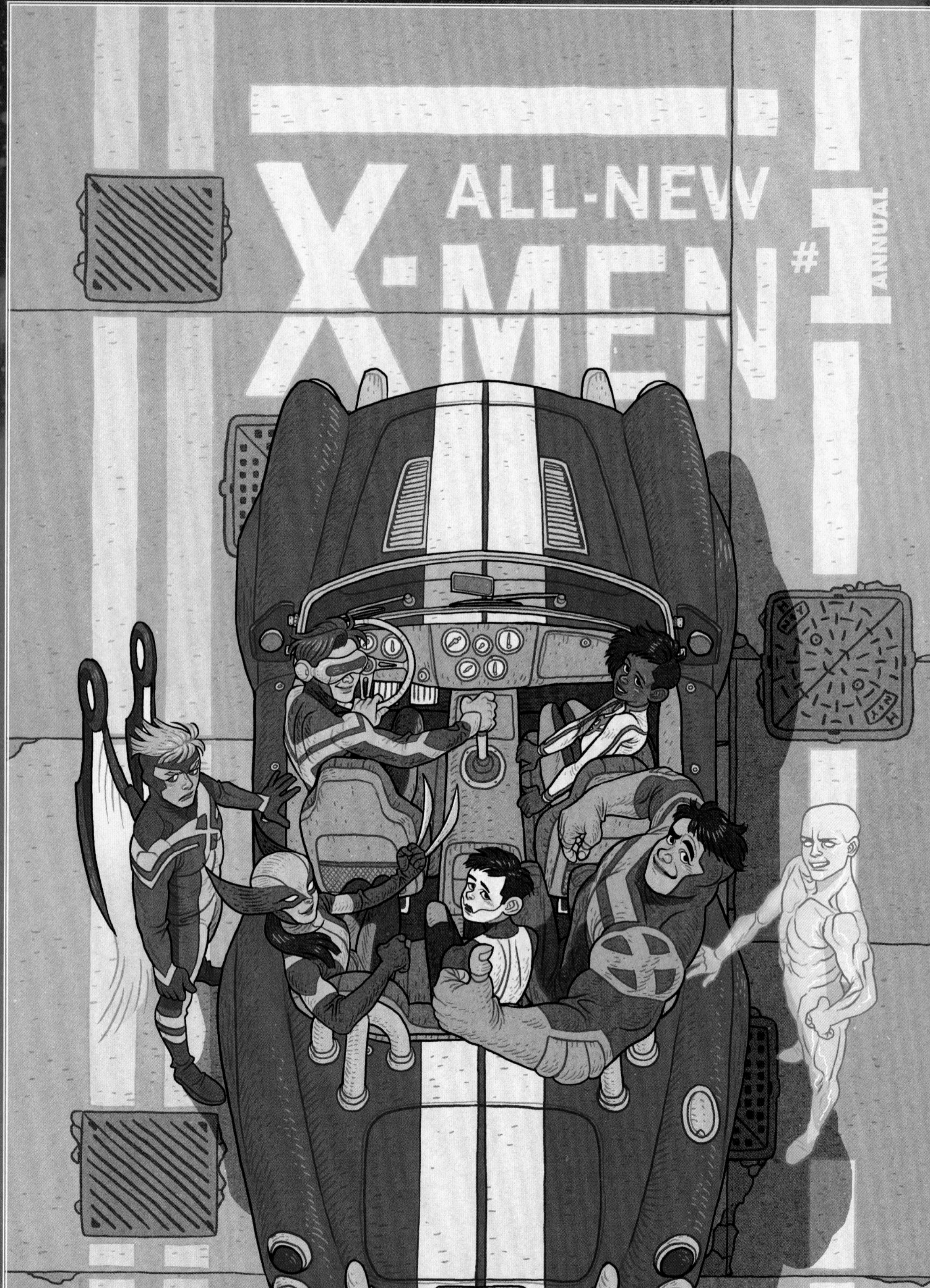
ALL-NEW
X-MEN
#1
ANNUAL
NEW YORK
ACY-1927
AFU
CHAN
2016

ANNUAL #1 VARIANT BY **AFU CHAN**

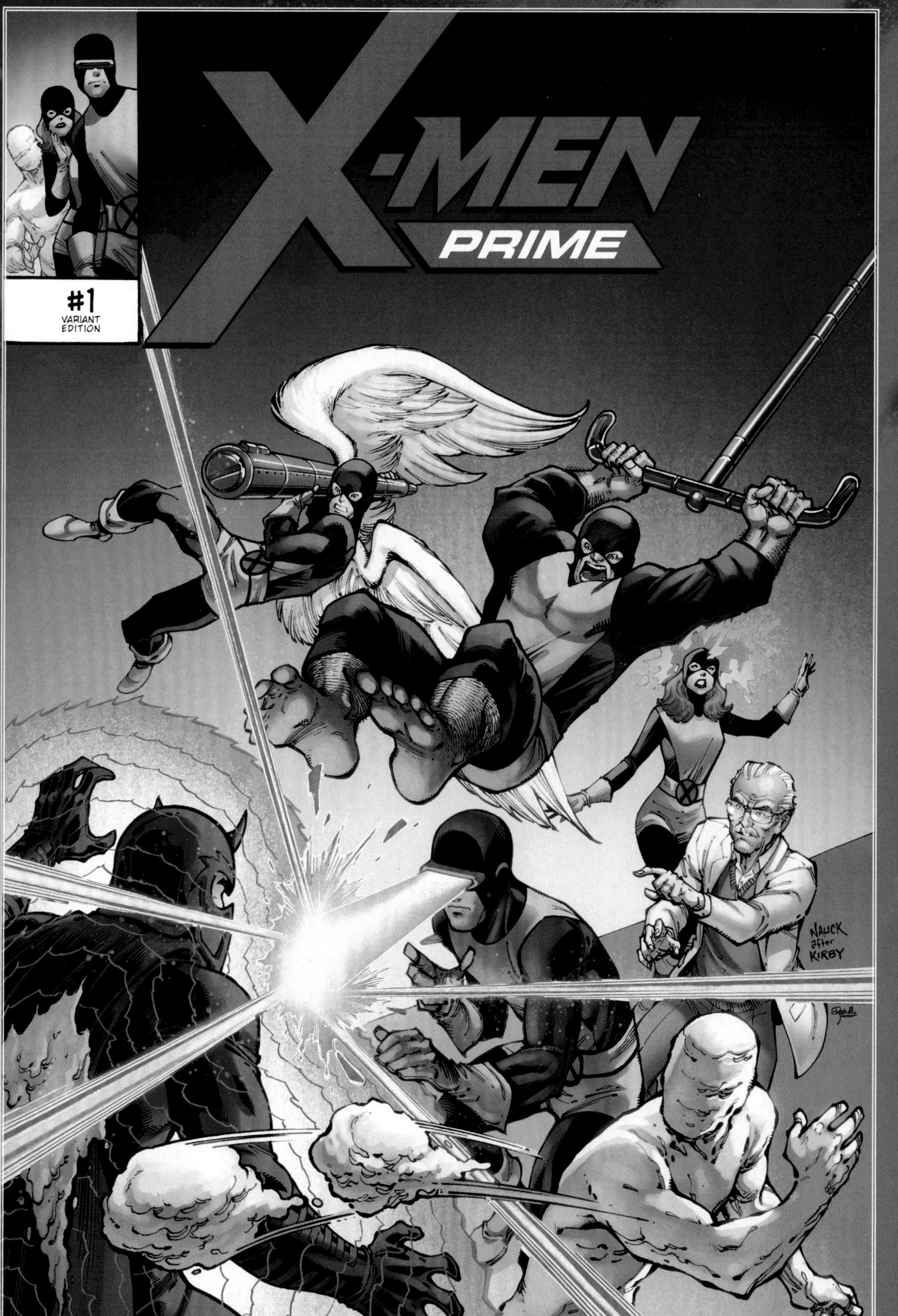
X-MEN
PRIME
#1
VARIANT EDITION
NAUCK after KIRBY

X-MEN PRIME #1 VARIANT BY **TODD NAUCK** & **RACHELLE ROSENBERG**

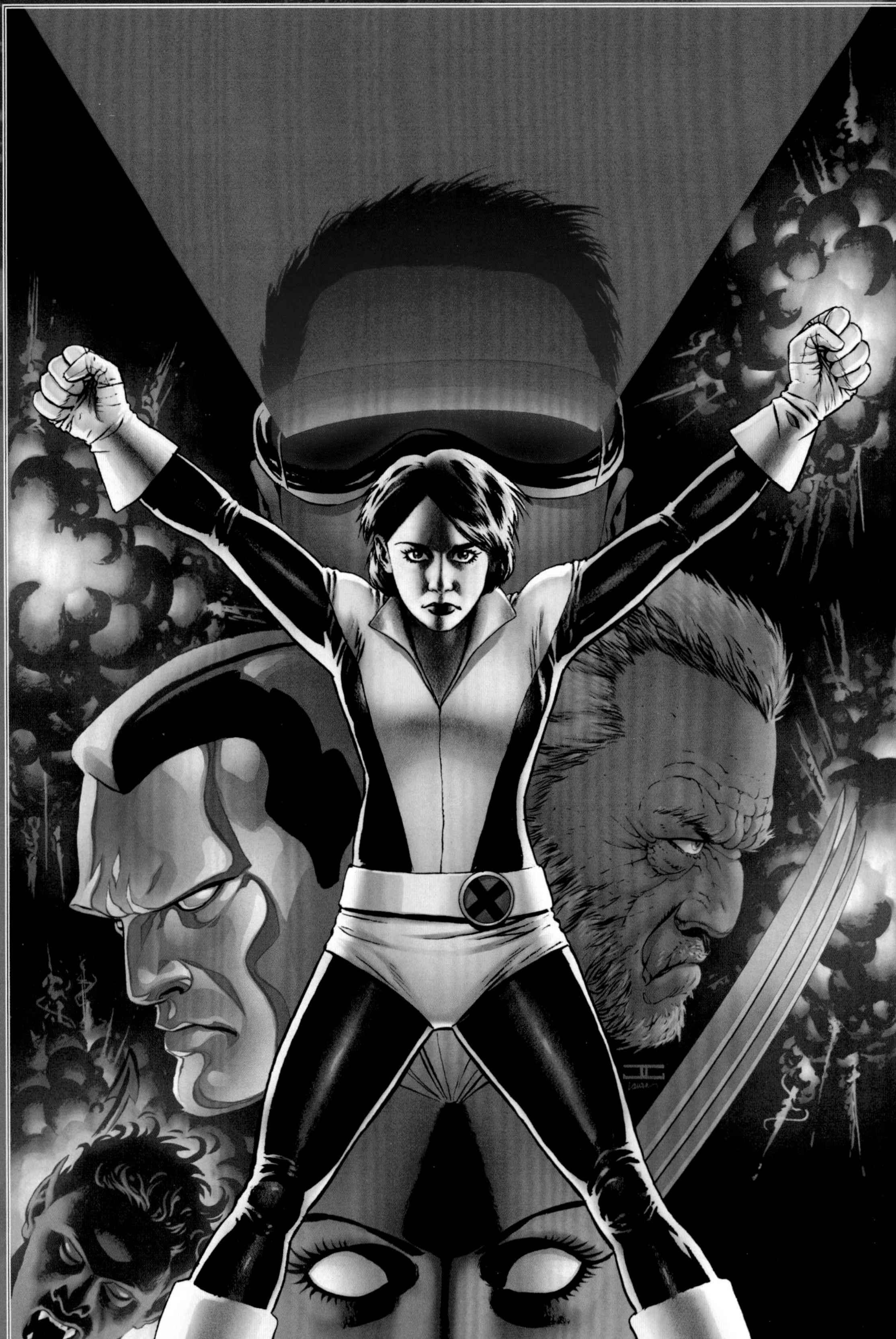

X-MEN PRIME #1 VARIANT BY **JOHN CASSADAY** & **LAURA MARTIN**

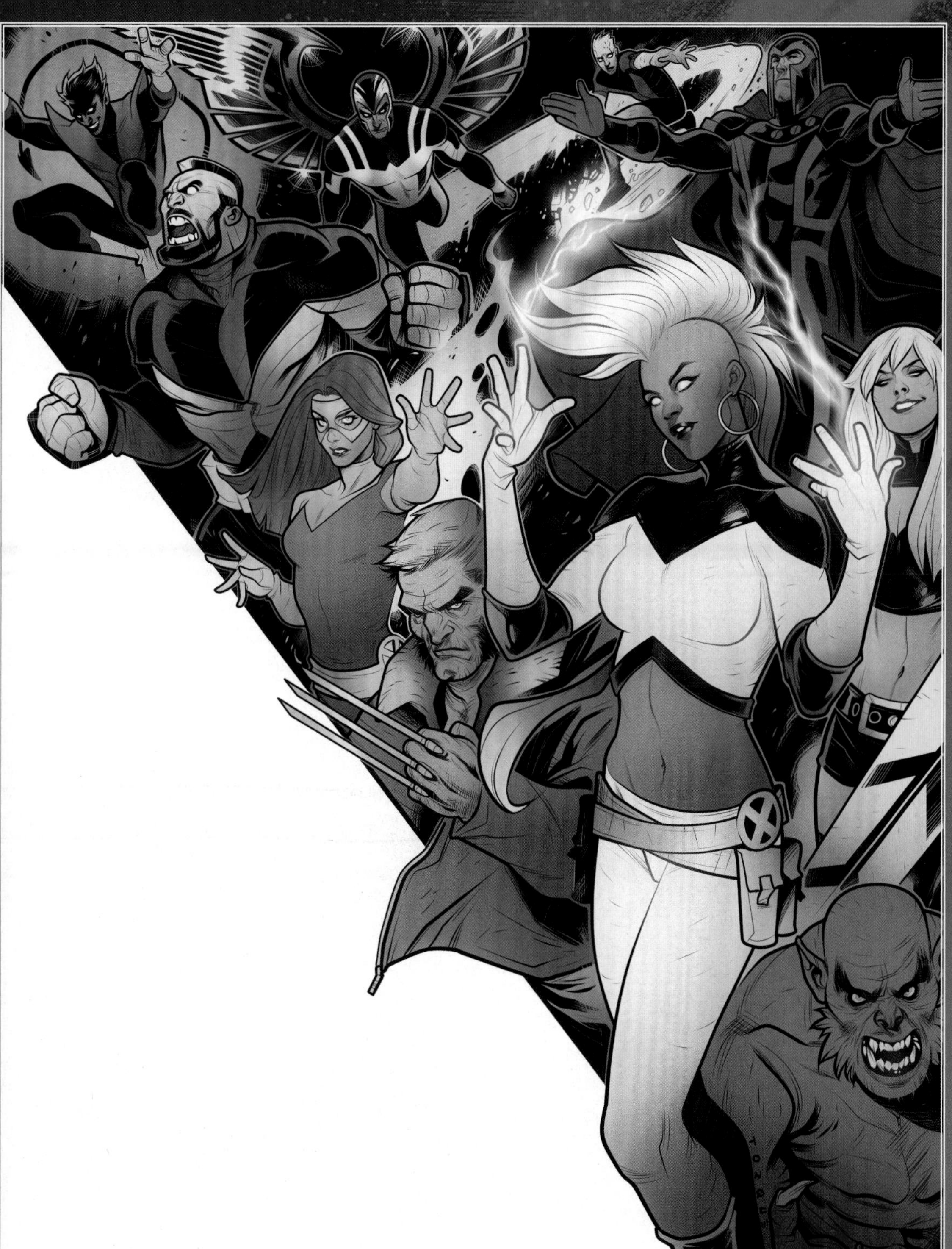

X-MEN PRIME #1 VARIANT BY **ELIZABETH TORQUE**

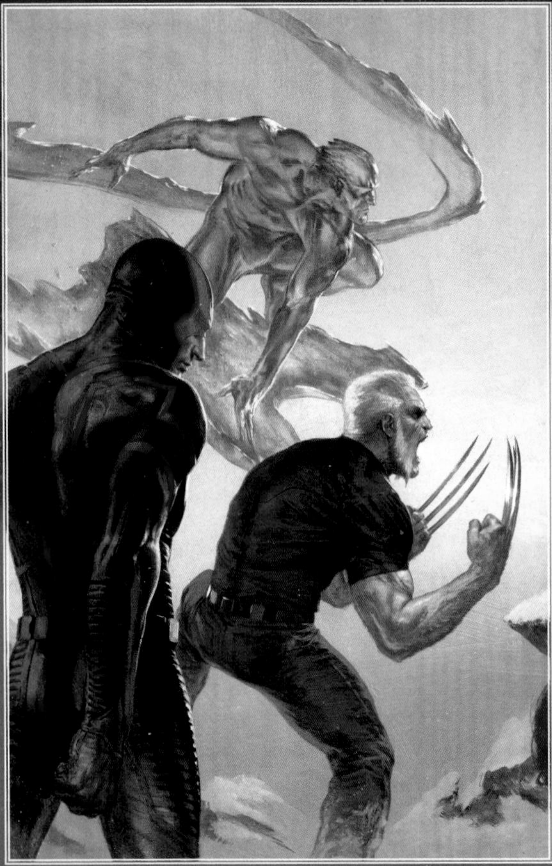

X-MEN PRIME #1 VARIANT
BY **GABRIELE DELL'OTTO**

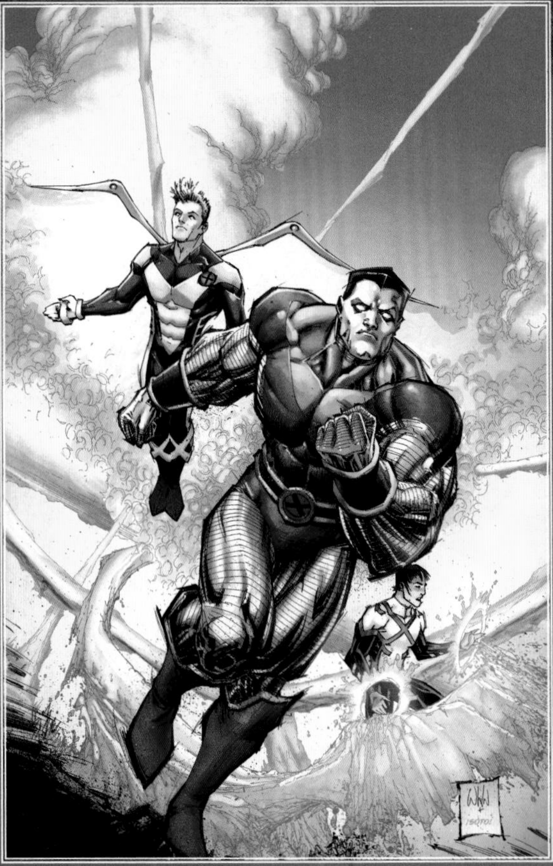

X-MEN PRIME #1 VARIANT
BY **WHILCE PORTACIO** & **CHRIS SOTOMAYOR**

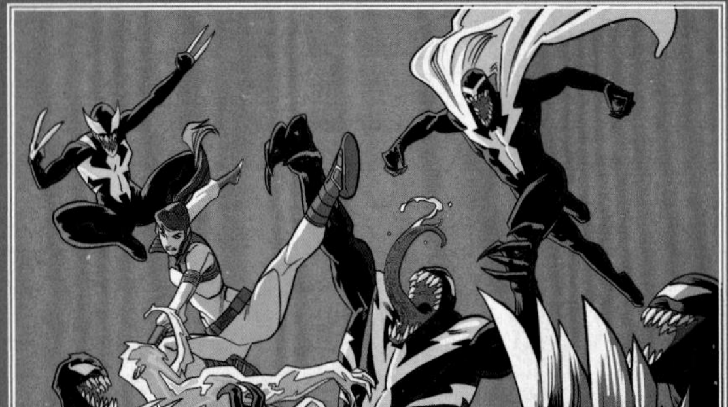

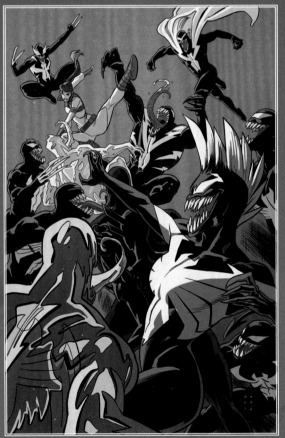

X-MEN PRIME #1 VENOMIZED VARIANT
BY **KRIS ANKA**

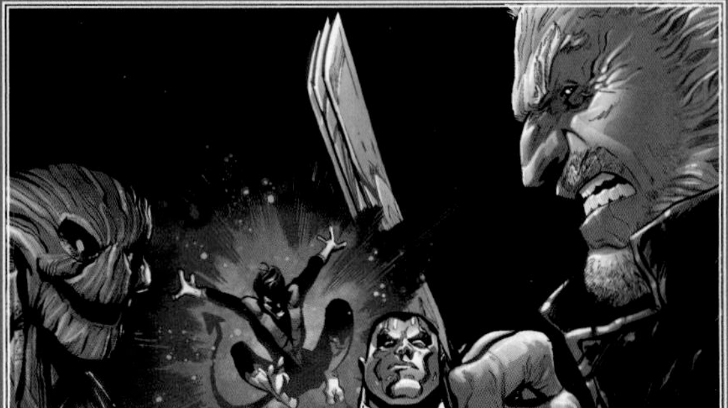

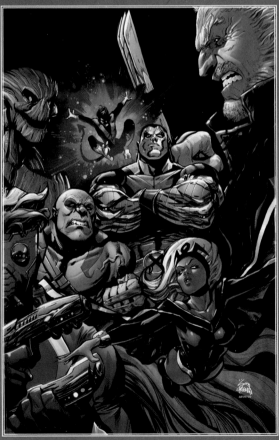

X-MEN PRIME #1 VARIANT
BY **RYAN STEGMAN** & **JESUS ABURTOV**